GIZINSKI

M&A
INTEGRATION

M&A INTEGRATION

A FRAMEWORK FOR EXECUTIVES AND MANAGERS

DAVID M. SCHWEIGER

McGraw-Hill

New York   Chicago   San Francisco   Lisbon   London   Madrid
Mexico City   Milan   New Delhi   San Juan   Seoul
Singapore   Sydney   Toronto

Library of Congress Cataloging-in-Publication Data

Schweiger, David M.
    M&A integration: a framework for executives and managers / David M. Schweiger.
        p.   cm.
    ISBN 0-07-138303-4
    1. Consolidation and merger of corporations.   2. Personnel management.   3. Human
    capital.   4. Management.   I. Title: Mergers and acquisitions integration.   II. Title.

    HD2746.5.S39   2002
    658.1'6—dc21   2001044892

McGraw-Hill

A Division of The McGraw-Hill Companies

    2 3 4 5 6 7 8 9 0   DOC/DOC   0 9 8 7 6 5 4 3 2

ISBN 0-07-138303-4

This book was set in Palatino. It was composed in Hightstown, N.J.

Printed and bound by R. R. Donnelley & Sons Company.

McGraw-Hill books are available at special quantity discounts to use as
premiums and sales promotions, or for use in corporate training programs. For
more information, please write to the Director of Special Sales, Professional
Publishing, McGraw-Hill, Two Penn Plaza, New York, NY 10121-2298. Or
contact your local bookstore.

This publication is designed to provide accurate and authoritative information
in regard to the subject matter covered. It is sold with the understanding that
neither the author nor the publisher is engaged in rendering legal, accounting, or
other professional service. If legal advice or other expert assistance is required,
the services of a competent professional person should be sought.
*—From a Declaration of Principles jointly adopted by a Committee of the American Bar
Association and a Committee of Publishers.*

 This book is printed on recycled, acid-free paper containing a
minimum of 50% recycled, de-inked fiber.

To:
Dianne, for the love and support,
Andrew and Evan, for giving my life meaning,
Mom and Dad, for the foundation and love, and
Bonnie and Zoe for the comic relief.

Without all of you, this and many other things
would not have been possible.

CONTENTS

PREFACE

The fact that you have picked up this book and are reading this preface suggests one of several things:

1. You are curious about the integration of mergers and acquisitions (M&As) and how the integration process impacts value creation.
2. You are getting ready to undertake your first merger or acquisition and want to make sure the integration is handled properly.
3. You have made one or several acquisitions in the past and are looking to improve how you handle the next one.

Regardless of the reason, you have just joined the growing rank of people who have come to understand the importance of integration to the success of M&As.

During the last 20 years I have conducted research on how integration impacts value creation. As a result of what has been learned, I have been able to help a number of companies develop and improve their integration process. When I first began working in the M&A arena, it was quite difficult to get the attention of executives. Most were exclusively focused on deal making. Topics such as valuation, strategic fit, pricing, and financing were their priorities. When asked about integration, most M&A leaders dismissed it as a secondary issue to be addressed after the closing. In their opinions, *integration* was not critical to the success of the deal.

Moreover, their advisers—investment bankers, lawyers, and consultants—were not very interested in integration either. For them, doing the deal was everything. Once the deal was done, they walked away and on to the next deal. Making the deal work and delivering value to investors after the closing were not their responsibility.

Sadly, however, many executives have learned over time that often the deals they have struck have not created the value they had promised their investors. In fact, the cumulative evidence from research by academics and consulting firms supports these intuitive conclusions. Simply put, *mergers and acquisitions, on average, are not profitable and do not create value for the buying company's shareholders.*

In spite of these results, M&A activity marches on. In fact, the last decade of the twentieth century can be characterized as the largest M&A boom in the history of the world. It is paradoxical that while M&A activity is so strong, the results are so poor.

A number of reasons have been advanced for the poor results. Increasingly, both experience and research are pointing to the importance of integration. Topics such as culture clash, selection and retention of key people, value leakage, integration teams, and "the soft side of due diligence" have entered the vocabulary of executives as they plan a merger or an acquisition. Why? Simply put, executives have come to realize that deal making is a theoretical exercise that attempts to forecast earnings and cashflow and thus the value of a target or merger partner. They have also come to realize that it is only after the closing when earnings and cashflow materialize.

Beyond this, they have found that:

1. Many deals require a premium to be paid to the target to get them to do the deal.
2. Premiums require synergies to justify the investment.
3. Synergies require changes to either the target or the acquirer.
4. An orderly, well-managed integration process can determine whether changes and synergies are captured, earnings and cashflow materialize, and investor value is created.

Research and experience indicate that integration is a critical management process that must be taken and managed seriously. Integration is not just a few random activities that can be handled after the closing, but a series of well-orchestrated activities that begin long before and continue long after the closing. There is a clearly defined process combined with a series of tested activities and approaches that can help executives ensure that a deal is theoretically sound, that it can be effectively integrated, and that the hypothesized results can be delivered.

As the M&A parade continues, the keys to success are to get the marching band to stop the drumming long enough to make sure all the players are in the right position, all the instruments are properly tuned, and each member is playing from the same sheet of music. It is to this end that I offer the thoughts in this book.

In the 10 chapters that follow, you will find an integrated framework with practical tools, checklists, models, and illustrations to help you effectively manage your integration process and create value for your investors. A more detailed description of the framework and the remaining chapters is presented in Chapter 1. My hope is that the ideas presented will stimulate your own, and that the resulting synergies will justify your investment in focusing on the value of integration.

As part of an ongoing commitment to improving our understanding of the integration process, I invite you to become involved in a continuous best-practices study and interactive learning community. The objective is to capture what companies are doing to more effectively manage integration in the pursuit of synergies and value and to share the aggregate findings with those participating in the study and with the scientific community at large.

If you are interested in participating in the study, please contact me at DMS@Schweiger-Associates.com.

ACKNOWLEDGMENTS

Integrating a merger or an acquisition is a complex process that requires the knowledge, insights, and energy of many people. So too is writing a book. Although I would like to take credit for all the ideas contained in this book, I cannot. There are many people and organizations that have contributed to my education, and without them I could not have written even one chapter. It is impossible to recognize every one of them, but you know who you are. There are, however, several that deserve special recognition.

I would like to begin by thanking several close friends and colleagues with whom I have worked closely over the years: Tugrul Atamer, Ernie Csiszar, Victoria Emerson, Rob Lippert, Peter Topping, and Philippe Very. Thank you for the stimulation, encouragement, and education.

Thanks also go to several key executives who have given me valuable feedback on this book: Dr. Roger Birkman (Birkman International), Glenn Tilton (Chevron/Texaco), Bill Rusak (BBA Nonwovens), Don Benson (Methodist Healthcare System), Harris Deloach (Sonoco Products), Gary Butler (Verizon), and Joel Smith (Moore School of Business). Thank you for the dose of reality.

I am grateful to the leadership of the Moore School of Business, University of South Carolina, who have given me the time, support, and freedom to acquire the practical skills and knowledge required to write this book. In particular, I would like to thank Joe Ullman, Susie VanHuss, and Hoyt Wheeler, who over the years have encouraged my efforts to integrate practice with academic research and theory. The Center for International Business Education and Research and the Riegel and Emory Human Resources Research Center at the University of South Carolina deserve recognition for their continued financial support of my research on mergers and acquisitions. Thank you all for creating a productive work environment.

And I would be remiss if I did not thank the many students I have taught in my graduate M&A classes and in my executive education seminars. You have provided me with stimulation and knowledge to undertake this project.

I would also like to thank the many clients and researchers who have over the years provided me with the knowledge and material for this book. Without you this would not be possible.

Last, but not least, I would like to thank my editor, Kelli Christiansen, my editing supervisor, Janice Race, and the editorial staff at McGraw-Hill for their support. I appreciate your confidence in me and your help in making this book better.

M&A
INTEGRATION

1

THE PROMISING WORLD OF MERGERS AND ACQUISITIONS

We believe that the merger of Chrysler Corporation and Daimler-Benz AG to form DaimlerChrysler is a historical step that will offer Daimler-Benz shareholders exciting perspectives. In addition to participating in the growth of two very profitable automobile companies, the merger offers the opportunity to benefit from the additional earnings potential that we believe will be generated by the merged activities of the new company.

We have already identified opportunities to increase sales, to create new markets for Daimler-Chrysler, to reduce purchasing costs and to realize economies of scale. We are well-positioned to capitalize on these opportunities to increase the earnings power of DaimlerChrysler AG. In the short term, we see synergies of $1.4 billion that we expect to more than double in the medium term. Even beyond that, given the creativity and inventiveness of our teams, we expect to be able to identify substantial additional benefits as the integration process accelerates.

Jurgen E. Schrempp, Chairman and CEO, Daimler-Benz AG[1]
Robert J. Eaton, Chairman and CEO, Chrysler Corporation

Telecommunications is the most dynamic and exciting industry that we will see in our lifetimes, and the rapid and dramatic changes around us have created tremendous opportunities for companies that are willing to seize the moment. GTE's proposed merger with Bell Atlantic works in this environment because it will help us capture those emerging opportunities more effectively than we could on our own. The challenge that faces us, of course, as we move toward merger completion is to meld two strong, dynamic companies into one that can keep growing and evolving without missing a beat. To do that, we must blend not only our management and our operations, but we must blend our cultures and work styles.

Chuck Lee, Chairman and CEO, GTE (Now Verizon)[2]

This is a merger that truly constitutes far more than the sum of the parts. The new company will be able to take advantage of uniquely complementary geographical reach, product portfolio, pipeline and R&D strengths. As a result of the merger, Pharmacia & Upjohn will have extensive financial and operating resources, market scope, and earnings potential. Consequently, we fully expect the new company to achieve additional growth in expected 1996 EPS as well as accelerate future earnings growth. Above all Pharmacia & Upjohn is expected to generate significantly enhanced value for shareholders.

John L. Zabrisie, Chairman and CEO, Upjohn

These comments made prior to the merger of Daimler and Chrysler, GTE and Bell Atlantic, and Upjohn and Pharmacia are typical of those made by many companies in the throes of mergers and acquisitions (M&As).[3] They capture the optimism reflected in these deals as CEOs court their shareholders and employees and encourage them to support the deal. The CEOs promise that synergies will be realized, customers will benefit, employees will be excited, and investors will prosper.

Yet in spite of all the pronouncements, the evidence suggests that much of the exuberance and promised synergies and value never come to fruition, only to leave customers, investors, managers, and employees disappointed. Nevertheless, M&A activity marches on!

THE NEVER-ENDING QUEST TO MERGE AND ACQUIRE

Since the beginning of the twentieth century, M&As have become a common part of the business landscape. During this relatively short period of time, trillions of dollars in deals have been struck and tens of millions of people have been affected. As the twentieth century opened, there was a wave of M&As characterized by horizontal consolidation. Since then, M&A activity has remained a consistent and growing part of business, characterized by a number of major and differing waves.

As we end the twentieth and begin the twenty-first century, we are again in the midst of another major wave. From 1992 through 2000 there have been eight straight record years of worldwide M&A activity, although such activity slowed at the beginning of 2001.[4] This wave is the largest in history and is being driven by globalization, technological change, and market deregulation and liberalization. The escalation in the price of many companies' stocks during the stock market boom of the 1990s also provided a currency that fueled the M&A boom. So far, the new millennium has not been as helpful for equity-based purchases.

Unlike the conglomeration movement of the 1960s, the latest wave appears to be strategic. Companies are attempting to improve their current and future strategic positions domestically, regionally, and globally, and are doing so by acquiring new technologies, products, and services; gaining access to new customers; expanding geographic presence; and consolidating within the markets in which they compete or hope to compete. Whether through mega-mergers or industry roll-ups, M&A activity goes on. Just a small sample of the deals transacted on a worldwide basis during the last five years of the twentieth century include:

- AOL –Time Warner
- Chevron-Texaco
- BP-Amoco-Arco
- Daimler-Chrysler
- Sandoz–Ciba Geigy
- SBC-Ameritech
- Bell Atlantic–GTE
- AT&T–TCI
- Vodaphone-Mannesman
- Travelers-Citicorp
- Bank America–Nations Bank

In addition to these mega-mergers, numerous other fragmented industries have been consolidating. Most of these deals involve larger players acquiring small and medium-sized companies as they attempt to "roll up" their industry. Some examples include the funeral home, security monitoring, and banking industries. It is almost impossible to find an industry where merger or acquisition activity is not taking place.

Given the pervasiveness and growth of M&A activity and the volume of capital involved, it is critical that we understand as much as we can about the dynamics underlying M&As and whether they create value for investors.

DO MERGERS AND ACQUISITIONS CREATE VALUE?

Numerous studies have investigated the relationship between M&As and financial performance. Using a variety of financial measures (e.g., profit, stock price) and nonfinancial measures (e.g., firm reputation) and time frames (e.g., premeasurement and postmeasurement, initial market reaction and four years after a deal), these studies demonstrate that, on average, M&As consistently benefit the target's shareholders, but not the acquirer's shareholders. In fact, there are varying results with respect to the buying firms' performance.[5]

For example, financial economists have found that, on average, M&As lead to no gain or a slight loss (over a variety of time frames) in both stock price and profit to the buying firm following closing. However, stock price gains to target shareholders average between 20 and 30 percent depending upon the particular study. Various consulting firms have also estimated that from one-half to two-thirds of M&As do not live up to the financial expectations of those transacting them, and many resulted in divestitures. One study even estimated that the merger and acquisition failure rate is equivalent to the marriage divorce rate in the United States!

Clearly the evidence for the shareholders of acquiring firms is not encouraging, at least not encouraging enough to make executives jump up and do as many deals as they can. As importantly, numerous studies and practical experience have also demonstrated that the impact of M&As on managers and employees can be traumatic. Studies have shown that M&As often result in job loss for people, as acquirers pursue cost synergies through the elimination of redundant jobs. Often the numbers of jobs lost in a particular deal can range into the thousands and even tens of thousands. Studies have also shown that M&As can affect employees' health, stress, loyalty to their organization, productivity, absenteeism, and the like, all elements that are essential to a well-functioning organization.

Given the evidence to date, is it unrealistic to expect that M&As can create value for investors? Is it ridiculous to conceive that M&As can be beneficial to employees, or at least do no harm? If the answers to these questions are no, then it would be crazy for executives to continue doing deals. But as in most cases, there are no simple answers. Most of the studies reported and summarized represent averages, and where there are averages there are variances. The bottom line—some M&As create value, whereas others do not. Thus, the key is to understand what differentiates those that do from those that do not.

VALUE CREATION AND DESTRUCTION[6]

Before going any further, it is important to briefly define value creation. For the purposes of this book, value will be defined as the extent to which the return on investment over a period of time exceeds the cost of capital for that investment. The cost of capital is a function of the risk of an investment. Return is a function of cashflow and amount of investment. A more detailed discussion of value and its formulation is presented in Chapter 2.

From the perspective of a merging or acquiring firm's shareholders, the decision to acquire should depend on whether an investment produces realistic expectations of potential future returns on investments. If not, it simply ought to be avoided. (Easier said than done!) Accordingly, the executives of merging or acquiring firms face two formidable tasks.

First, they must determine what returns a merger or an acquisition can be expected to create. This is not an easy task since it requires executives to predict, with considerable accuracy, the sources of value and the future cashflows of three different entities: the target, the acquirer, and the combined firm. Also included in these predictions is an equally difficult assessment of the likelihood that these future cashflows will indeed be realized over an appropriate time horizon.

Second, executives must convince shareholders that a merger or an acquisition will add the value that management expects. The executives can achieve this in one of two ways: by convincing shareholders to share their positive expectations or, absent such shared expectations, by proceeding with the deal and succeeding in creating the value they promised. The statements made at the opening of this chapter reflect such expectations, as executives attempted to convince their shareholders, employees, and customers of the inherent value of a merger and ensure that such value would be realized after the deal was closed. Neither would be an easy challenge.

Not meeting these expectations destroys whatever increase in value might have been achieved as a result of the initial (and ultimately false) expectations; and not realizing the value that management expected, obviously, damages the acquirer or merging partners. Moreover, unmet expectations are likely to generate reservations about management's competence and, hence, are likely to fuel adverse expectations with respect to management's future performance. Neither bodes well for an executive's career.

How, then, can the executives of an acquiring firm determine what value to expect from an acquisition? What can they do to ensure their expectations are met? What is the nature of the process whereby value can be created? These questions have been debated by both practitioners and academics for years and have resulted in many proposed answers.

A FRAMEWORK FOR CREATING VALUE

Two sources of value are possible in a merger or an acquisition:

- Value from the purchase of a target for less than its intrinsic or stand-alone value (i.e., an undervalued target)
- Value from synergies that can be created by integrating two firms

Whether a "good deal" can be had or synergies can be realized is a function of inflows and outflows of value that occur during a merger or an acquisition. If the inflows exceed the outflows, then a merger or an acquisition will add value to an acquirer. If the reverse holds true, a negative impact on value is to be expected. Accordingly, it is necessary to specify the inflows and the outflows that an acquiring or merging firm can expect. These are summarized in Figure 1-1.

Inflows of Value

There are two categories of inflows: the intrinsic value of a target and synergy value.

Intrinsic Value of a Target

This is the true stand-alone value of a target firm. It is determined by the actual cashflows, adjusted for risk, that a firm generates. The true intrinsic value of a firm at any given time can only be established retrospectively, as time unfolds and expectations of future cashflows turn into historical events. The best an acquiring firm can do is to approximate intrinsic value by formulating realistic expectations about the future cashflows of a target.

Since neither a buyer nor a seller can know for certain what a target's true value is at the time of a transaction, both parties are subject to the potential for error. When a target errs by underestimating its own true value, an acquiring firm has an opportunity to create value for itself by taking advantage of the error. More specifically, this opportunity arises when a target underestimates its full prospective cashflow potential or overestimates the risks that attend these cashflows. If an acquiring firm can realistically expect to exceed a target's self-assessed expectations of its future cashflows, value can be created.

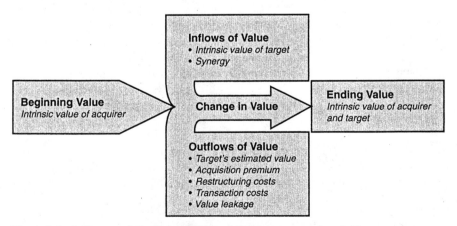

Figure 1-1   Inflows and Outflows of Value in a Merger or an Acquisition

While such a situation is theoretically possible, in actual practice it is exceedingly difficult to achieve. In the case of a publicly traded target, for example, an acquiring firm would have to outguess the market with respect to a target's prospects. One need not assume a fully efficient market to suggest that the presence of highly sophisticated market participants make such an outcome extremely unlikely. Perhaps the case of an undervalued private target is easier to imagine. However, the strong emotional attachments that private owners have to their firms, often the product of several generations' work, typically lead these owners to overestimate rather than underestimate the value of their firm.

Synergy Value
An acquisition can create opportunities to increase revenues, reduce costs, reduce net working capital, and improve investment intensity. In order to assess the opportunities created by synergy, an acquiring firm must not only identify the changes that are likely to enhance cashflows but also estimate the probability of implementing these changes. Yet many firms satisfy themselves with very broad or global assessments of this potential, as in the opening statements of this chapter. Such vague assessments, even if quantifiable, are much too general to permit the formulation of realistic expectations with respect to an acquisition, particularly expectations about how such "synergies" might eventually be implemented.

Acquiring firms could profit from more accurate and refined calibrations of this potential, whether that be by gaining a more realistic appreciation of the value that can be expected to be delivered or by determining that the transaction is not worth the price. More is said about this in Chapter 2.

Outflows of Value
There are five categories of outflows. They include the target's estimated value, acquisition control premium, restructuring costs, transaction costs, and value leakage.

Target's Estimated Value
For a publicly traded target, the market sets a benchmark for estimating its value. For a privately held firm, no such benchmark is available. Regardless of whether a target is a public or a private company, however, both a target and an acquirer need to estimate the intrinsic value of the target if for no other reason than to establish the parameters for a fair acquisition price. These estimates will be based on each firm's assessment of a target's prospective cashflows. Since these estimates are likely to derive from differing perceptions of a target's future performance and valuation methodologies, the possibility exists that a target will overestimate its intrinsic value. In this case the difference between this value and the intrinsic value will result in an outflow.

Acquisition Premium

Mergers and acquisitions typically require an incentive payment in order to induce the owners of a target to sell their interest in a firm. In a publicly traded firm, this premium is simply the portion of the purchase price that exceeds the firm's market value. With a private firm, the parties are more likely to conceive of the transaction in terms of a "bulk" purchase price. Nonetheless, it is important for executives of acquiring firms to develop a clear distinction between that portion of the price that represents its estimate of a target's intrinsic value and the portion that represents the premium. The importance of this distinction lies in the fact that if value is to be created, the premium most likely must be recovered from something other than the intrinsic value of a target (i.e., synergy).

Restructuring Costs

These are the costs incurred in implementing the changes that are necessary to realize the potential value added by combining two firms. These may include such costs as severance benefits and the costs incurred in bringing certain facilities up to OSHA standards.

Transaction Costs

Transaction costs arise from the transaction itself, including attorneys' fees, investment bankers' fees, financial commitment fees, consultants' fees, etc.

Value Leakage

Value leakage occurs when there is a loss of cashflow during the M&A process. Two possibilities give rise to the potential for value to leak during a merger or an acquisition. These include the dissipation of the potential value of combining due to:

1. The potentially negative impact the act of acquiring has on the intrinsic value of either firm (e.g., loss of productivity, employees, and customers)
2. External environmental changes before implementation (e.g., economic downturns)

To summarize, a merging or an acquiring firm must determine which of these potential inflows and outflows of value are applicable to a particular merger or an acquisition. The difference between the sum of the inflows and the sum of the outflows determines the change that an acquiring firm should expect from a merger or an acquisition. The objective in a value-creating merger or acquisition is to ensure inflows exceed outflows. Ensuring that this happens is the core responsibility of executives and depends upon a number of critical factors:

1. An appropriate merger or acquisition candidate must be targeted, and a basic understanding of how value can be created from a deal is developed.

2. Realistic expectations (i.e., pro forma) of a future target's revenues, costs, net working capital, investments, and the sources of them must be estimated.

3. Pro forma financial statements must be established based on detailed assessments of how specific functions of the target will be integrated — or, at least enough functions to recover any premium paid.

4. Based on pro forma statements and other methods (e.g., market multiples, asset values), values for a target must be developed.

5. Estimates of value from a target must be continually refined based on securing due diligence information (legal, strategic, financial, organizational).

6. Effective bargaining and negotiating with a target must be undertaken to ensure that the right price based on the valuation models is paid. Poor negotiations can lead to overpayment.

7. Actions must be undertaken to ensure that the acquisition process does not destroy existing value of either a target or an acquirer (e.g., uncertainty or confusion about the implications of the acquisition may lead to the defection of key employees or customers, productivity losses, poor customer service, etc.).

8. Actions must be taken to ensure that integration is achieved and that synergy value is realized.

Throughout this chapter, I have outlined a balanced view of the many elements that affect value creation in M&As and the challenges executives face in managing them. Although all the elements are important, one in particular, integration, has historically been among the most neglected, most underestimated, but the most difficult process to manage by executives.

THE IMPORTANCE OF INTEGRATION

Why is integration so important? As the discussion above suggests, most of the elements in the M&A process take place prior to the closing of a deal. They are theoretical activities to help arrive at and negotiate a "reasonable" purchase price. Once the deal is closed, the challenge first begins. Now the organizations and the people of the combining organizations have to be managed in such a fashion that all the assumptions about synergies, cashflows, and earnings are converted to reality. Enamored with the excitement of doing deals and preoccupied by financial and strategic issues, executives have not, historically, focused much attention on integration. Increasingly, however, that has been changing. Burned by a lack of results, many executives have come to appreciate the importance of the roles integration and people play in the success of M&As and their ability to create value for investors. Growing research in this area has also demonstrated that many disappointing mergers and acquisitions may be attributed to failure to plan for and execute integration. [7]

MANAGING THE INTEGRATION PROCESS

Figure 1-2 illustrates the key elements of the integration process and serves as the framework for the rest of this book. The process starts with the strategic and financial objectives underlying a merger or an acquisition. The first major premise of this book is that for value to be created, the integration process must be aligned with and be driven by these objectives. These objectives are discussed in depth in Chapter 2.

The second major premise of this book is that integration activities should not begin after closing. Integration begins at the point at which a target or merger partner is considered and continues until well after closing when a merger or an acquisition is actually integrated. To better understand the complex integration process, the discussion will be divided into three interrelated stages: transaction, transition, and integration. Each stage and the activities to be performed during them are briefly described below and are discussed in depth in Chapters 3 through 8.

The last element in the framework focuses on evaluation. It is the third major premise of the book that continuous evaluation and improvement are critical to success during integration and that what is learned is applied to future deals to improve subsequent integration efforts. Evaluation is discussed in Chapter 9.

THE STAGES OF THE M&A PROCESS

Let's begin by eliminating a myth: namely, that the integration process should begin after the deal is closed. Most experienced and successful acquirers recognize that the process should begin as early as possible in the life of a deal (e.g., when a target firm is being considered). The earlier that information pertinent to the integration is collected and the planning of the integration is begun, the better! These steps create the speed and momentum needed to integrate the firms after closing. However, this is not always possible. Two elements drive the timing of integration activities: availability of accurate and relevant information and access to and cooperation with a target.

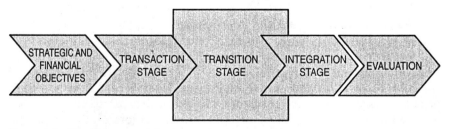

Figure 1-2   Key Elements of the Integration Process

Accurate and Relevant Information

As noted earlier, a buyer's ability to forecast earnings and cashflows is central to an accurate valuation. Being able to analyze and understand the issues (e.g., cultural fit, retention of key people, information systems compatibility) that might affect the success of the integration is more likely to lead to an accurate valuation. After all, cashflows and earnings can only be realized after closing! For example, a buyer forecasts a certain cashflow in the first year after the closing, which typically serves as the basis of future cashflows and the terminal value. Let us assume that such a forecast is based on revenue synergies that presume cross-selling of products between complementary sales organizations. To the extent that a buyer understands the likelihood that cross-selling can be implemented and effectively managed in the merging sales forces or distribution channel, the greater the likelihood that the valuation will be accurate. Failure to anticipate and understand the integration issues that affect cross-selling will probably lead to a poor forecast and the likelihood of overpayment—if, of course, the price assumed the presence of sales synergies. These assumptions point to the importance of obtaining early information and analysis. This gives the time needed to devise strategies for ensuring that plans are put in place to manage these issues once a deal has closed.

If integration information is not available during the selection of a target, then it is essential that a buyer attempt to gather it during due diligence. Knowing that sales synergies are critical to the valuation, the buyer needs to conduct a proper investigation to verify the presence and likelihood of that synergy. Chances are that this will include questions concerning the capabilities of the sales staff, the customers they serve, the likelihood that products or services are transferable, and the incentives that are provided to the sales staff. If such questions cannot be answered until after the deal is closed due to lack of availability or access to information, then two problems are created.

First, the presence of synergies becomes a guessing game, as does deciding on the price that should be paid. Second, the buyer then has to wait until after a deal has closed to determine whether synergies exist and how to capture them. When this happens, there is a tremendous slowing of momentum of the integration and a lower probability that the earnings and cashflows that were forecasted earlier in the process will be realized. Moreover, the buyer may have to find unanticipated ways (e.g., cost cutting), with unanticipated consequences, to improve earnings and cashflows after the deal is closed. After all, no one wants to fail to meet expectations.

Information Access

Access to information about a target and the timing of when that information can be secured is essential to effective integration. Obviously, with a publicly traded target, information is more readily available. This is also likely to be the case with a large and visible target. The greatest difficulty is with small, privately held companies. Access to information is often a function of:

- The trust an acquirer can generate with a target's management/owners and assurances as to the acquirer's "seriousness" about doing a deal
- A target management's concerns about employees learning that the target is up for sale

An acquirer must be prepared to conduct assessments during this phase with varying levels of access and to decide what risks to take if not permitted sufficient access. Note that some of the risks may be mitigated through warranties, representations, and indemnification clauses written into the acquisition agreement.[8]

Stages of Information Gathering and Analysis

It is important to keep in mind that there are two separate stages of information gathering and analysis: assessing the target before formal contact and after formal contact.

Stage 1: Assessing the Target Prior to Formal Contact

This would involve discreetly collecting information through primary sources (e.g., knowledgeable personal contacts) or secondary sources (e.g., public databases and periodicals). On the basis of such an analysis, a buyer can develop a preliminary understanding of the target.

Information gathered at this stage may be related to product lines and markets (including customers, distribution channels, etc.), functional area capabilities, work processes and strategies, support area capabilities (e.g., MIS, accounting, human resources), financial situation, legal situation, organizational culture, organizational structure and staffing, and key management and employees. Although preliminary, this information prepares an acquirer for integration issues that may require further analysis.

As soon as contact with a target is established, the integration process begins. It starts before the closing, beginning at the time of the initial entrée, and continuing through negotiations, due diligence, integration planning, and the integration process itself. Why is this the case? From the point at which contact begins, a buyer and target establish a relationship and create a history. They learn about each other's values, culture, behaviors, etc., all of which send signals about what life is going to be like after a deal is closed. Moreover, the parties will remember how the other treated them, which will establish a base for future cooperation, or conflict. For example, if the people sent by the buyer to conduct due diligence are insensitive to the target's people, or treat them like second-class citizens, the latter will likely remember it after the closing—if, of course, they decide to stay around. It will not take them very long to become defensive and will not create the cooperative atmosphere needed for the success of the subsequent integration.

The discussion above suggests three important elements. First, collecting integration information early in the M&A process helps ensure that the valuations and needed integration are aligned. Second, establishing a cooperative atmosphere early in the M&A process facilitates the ensuing integration. Third, beginning the integration planning as early as possible creates the momentum to integrate after the closing.

Stage 2: Assessing the Target after Formal Contact and Cooperation Have Been Established

This may not happen until the transition or integration stages. This would involve in-depth assessments of the current state of the target and/or similarities and differences between it and the acquirer.

PREPARING FOR SUCCESS DURING THE TRANSACTION STAGE

The transaction stage characterizes the period after which an acquirer identifies a target and culminates when there is commitment to "do a deal." This commitment is typically reflected in the signing of a merger or an acquisition agreement and the announcement of a deal.

During this stage the acquirer or merger partner attempts to gather enough information to decide whether to do the deal and what issues must be managed to successfully close the deal. Information pertains to valuation, pricing, due diligence, and negotiations. Typically, acquirers and merger partners focus on strategic, financial, and legal considerations during this stage. Rarely do they seriously consider significant organizational issues that affect integration, especially in the case of an inexperienced acquirer. Organizational issues, with the exception of payroll and benefits costs, are often considered too soft and difficult to quantify and as such are given less attention. Increasingly, however, experienced buyers have come to realize the importance of organizational issues (e.g., cultural fit, the caliber of key personnel, etc.) and the impact those issues can have on the success of the deal, and have begun incorporating them into the transaction stage. A study of 350 European mergers and acquisitions[9] supports the conclusion that the issues listed below were insufficiently considered prior to closing:

1. Communication plans
2. Organization of the new entity
3. Culture
4. Assessing target management

Transaction-Stage Objectives

During the transaction stage there are four objectives that an acquirer or merger partner should focus on. These are:

1. Gather and analyze information (i.e., due diligence) to learn as much as possible about a target. In particular, the acquirer must decide whether the target and the deal make sense from four perspectives:
   a. *Strategic.* Will the deal allow the company to achieve some or all of its strategic objectives? Can enough synergies be documented to support the strategic objectives and justify the price being paid?
   b. *Financial.* Will the deal likely deliver the financial results hoped for? Are the cashflow and earnings forecasts accurate? Is the valuation model correct? Do we have an accurate assessment of the assets and liabilities?
   c. *Legal.* Do we understand all of the target's off-balance sheet liabilities and their impact? Have we complied with all laws and regulations?
   d. *Organizational.* Do we have an accurate assessment of the people and organizational cultures? Do the two organizations fit together enough to ensure that the deal can be integrated and synergies can be captured?
2. Negotiate the right price. Based on all the information gathered, the acquirer must not pay a price beyond what a target is worth. This requires accurate valuation and objectivity during the negotiation process.
3. Ensure both that the behaviors of all acquirer personnel who come in contact with the target and that the activities conducted during this stage create a constructive environment for successful integration and preserve the value of the acquirer and the target.
4. Anticipate roadblocks that need to be managed for effective integration. These may include technical, political, or cultural issues.

Transaction-Stage Activities

Several key integration activities should be performed during the transaction stage. Although numerous activities are required to close a deal, our discussion will focus only on those that pertain directly to integration. These include:

1. *Organizing for information gathering and analysis.* Creating, developing, and managing teams of people to perform an effective and efficient due diligence is critical, especially if time available to do so is limited. The information gathered here provides an early view of the integration issues to be managed.
2. *Assessing the culture of the target.* It is increasingly becoming common knowledge that differences in culture between merging firms are a

major source of conflict in M&As. As such, it is necessary that an acquirer assess the cultures of both a target and itself to:

   a. Determine whether culture is important to a deal

   b. Determine whether differences are so severe that a deal should be killed

   c. Employ interventions that can ensure that differences become a source of value rather than destructive conflict

3. *Assessing key target people.* As will be demonstrated throughout the book, identifying and assessing people in both an acquirer and a target who might be important to either the success of the transition or the long-term viability of the combined organization is essential. Without qualified people an organization cannot function effectively.

4. *Guiding the behaviors and attitudes of negotiators, due diligence teams, and negotiators.* As noted above, the integration process begins the minute that people from an acquirer and a target come in contact with each other. Thus acquirer's people should be trained in how to properly interact with the target and create a context for cooperation.

PREPARING FOR SUCCESS DURING THE TRANSITION STAGE

The transition stage begins when the acquirer and the target or merger partners formally announce a deal and sign a merger or acquisition agreement. At this point there is likely to be significant speculation by both employees and customers about the implications of the deal and its impact on them and their organization. There will also be greater interaction among people from both organizations, and the acquirer will have access to the target. As noted above, this stage may involve completing the activities that were not finished during the transaction stage due to limited access to the target.

Transition-Stage Objectives

There are four objectives during the transition stage:

1. Ensure that the activities conducted during this stage continue to create a constructive environment for successful integration.

2. Ensure that the value of both the acquirer and the target or merger partners is preserved.

3. Ensure that any preliminary integration analyses and assessments begun during the transaction stage are either completed or conducted in more depth.

4. Conduct the integration planning process.

Transition-Stage Activities

Several integration activities need to be performed during this stage. These include:

1. *Create an integration transition structure.* A structure to manage the process of taking two independent companies and creating one can help create an orderly integration. The complexity of the structure will vary depending upon the nature and level of the integration process.
2. *Articulate integration guiding principles.* Numerous activities are performed during this stage, and many people are involved. Thus, it is impossible to control everything tightly. Guiding principles are broad enough to help ensure that the basic philosophy underlying the integration is understood and that the decisions and behaviors of those involved are in concert.
3. *Decide what to integrate and how to do it.* What areas to integrate and how best to integrate them needs to be defined. Considerations at this point include using best practices or innovating new practices.
4. *Develop an integration project plan to drive implementation.* It is almost impossible to manage the many activities involved in integration unless there is a coherent and organized plan for doing so. Project planning methodologies can be of great help.
5. *Manage communications with all stakeholders.* Although discussed in the transition stage, communications should be a key component in every stage of the integration process. From the point at which rumors begin to circulate about a possible merger or acquisition throughout the integration stage, communication with stakeholders will be critical, especially if the changes being created impact them.

PREPARING FOR SUCCESS DURING THE INTEGRATION STAGE

The integration stage begins after closing and continues until after the target or merger partners are integrated. Closing is a critical event since it is the point at which the acquirer formally owns the target or a new merged entity is created, control has shifted, and changes can "officially" be made. Prior to that point an acquirer or a merger partner can only recommend changes to the other management team.

Integration-Stage Objectives

There are three objectives during integration. These include:

1. Complete any analytical activities that were not completed prior to the closing.
2. Execute actions to physically integrate the target or merger partner.

3. Rebuild the organization into a stronger, more competitive entity capable of realizing financial and strategic objectives.

Integration-Stage Activities

Several integration activities need to be performed during this stage. These include:

1. *Demonstrating a committed and open-minded leadership.* Since integration involves change, it often requires a strong leader to drive the effort. In fact, strong and committed leadership is often cited as a key element in any change effort.[10]
2. *Building teams and work units.* Often in a merger or an acquisition, teams of people who have never worked together are created. Creating a cooperative context in which this can happen can help facilitate the ease and speed of the integration.
3. *Focusing on financial and strategic objectives.* It is very easy for people to take their eyes off the business during the integration process as they deal with their many personal issues. Moreover, as work units change, it is very easy for them to fall out of alignment with the broader organizational financial and strategic objectives. Alignment must therefore be managed to ensure this does not happen.
4. *Remaining flexible—things change.* No matter how well transition planning was conducted, many elements cannot be forecasted accurately. Executives and managers must therefore be prepared to make adjustments to plans as events change.
5. *Developing capable and motivated people.* It is a mistake to assume that people will be able to step into new positions and perform well after a merger or an acquisition has closed. It is essential that executives put into place elements that help people develop the proper capabilities and motivation.
6. *Assimilating new people.* Many people in a merger or an acquisition want to succeed in the new organization. Care must be taken that they are properly assimilated and are provided proper coaching and information on how they can succeed in their new positions.
7. *Achieving cultural integration.* As new units and teams are created with people from different organizations, the opportunities for culture clash are significant. Rather than wait for a clash, there are approaches that executives and managers can employ to ensure cultural learning and cooperation. These can greatly improve the speed of and the impact of the integration effort on the financial and strategic considerations.

EVALUATING THE INTEGRATION PROCESS

Central to the effectiveness of the integration is the need to continually improve the process. This must occur in two ways. First, a process must be developed where learning and improvement can take place during the integration effort. Thus, when deviations from the plan are found or problems arise, they can be corrected. After the merger or acquisition is "completed," it may be too late. Value may have leaked, and synergies may have not been realized.

Second, there are many opportunities for executives to learn from each integration effort and improve subsequent efforts. I have learned over the last 20 years from research and consulting that there is always something new to learn and new ways to improve the integration process. Unfortunately in most organizations there is no process for institutionalizing learning. What has been learned often resides in the minds of a few people. Sometimes they share what they have learned, and sometimes they do not. Sometimes they leave before they have had the opportunity to do so. The result is that companies repeat mistakes and miss opportunities.

THE LAST CHAPTER

Thus far I have presented the conceptual framework for the book and the 9 chapters that support it. However, there is one last chapter. While it does not directly fit within the framework, it nevertheless is of importance to the success of the integration effort and to those who participate in it.

Chapter 10 presents a personal perspective on M&As and strategies for how executives, managers, and employees can personally prosper during them. Many of the insights in this chapter are drawn from psychological disciplines, personal experience, and interactions with thousands of people who have both prospered and suffered during M&As.

This chapter is important for two reasons. First, I learned a long time ago that if people cannot successfully manage how they deal with challenging events, they have little chance in successfully managing others going through them. Second, many people needlessly suffer during M&As and other traumatic organizational changes. The hope is that this chapter will provide some insights to help manage oneself and others during these challenging times.

Now that the overview of the book is complete, we will turn our attention to creating value through the integration process. The next chapter will focus on the strategic and financial objectives driving integration.

2

STRATEGIC AND FINANCIAL OBJECTIVES: THE DRIVERS OF INTEGRATION

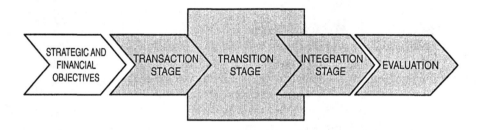

The financial and strategic objectives underlying a deal must first be understood before an approach to integration is chosen. This chapter specifically illustrates how both objectives shape the integration process.

For M&As to succeed, they must be driven by a sound business strategy. Contrary to what some executives might think, M&As are not strategies in and of themselves. They are only tools of implementation, much like joint ventures, alliances, licensing agreements, and internal investments. Although each has different attributes and pros and cons, they are essentially interchangeable. Of importance is what they accomplish for a firm. For example, do they allow a firm to extend its geographic scope of operations; sell to new customer groups; improve its cost position through economies of scale; acquire new products, services, and technologies; control supply and distribution; or all of the above? Essentially, do they allow the firm to grow revenues profitably and improve competitive advantage? If not, then it is unlikely they will create value for investors.

Strategy alone is not sufficient to create value for investors. M&As must satisfy financial objectives as well. If the strategy is sound but the deal is unable to provide the right return, value for investors will be lost. Throughout the remainder of this chapter I discuss how strategic and financial objectives shape the integration process. Additionally, I demonstrate that the true purpose of the integration process is to ensure that both strategic and financial objectives are indeed realized and provide a framework for guiding the integration process.

CREATING VALUE—THE VALUE OF A COMPANY AND THE PRICE PAID

It is essential to understand the relationship between valuation and pricing. Although a simple idea, it is quite complex in practice. When making an acquisition or undertaking a merger, most companies employ several methods to valuation. The two most influential are (1) cashflow models such as discounted cashflows (DCF) and real options and (2) market-based models such as comparable company and comparable acquisition transaction analyses. Publicly traded companies also examine earnings-per-share (EPS) dilution effects. These are critical drivers of the results that must be achieved during the integration and ultimately determine the success or failure of a merger or an acquisition. In this section I briefly review valuation methods and illustrate how they affect integration.

Market-Based Measures

Market-based measures usually rely on multiples such as price to trailing 12-month earnings, EBITDA (earnings before interest, tax, depreciation, and amortization), or cashflow. Typically a particular merger or an acquisition is compared with a recent comparable transaction or with a publicly traded company to determine what an "acceptable" multiple is (e.g., 10 times EBITDA). A market-based multiple only suggests what other comparable companies are valued at or have sold for in the marketplace and often establish the purchase price for a target. It does not indicate what a company might be worth to a particular buyer; it may be worth more to one buyer than to another due to differences in their organizational capabilities and the role that a target plays in enhancing the buyer's competitive position. In other words, there may be synergies available to one acquirer but not to another. Moreover, a market multiple may change without any fundamental change in a target's intrinsic or stand-alone value.

Earnings-per-Share Approach

An EPS approach is typically used by publicly traded acquirers. EPS is an important measure that shareholders and analysts use to assess a firm's performance. It is not a valuation measure but does demonstrate the impact of price paid as an important predictor of stock price. Essentially, the acquirer examines an acquisition to determine whether it will be dilutive or accretive. A dilutive acquisition is one in which the initial and subsequent combined earnings of the acquiring and acquired firms do not at least sustain the acquirer's EPS. An accretive acquisition is one in which EPS is improved. In publicly traded companies, where EPS seems to influence stock price, this is an important consideration. This is especially important in cases where an acquirer has issued stock as currency to make an acquisition. For example, this was a critical part of Worldcom's growth strategy. As the multiple paid increases, so do the earnings needed to sustain EPS. An example of dilution-accretion is as follows.

Telecom is interested in buying Terrestrial Communications. Both companies are publicly traded. Telecom will purchase 100 percent of Terrestrial Communication's stock by issuing new shares of its own stock. However, Telecom is concerned about possible dilution. Table 2-1 presents some basic statistics on both companies' financial situations.

To examine possible dilution, Telecom conducts the following analysis. First Telecom must determine how many shares of its stock it must issue to acquire all of Terrestrial's stock. After initial valuation and negotiations, Telecom offers $65 per share. To determine how many shares of its own stock Telecom must exchange, the following calculations are made:

Exchange ratio = offer price per share for target/share price of acquirer

Exchange ratio = $65/$150 = 0.43 share

Given Telecom's stock price and the offer price, Telecom will offer 0.43 share of Telecom for each share of Terrestrial Communications.

Total shares = (offer price)(total target shares outstanding)/price of acquirer

Total shares = ($65) (2,000,000)/ $150 = 866,667.67 shares

Given that there are 2,000,000 shares of Terrestrial outstanding, the total number of shares of Telecom required is 866,667.67. The following analysis allows us to calculate initial dilution-accretion.

Initial EPS of Combined Firm

Combined earnings = $50,000,000 + $10,000,000
Total shares outstanding = 5,000,000 + 866,666.67
Preacquisition EPS = $10
Postacquisition EPS = $60,000,000/5,866,666.67; Postacquisition EPS = $10.23

In this case the merger is accretive since the EPS increases after the deal is done. The sensitivity of the initial EPS to offer price is as follows:

At $65   EPS = $10.23

At $90   EPS = $9.68

In general, dilution occurs whenever the P/E paid for the target exceeds the P/E of the buyer.

Table 2-1   Financial Statistics for Telecom and Terrestrial Communications

	Telecom	Terrestrial Communications
Present earnings	$50,000,000	$10,000,000
Shares outstanding	5,000,000	2,000,000
EPS	$10	$5
Stock price	$150	$50
Price/earnings	15	10

$$P/E \text{ paid} = \$65 / \$5 = \$13 < \$15$$

$$P/E \text{ paid} = \$90 / \$5 = \$18 > \$15$$

The following calculation determines the maximum offer price where there is no dilution:

Maximum nondilution offer price = (buyer P/E) (target EPS)

$$= (\$15) (\$5) = \$75 \text{ per share}$$

The above analysis can be applied to forecasted earnings for subsequent years following the initial combination as well. If forecasted earnings of the combined firm decline or do not increase (given initial dilution), then the deal will likely lead to future dilution and will be value-destroying. If it increases, the deal will likely be value-enhancing. Why is this important? It clearly indicates the level of earnings that will be required after the deal to avoid dilution. If the target's earnings are not sufficient to sustain EPS, then dilution will occur. To avoid this, earnings will need to improve. The result: The need for synergies. The implication: The need for successful integration.

Discounted Cashflow Approach

Often, companies rely on some form of discounted cashflow to value a target.[1] Under this approach the value of a target is essentially the stream of its future cashflows (usually five years) plus a terminal value discounted at the combined firms' weighted cost of capital. Cashflows for the projected time period and the terminal value are discounted and added to determine the total value of the target firm.[2]

From this perspective it is apparent that value creation is dependent upon the total capital invested (i.e., purchase price) in an acquisition and the cashflows generated from it. If the DCF value is less than the purchase price, then value is destroyed. If it is greater, then value is created. Based on this model, economic value is created when the return on capital employed in an acquisition exceeds the target's weighted-average cost of capital.[3] The final valuation will vary depending upon the weighted-average cost of capital, the forecasted cashflows, and the terminal value chosen.[4]

To illustrate this, an example of a privately owned company that is being acquired as part of an industry roll-up is presented. The industry is growing at a modest 2 percent rate and is highly fragmented, with small, privately held companies. There is some overcapacity in the market, prices have been declining, and cost of goods sold is growing annually at a 1 percent rate. Thus, margins have been shrinking. Most of the companies have been around for many years and increasingly have come up for sale. The buyer sees a number of synergies that can be accrued from consolidation and has embarked on an active program to do so.

A DCF model is built from the income statement and elements of the balance sheet (see Part A of Table 2-2). First, beginning with a partial income statement, a five-year pro forma is developed. Critical to the pro forma are forecasts of sales volume and pricing; cost of goods sold; sales, general, and administrative expenses; and profit margins. With the use of the partial balance sheet, a net working capital (i.e., inventory plus receivables minus accounts payable) and an investment pro forma are then developed.

A pro forma is first developed for the target as a stand-alone company, i.e., as an ongoing business without any synergies created through acquisition.[5] Then forecasts are developed for each synergy that is hypothesized. Essentially, a pro forma is developed to reflect the incremental value created by each synergy. The purpose of this exercise is to understand what incremental values are related to the achievement of specific synergies, and ultimately what integration issues are related to the achievement of specific synergies.

Based on the income statement and balance sheet, cashflow statements are then developed. As noted below, cashflow analyses are developed for the stand-alone value and for each potential synergy. The weighted-average cost capital for the target, which is used as the discount factor, is 10 percent based on its capital structure, the cost of its debt, and the cost of its equity.

As can be seen from the DCF analysis in Part B of Table 2-2, the stand-alone value of the company is $35,526,770. Synergy values are derived from a number of sources. The first source is a 5 percent cut in sales, general, and administrative costs through the elimination of duplicate corporate offices and services and some limited pruning in the sales organization. The second is a 3 percent increase in sales due to opportunities to cross-sell products. In particular, the buyer has a number of products that it has developed that can be sold through the target's distribution channels. The third is a price increase of 1 percent through the elimination of some capacity from the marketplace. The last source is a 5 percent cost saving in raw materials through the superior purchasing power of the buyer. As illustrated in Part C of Table 2-2, the total value of the synergies is worth $13,388,540.

From the example presented above, it is clear that the analysis yields a range of values. The values depend upon the assumptions made concerning the drivers of cashflow. For example, in Table 2-2, Part A, it is assumed that sales volume would grow 2 percent; cost of goods would grow 1 percent; sales, general, and administrative expenses would remain at 5 percent of sales; and investment would equal the rate of depreciation. The numbers were derived from historical averages. Clearly, there are numerous ways in which to forecast these numbers. In the stand-alone case, the valuation is based on the target firm as an ongoing concern with no synergies created by the acquirer. In this case, the greatest managerial challenge is to do no harm to the target, sustain the projected cashflows, and thus realize the value that is inherent in the business.

If the buyer can acquire a target for the stand-alone value ($35,526,770) or less, the implementation challenges are fewer. Synergies are not required to create value. However, valuation is subject to the

Table 2-2 Financial Statements, Part A (All numbers reported in $,000)

Partial Pro Forma Income Statement

	Year 0	Year 1	Year 2	Year 3	Year 4	Year 5	
Revenue	$40,000.00	$38,760.00	$39,044.58	$39,330.98	$39,619.19	$39,803.10	
Price	$ 20.00	$ 19.00	$ 18.95	$ 18.90	$ 18.85	$ 18.75	2% growth
Volume	$ 2,000.00	$ 2,040.00	$ 2,060.40	$ 2,081.00	$ 2,101.81	$ 2,122.83	1% growth
Cost of goods sold	$30,000.00	$30,300.00	$30,603.00	$30,909.03	$31,218.12	$31,530.30	
Gross margin	$10,000.00	$ 8,460.00	$ 8,441.58	$ 8,421.95	$ 8,401.07	$ 8,272.80	
Sales, general, administrative costs	$ 2,000.00	$ 1,938.00	$ 1,952.23	$ 1,966.55	$ 1,980.96	$ 1,990.16	5% of revenue
Depreciation	$ 1,000.00	$ 950.00	$ 800.00	$ 600.00	$ 800.00	$ 900.00	
Earnings before interest and taxes	$ 7,000.00	$ 5,572.00	$ 5,689.35	$ 5,855.40	$ 5,620.11	$ 5,382.65	
Interest	$ 1,000.00	$ 958.00	$ 1,011.00	$ 1,032.00	$ 980.00	$ 650.00	
Earnings before taxes	$ 6,000.00	$ 4,614.00	$ 4,678.35	$ 4,823.40	$ 4,640.11	$ 4,732.65	
Taxes @34%	$ 2,040.00	$ 1,568.76	$ 1,590.64	$ 1,639.95	$ 1,577.64	$ 1,609.10	
Net income	$ 3,960.00	$ 3,045.24	$ 3,087.71	$ 3,183.44	$ 3,062.48	$ 3,123.55	

Additional Information

		Year 1	Year 2	Year 3	Year 4	Year 5	
Capital expenditures		$ 950.00	$ 850.00	$ 600.00	$ 800.00	$ 900.00	Equal to depreciation
Changes in net working capital		$ 8.00	$ 3.56	$ 119.63	$ 126.26	$ 133.49	

Partial Pro Forma Balance Sheet

		Year 1	Year 2	Year 3	Year 4	Year 5	
Assets:							
Inventory		$ 5,050.00	$ 5,100.50	$ 5,151.51	$ 5,203.02	$ 5,255.05	
Receivables		$ 1,008.00	$ 1,016.06	$ 1,024.19	$ 1,032.39	$ 1,040.65	
Fixed assets		$10,000.00	$10,050.00	$10,050.00	$10,050.00	$10,050.00	
Total assets		$16,058.00	$16,166.56	$16,225.70	$16,285.41	$16,345.70	
Liabilities and equity:							
Accounts payable		$ 550.00	$ 605.00	$ 665.50	$ 732.05	$ 805.26	

Table 2-2 Financial Statements, Part B (All numbers reported in $,000)

		Stand-Alone Value				
	Year 0	Year 1	Year 2	Year 3	Year 4	Year 5
EBIT	$ 7,000.00	$5,572.00	$5,689.35	$5,855.40	$5,620.11	$5,382.65
Taxes	$ 2,040.00	$1,568.76	$1,590.64	$1,639.95	$1,577.64	$1,609.10
EBI after taxes	$ 3,960.00	$3,045.24	$3,087.71	$3,183.44	$3,062.48	$3,123.55
Depreciation	$ 1,000.00	$ 950.00	$ 800.00	$ 600.00	$ 800.00	$ 900.00
Cashflow from operations	$ 4,960.00	$3,995.24	$3,887.71	$3,783.44	$3,862.48	$4,023.55
Change in net working capital		$ 8.00	$ 3.56	$ 119.63	$ 126.26	$ 133.49
Capital expenditures		$ 950.00	$ 850.00	$ 600.00	$ 800.00	$ 900.00
Free cashflow		$3,037.24	$3,034.15	$3,063.81	$2,936.22	$2,990.05
Free cashflow		$3,037.24	$3,034.15	$3,063.81	$2,936.22	$2,990.05
Terminal value						$42,715.036	$24,097.06
Discount factor =10%						
Present value per year		$2,761.13	$2,507.06	$2,301.19	$2,004.67	$1,855.66
Stand-alone value	$35,526.77					

25

Table 2-2 Financial Statements, Part C (All numbers reported in $,000)

	Year 1	Year 2	Year 3	Year 4	Year 5	Synergy Values
SGA Expenses Cut of 5%						
Incremental EBIT	$ 96.90	$ 97.61	$ 98.33	$ 99.05	$ 99.51	
Taxes	$ 32.95	$ 33.19	$ 33.43	$ 33.68	$ 33.83	
Incremental free cashflow	$ 63.95	$ 64.42	$ 64.90	$ 65.37	$ 65.68	
Terminal value increment						938.2160083
Present value per year	$ 58.14	$ 53.23	$ 48.74	$ 44.63	$ 40.76	$ 529.28
SGA increment total	$ 774.79					
Increase Sales Volume 3%						
Incremental EBIT	$ 60.00	$ 61.20	$ 61.81	$ 62.43	$ 63.05	
Taxes	$ 20.40	$ 20.81	$ 21.02	$ 21.23	$ 21.44	
Incremental free cashflow	$ 39.60	$ 40.39	$ 40.80	$ 41.20	$ 41.62	
Terminal value increment						594.5131142
Present value per year	$ 36.00	$ 33.38	$ 30.64	$ 28.13	$ 25.83	$ 335.39
SGA increment total	$ 489.36					
Increase Prices 1%						
Incremental EBIT	$ 0.20	$ 0.19	$ 0.19	$ 0.19	$ 0.19	
Taxes	$ 0.07	$ 0.06	$ 0.06	$ 0.06	$ 0.06	
Incremental free cashflow	$ 0.13	$ 0.13	$ 0.13	$ 0.12	$ 0.12	
Terminal value increment						1.777285714
Present value per year	$ 0.12	$ 0.10	$ 0.09	$ 0.09	$ 0.08	$ 1.00
SGA increment total	$ 1.48					
Reduce Cost of Goods Sold 5%						
Incremental EBIT	$1,500.00	$1,515.00	$1,530.15	$1,545.45	$1,560.91	
Taxes	$ 510.00	$ 515.10	$ 520.25	$ 525.45	$ 530.71	
Incremental free cashflow	$ 990.00	$ 999.90	$1,009.90	$1,020.00	$1,030.20	
Terminal value increment						14717.11386
Present value per year	$ 900.00	$ 826.20	$ 758.52	$ 696.39	$ 639.35	$ 8,302.44
SGA increment total	$12,122.91					
Total synergy value	$13,388.54					

vagaries of predicting revenues, costs, margins, net working capital, and investments. Once the buyer has to pay above the stand-alone value, the challenge becomes more interesting.

PAYING PREMIUMS AND ACHIEVING SYNERGIES (PRICING AND VALUE)

The real challenge in creating value is to ensure that the price paid for an acquisition does not exceed its value to the buyer. As Figure 2-1 illustrates, there are three key elements to consider. First is the stand-alone value of a target. Second are the synergies that can be accrued from the acquisition. Third is the price a buyer will have to pay to gain control of the target.

If the price (Price 1) is lower than or equal to the stand-alone value (e.g., $35,526,770 in the example), then the buyer is likely to have few difficulties in creating value (unless, of course, the buyer overestimated the stand-alone value, has value leakage, or did not uncover critical hidden liabilities during due diligence that lower future cashflow projections).

If the price (Price 2) paid is higher than the stand-alone value, then the buyer must capture synergies to justify the price. In the example, this

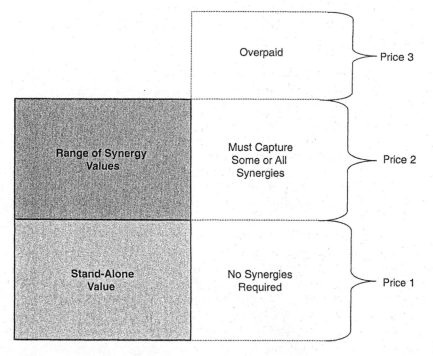

Price Paid for Target

Figure 2-1   Pricing, Synergy, and Value Creation

incremental value of synergies ranges from $1,480,000 to $12,122,910 and totals to $13,388,540. Failure to do so clearly leads to overpaying. Theoretically, the target is worth anywhere from $35,526,770 to $48,915,320. At the high end, all synergies must be captured through effective integration.

As Mark Sirower,[6] a consultant and former professor at New York University found, however, that firms almost always pay a premium (above the stand-alone value) to gain control of a company, and thus have to find synergies. The capture of synergies is not an easy task. Those that can be easily documented and captured immediately are the ones a firm is most likely to realize. These often are immediate and obvious cost reductions. As a buyer has to realize more difficult synergies (e.g., cross-selling among sales organizations or distribution channels), the challenges become greater and the likelihood of success becomes lower. Sirower also noted that for M&As where a premium has been paid, the likelihood that value will be created is lower.

Finally, if the price paid (Price 3) exceeds the combined stand-alone and synergy value that can "reasonably be expected" (e.g., $48,915,320), then the buyer has overpaid. In such cases there is little hope that value can ever be created, unless of course the stand-alone cashflows or synergies that were forecasted were underestimated. Rarely is this the case, especially when a buyer is eager to do a deal.

As consultants Robert Eccles, Kersten Lanes, and Thomas Wilson note, "Ultimately, the key to success in buying another company is knowing the maximum price you can pay and then having the discipline not to pay a penny more."[7]

Now you might be thinking why anyone would do anything so foolish. There are several reasons. First, a buyer may get caught up in a competitive bidding process and just pay too much. This has come to be known as the "winner's curse." The bidder won, but value was lost. That happened in the security monitoring business in the late 1990s. Both SecurityLink from Ameritech and ADT were rolling up this highly fragmented industry. Over time it became clear to sellers that these two companies were eager to do deals. Within one year prices for the targets (based on market multiples of recurring monthly revenues) doubled, without any appreciable increases in the stand-alone values of the firms (i.e., earnings and cashflows). The pressure for synergies just escalated!

Second, many acquisition negotiations create an escalation of momentum. This is a psychological state whereby the buyer has invested time, energy, and resources (e.g., legal, investment banking, and consulting fees). Given these sunk costs, it becomes increasingly more difficult to walk away, even when it might be prudent to do so.[8]

Third, a buyer wants to do a deal because he is convinced of the strategic reasons regardless of what the "numbers say." When this happens, objectivity is dismissed and the numbers are crafted to justify the deal. It is not uncommon in such cases for buyers to adjust forecasts in a DCF model to generate a value that supports the price demanded by a target.

Finally a buyer underestimates the difficulties involved in integrating the firms, and so synergies are never realized. Although many synergies are identified, they cannot be achieved due to problems such as culture clashes, loss of key people, and loss of customers. (A more comprehensive discussion of these issues is presented in Chapters 3 to 8.)

To create value the buyer must be realistic about the synergies that can be realized. Buyers should not pay a premium above the intrinsic and synergy values, and they should develop and implement an integration process to ensure orderly capture of synergies.

Value Creation and the Timing of Cashflows

Of critical importance to valuation models is the timing of the forecasted earnings and cashflows. For example, if certain synergies are forecasted to take place during the first year after the closing but are not realized until the second year, the results can be dramatically different. For instance, in Table 2-2 if the cost of goods sold take an additional year to realize due to integration problems, the value of the synergy drops from $12,122,910 to $11,222,910. This clearly suggests that forecasted synergies are quite sensitive to the realization and timing of synergies, which in turn are dependent upon the management and success of the integration process.

STRATEGIC OBJECTIVES AND POTENTIAL SOURCES OF SYNERGY

Now that the financial objectives underlying M&As have been examined, it is important to focus on strategy. Various strategies represent different potential sources of synergies and the opportunity to realize value. Regardless of how good a strategy may appear, it is dangerous to argue that a deal should be done based on "conceptual definitions" of strategy and synergies alone. The business landscape is lined with many M&As that made conceptual sense, "were made in heaven," and delivered no value. The following comments reported in Eccles, Lanes, and Wilson summarize my key points perfectly:

> Assume that the numbers don't add up, but people in the company still claim there are compelling strategic reasons for doing the deal anyway. What's next? The most disciplined thing to do is walk away.
>
> Doubtless there are deals that should happen for strategic reasons even when the numbers don't sound promising, but they are few and far between.

"We have a rule on the Executive Committee," says Harry
Tempest of ABN AMBRO. "When someone says 'strategic,' the
rest of us say, 'too expensive.'"

This is not to argue that the numbers should drive the decision. The
very specific strategic benefits that a deal delivers and how that translates
at some point into earnings and cashflow must also be taken into consideration.[9] Even if it may take 10 years to realize the benefits of a strategy, an
attempt must be made to quantify and capture it. Although DCF models are
as much art as they are science, they do force managers to articulate their
assumptions about industry and organizational factors that drive cashflows
and earnings. This exercise is often sobering and useful, especially if
attempted with some level of objectivity.

As illustrated below, a number of strategic objectives drive a deal.
Each has the potential to deliver certain synergies. These are key to creating
value—of course, depending upon the price paid!

Sources of Synergy

There are basically four sources of synergy: cost, revenue, market power,
and intangibles. Cost synergies are often the easiest to document and capture in a merger or an acquisition. Revenue, market power, and intangibles,
on the other hand, are increasingly more difficult. Each is described below.

Cost Synergies

Reducing costs is one clear way to increase earnings and cashflows. It has
historically been the most common form of synergy and is often the easiest type to capture. There are two types of cost synergies:

1. Fixed-cost reduction
2. Variable-cost reduction

Fixed-cost reduction is often associated with economies of scope
and scale and productivity. It is also associated with reducing general,
administrative, and sales expenses through headquarters and support
function consolidation; gaining economies of scale in operations, sales
force, and distribution optimization; and reducing transaction costs in
the supply chain. Variable-cost reduction is associated with increased
purchasing power and productivity. Both forms of cost reduction often
come with the physical consolidation of activities between the combining
companies. The synergies that can be accrued here depend very much
on the nature of the cost structure of the business model being employed
by an acquirer.

Cost synergies are present in almost every M&A. They have been central elements behind deals transacted in the banking, pharmaceutical,
automobile, airline, and security monitoring industries, to name just a few.

Revenue Synergies

Revenue synergies are often hoped for but rarely realized in M&As. Typically, revenue synergies are associated with cross-selling products or services through complementary (i.e., nonoverlapping) sales organizations or distribution channels that serve different geographic regions, customer groups, or technologies. A key assumption underlying this source is that complementary markets desire the same products and services.

In addition, revenue synergies can be derived from broadening a company's products and services to provide needed bundling or a more complete offering. Critical to this synergy is to leverage complementarity without adding additional costs. This includes:

1. Increased sales productivity by selling more volume with the same number of or fewer salespeople (this may also create cost synergies)
2. Cross-selling products through complementary sales organizations and distribution channels
3. Reducing fixed new-product development costs by utilizing complementary products (i.e., reducing the per unit cost of each product or service through increased volume)

In the 1999 merger between SBC and Ameritech, revenue synergies were captured. In particular, new products were brought from SBC to Ameritech in the directory services (i.e., Yellow Pages) business. Revenues per employee were increased in the Ameritech organization without any additional new-product development or fixed sales expenses.

Revenue synergy was also a critical element behind the Pharmacia and Upjohn merger, where there was geographic complementarity. Pharmacia had a strong presence in Europe, whereas Upjohn had one in the United States. This provided a potential opportunity to cross-sell products. There were differences in customers served and local regulations, however, that limited the benefits that could be realized.

In the 1998 Travelers and Citicorp merger, complementarity existed in customer groups served and in distribution channels employed. Originally, Travelers' insurance products focused on mature adults, whereas Citigroup's banking products emphasized younger customers.

Hilton Hotels has taken advantage of its worldwide reservation systems to cross-sell room inventory for all the brands it acquires. Hilton has used five U.S. call centers to cross-sell through manual call transferring, accounting for more than $100 million in incremental revenue. The centers have become a leverage point for additional acquisitions.[10]

Of course, revenue synergies assume that sales and distribution channels are capable and motivated to sell complementary products. This, however, is not always the case.

Market Power Synergies

This type of synergy results from the elimination of competitors and capacity from a market. This synergy has been a critical element in many mature market consolidations where there is overcapacity. It allows an acquirer to maintain or increase prices in the market, thereby improving margins. An excellent example of this has been the paper core and core board market in Northern Europe. With the market fraught with overcapacity, prices declined in the late 1990s. Through consolidation, capacity could be taken out of the market and competitors eliminated. The net result was increased market power, prices, and margins for the remaining players.

Intangible Synergies

This type of synergy is the most difficult to achieve. It does not easily lend itself to quantification. Intangibles include brand name extensions and the sharing of knowledge and know-how. Rarely do they accrue through the physical consolidation of activities. They rely on the ability to transfer the intangible capabilities of one firm to the other.

This source of synergy was the basis of many acquisitions made by the French company LaFarge, one of the largest cement and concrete manufacturers in the world. In its acquisitions, little opportunity for physical consolidation and economies of scale in operations existed since cement manufacturing is highly localized and decentralized due to transportation costs. What their acquisitions did, however, was to provide excellent opportunities for the transfer of best practices to improve the operations of each manufacturing facility acquired.

Negative Synergy

All the types of synergies described above focus on the creation of value. However, it is important to note that M&As are interventions in organizations that can create disruptions that destroy the intrinsic value of a firm. We call this *value leakage* or *negative synergy*. Thus, while it is critical to manage for positive synergies, it is also important to manage against negative synergies by developing a value preservation plan.

This was an issue, for example, in the sale of a privately held company in California (i.e., the target) that manufactured and sold fans for cooling the chips in personal computers. The target was sought by a Japanese company that wanted access to the U.S. market. Upon examination of the target's balance sheet, it was clear that the price being asked for the target was far greater than its tangible assets. The value provided by the target was its ability to generate cashflows through its extensive distribution network and design and engineering capability. Inability to maintain these, especially during due diligence, would have led to a leakage of value. This was especially critical since key employees and distributors were concerned about the impact of dealing with a large Japanese owner. In fact, the loss of one key distributor may have represented a loss of 10 percent of sales volume, without any clear alternative for regaining it. To combat this, a value preservation plan that included communications and incentives was put into place.

Rarely in a merger or an acquisition is only one form of synergy present or sought. Depending on the particular deal, the number and importance of possible synergies will vary. Moreover, the realization of each form of synergy cannot be assumed. The integration process must be managed with the achievement of each synergy in mind.

ASPECTS OF INTEGRATION

At this point it is necessary to take a closer look at the concept of integration. All too often integration is viewed as a simple concept that implies two organizations are either integrated or left autonomous.[11] In practice the term *integration* is not that simple. It has different meanings, and therefore different implications for how two firms might be combined. There are four primary dimensions of integration. These are:

1. *Consolidation*. The extent to which the separate functions and activities of both the acquirer and the target firms are physically consolidated into one.
2. *Standardization*. The extent to which the separate functions and activities of both firms are standardized and formalized, but not physically consolidated (e.g., separate operations may be maintained, but the operations are made identical). This is typical when acquirers formally transfer best practices across firms.
3. *Coordination*. The extent to which the functions and activities of both firms are coordinated (e.g., one firm's products are sold through the other firm's distribution channels).
4. *Intervention*. The extent to which interventions are made in the acquired firm to turn around poor operating profits and cashflow, regardless of any inherent sources of synergy value (e.g., change management, drop unprofitable products).

STRATEGIC OBJECTIVES, SYNERGIES, AND INTEGRATION: PUTTING IT TOGETHER

Based on the discussion above, it is important to understand how the strategic objectives driving a merger or an acquisition are related to the achievement of synergies and thus the different dimensions of integration. Simply put, different strategies result in different sets of potential synergies and require different dimensions of integration. Presented below are a series of strategic objectives and the synergies underlying them. Also discussed are some of the integration implications associated with achieving these synergies. It is important to note that an acquirer may be seeking multiple strategies and synergies in a particular merger or acquisition. More will be said about this later.

Consolidate Market within a Geographic Area

When this objective is employed, the basic goal is to acquire competitors in the same geographic market. Depending upon the nature of the market, it may include a region within a country, a country itself, a continent, or the globe.

For example, this was the strategy employed by a major U.S. paper manufacturer in Northern Europe. The market was fragmented with many small, privately owned companies and suffered from overcapacity and high fixed costs. As a result, prices were crashing. In a high-fixed-cost business, volume is critical to success.

Consequently, the company began a process of consolidation through acquisition. The objectives were to take capacity out of the market by closing inefficient plants, eliminate redundant sales organizations, reduce general and administrative overhead, increase power vis-à-vis suppliers and customers, and utilize complementary products. The net results were better gross profit margins through higher prices and reduced raw material costs, lower fixed costs through elimination of redundancy, better capacity utilization through increased market share, and thus better return on net assets (i.e., return on capital employed).[12]

On a global level, consolidation has been a driving force in the auto industry. Due to overcapacity, many of the auto companies have made acquisitions, not only to broaden product lines, but also to eliminate capacity and increase economies of scale from manufacturing, product development, and distribution. They have also attempted to reduce general and administrative overhead and increase purchasing power through transactions with suppliers. This has been an objective behind many of the banking and security monitoring M&As that have taken place as well.

The potential sources of synergy in this strategic objective thus include:

- Lower variable costs of raw materials through increased purchasing power
- Lower fixed costs through the elimination of redundant functions, e.g., corporate staff, information technology, sales staff
- Lower fixed costs through better utilization of fixed assets, i.e., economies of scale
- Higher prices through elimination of capacity from the marketplace
- Economies of scope in the sales organization through sharing of products and services developed by each organization

Market consolidation requires high levels of organizational consolidation, standardization, and coordination. This means that:

- Most, if not all, organizational functions and activities will be consolidated and standardized.
- High levels of redundancy of management and employees exist, and reduction in force will likely take place at all organizational levels. Retention of key people in nonconsolidated areas, or highly competent people in general, may be important.
- Differences in organizational culture, identity, and management practices between the acquirer and the target will have to be resolved.
- Differences in strategy, policies, operations, brand names, etc., will have to be resolved.

Extend or Add Products, Services, and Technologies

Typically, opportunities exist to increase competitive capabilities in the marketplace by acquiring new products and services, skills and technology, and access to complementary distribution (if products or services utilize different distribution channels).

This strategy has been a primary driver of many companies in telecommunications equipment manufacturing. For example, Cisco, Alcatel, and Lucent have used acquisitions to expand their technological capabilities and products in Internet protocol and optronics (e.g., optical switching). In industries where numerous start-up firms are developing new technologies, acquisition is often a relied-upon vehicle utilized by larger players in the market. On the telecommunication-provider side, AT&T has relied upon acquisitions to enter both the wireless and cable businesses. Where companies are seeking bundling (i.e., providing a full range of products and services to customers), acquisition remains an important tool.

The elimination of the Glass-Steagall Act has led also to large consolidation in financial services. Today many commercial banks are merging with insurance companies and investment banks. Such mergers eliminate many backroom fixed costs and provide bundled products and services that allow both cross-selling opportunities and "one-stop shopping" for customers.

This strategy has also been employed by many consumer goods companies that have sought to round out their product offerings and by pharmaceutical companies that have attempted to improve their pipeline of new products.

The potential sources of synergy in this strategic objective thus include:

- Lower variable costs through increased purchasing power, where acquired products and services utilize the same basic raw materials

- Lower fixed costs through elimination of redundant functions, e.g., corporate staff, human resources, and information technology
- Lower fixed costs through better utilization of fixed assets (i.e., economies of scale) where products share basic platforms
- Lower fixed costs through better utilization of fixed investments such as advertising and brand development, i.e., economies of scope
- Increased revenue through sharing of products and services developed by each organization
- Increased market share (i.e., volume and revenue) by providing a more competitive lineup of products and services

Extension requires moderate levels of organizational consolidation and standardization and high levels of coordination. This means that:

- Some functions and activities, especially with respect to general and administrative overhead (e.g., MIS, accounting, human resources, and sales), may be consolidated and standardized. Operations may be consolidated and standardized depending upon the extent to which new products and services can be provided within the existing operating infrastructure.
- Redundancy of management and employees and reduction in force will likely take place in those areas being consolidated. Retention of key people in nonconsolidated areas, or highly competent people in general, is important. This may especially be the case where the value of the target is largely tied up in intangible assets such as people.
- High levels of coordination may be required across organizations and sales forces if cross-selling is required.
- Differences in organizational culture, identity, and management practices between the acquirer and the target will have to be resolved.
- Differences in strategy, policies, operations, brand names, etc., will have to be resolved.

Enter a New Geographic Market

In this case, the objective is to extend the business into geographic areas where the firm has had no presence. Typically, this objective is employed by firms that are rolling up a fragmented industry and by firms that are taking advantage of market deregulation and liberalization.

In roll-ups the market is highly fragmented and characterized by numerous small firms with very small market shares. Usually, one or several firms see an opportunity to grow revenues and profitability. Often roll-ups begin by consolidation within a geographic area and then by geographic extension. This has clearly been the case in the banking industry. Nations Bank, for example, first began rolling up retail banks within state (e.g., North Carolina) and then across states (e.g., Florida, Missouri). Today, it is found across regions of the United States (through its merger with Bank of America). In this example there was an excellent opportunity to consolidate the fixed costs associated with information technology and backroom activities and to expand geographic presence.

Geographic expansion has also been behind the acquisitions driving the security monitoring business within the United States. Historically, the security monitoring industry was made up of many small, privately held firms that provided basic services within a specific geographic area (e.g., a city). The typical firm provided sales, installation, customer service, and security monitoring. Two large players, ADT and SecurityLink from Ameritech, saw an opportunity to consolidate this market and grow on a national level. Not only could they expand their geographic reach, but they could also significantly improve profitability. First, there was an excellent opportunity to better manage fixed cost. Many of the small firms had their own security monitoring call centers. In general, they were not very efficient. By acquiring enough firms the large players could build a nationally scaled centralized monitoring center. They could much more effectively amortize the costs of the center by acquiring volume than the small firms could. The same opportunity existed for support functions such as payroll, accounting, and sales and billing systems. They could also transfer the knowledge they accrued to bring best practices to the geographically decentralized sales, installation, and customer service organizations. The net result was growth and improved profitability.

This strategy was also employed in the hospital management industry. Columbia/HCA, for example, acquired numerous hospitals throughout the United States. In doing so, it was also able to reduce fixed costs throughout many administrative functions. It was also able to reduce variable costs through increased power over hospital supply companies. It was a lot different negotiating for 300 hospitals than for just 1 or 2.

Market deregulation and liberalization have influenced numerous industries. Essentially the regulatory changes have opened previously closed markets. An excellent example is the telecommunications industry. In an attempt to grow beyond their regulated markets, many U.S. telecoms began making acquisitions (and taking equity interests) in international companies. All these opportunities were driven by host governments' privatizing previously owned government utilities. Some acquirers took portfolio positions (i.e., purely investment positions), whereas others brought technology and knowledge to the target to improve operations and profitability. Many of these acquisitions were purely opportunistic with few synergies present. The acquirers were responding to privatization opportunities. In the future, however, as the industry globalizes, the game may change. For example, serving the needs of international business customers will mean that many providers such as Verizon, MCI Worldcom, and AT&T will have to provide seamless data service throughout the major markets in the world. This will require strategic acquisitions in key countries and integrated operations to achieve that kind of service.

Geographic expansion has been a critical competitive issue in the mobile telephone business as well. Several years ago a mobile telephone provider could survive by serving a small regional area. Today, survival requires that it be able to serve the entire United States without roaming and long distance charges. In the future, as technological standards are harmonized, the market may likely be the globe! It is unlikely that geographic reach will be achieved through organic growth. It will require mergers, acquisitions, joint ventures, and alliances.

The potential sources of synergy in this strategic objective thus include:

- Lower variable costs through increased purchasing power, where acquired products and services utilize the same basic raw materials. This will now be accomplished on a larger geographic scope than before.
- Lower fixed costs through the elimination of redundant functions, e.g., corporate staff, human resources, and information technology.
- Lower fixed costs through better utilization of fixed investments such as advertising and brand development over a broader geographic scope.
- Increased revenue through sharing of products and services developed by each organization.
- Increased sales volume through geographic expansion.
- Increased competitiveness by being better able to serve customers with needs for broader geographic coverage.

Market entry requires low levels of organizational consolidation where there is little geographic overlap, but may require high levels of standardization and coordination. This, however, is dependent upon the extent to which the firms can take advantage of doing things the same way across geographic markets. If each market is relatively independent due to strong pressures for localization, there may be few if any opportunities for synergies. If markets are interconnected in some fashion, synergistic opportunities increase dramatically. Certainly standard products across markets would lead to significant efficiencies in new-product development and operations, as well as development of a standard for a best practice.

This means that:

- Very few functions and activities will be consolidated. Some aspects of general and administrative overhead (e.g., MIS, accounting, human resources, sales) may be consolidated and standardized.
- Operations will not be consolidated, depending upon the economics of the business. They may, however, be standardized to the extent that one basic approach (e.g., best practice) for providing the product or service across all markets makes sense.
- High levels of consolidation and standardization within new markets (e.g., as in market consolidation) may take place if geographic entry is the first step in a regional market concentration strategy.

- Redundancy of management and employees and reduction in force will likely take place in those areas being consolidated. Retention of key people in nonconsolidated areas, or highly competent people in general, may be important. In geographic expansion, retention of people is important in nonredundant areas since acquirers neither have the internal talents available to staff the new operation nor have "deep knowledge" of the local area.
- High levels of coordination may be required across organizations and sales forces if cross-selling is required.
- Differences in organizational culture, identity, and management practices between the acquirer and the target will have to be resolved unless each geographic area is different.
- Differences in strategy, policies, operations, brand names, etc., will have to be resolved, depending upon the degree of standardization.

Vertically Integrate

In this case, the objective is to enter into either sources of supply or distribution. Such moves are made to increase value added into the business or gain control over more aspects of the business. Vertical integration requires very low levels of organizational consolidation and standardization but high levels of coordination. Companies such as Home Depot have acquired lighting, heating, and plumbing companies to better control sources of supply.

The acquisition of Medco by Merck is another excellent illustration. Merck, a traditional pharmaceutical company, acquired Medco, a distribution intermediary (i.e., pharmacy benefit manager). Medco represented third-party payers and self-insured companies that were trying to lower the cost of ethical drugs. The acquisition gave Merck access to Medco's mail-order business and patient treatment database. The latter allowed Merck to better understand the effectiveness of treatments and to guide product development. The former gave Merck access to an emerging distribution channel for chronic-care drugs, thus increasing the market share.

The acquisition of Citgo by PDVSA, the Venezuelan oil company, was also driven by vertical integration. PDVSA was looking for a source of refining and distribution for its heavy crude oil. Not comfortable with long-term contracts, it decided to acquire the downstream activities of Citgo.

Vertical integration is also the key element in the America Online (AOL) and Time Warner merger. It melds the content of Time Warner (e.g., entertainment, news) with the Internet distribution power of AOL.

The potential sources of synergy in this strategic objective thus include:

- Lower variable costs of raw materials through control over raw materials and value added retained within the new company. Accounting for the costs will depend on the transfer pricing agreements established within the new company.

- Lower overall costs through improved product development and manufacturing interfaces.
- Lower fixed costs through the elimination of redundant functions, e.g., corporate staff, information technology, sales staff. Costs associated with managing the new vertical relationship internally will replace costs of managing the external relationship (e.g., purchasing function).

This means that:

- No functions and activities will be consolidated, with the exception of cash management, treasury functions, and financial statements. Moreover, the senior management of the target will likely report into the acquirer's structure.
- Operations will be neither consolidated nor standardized.
- Key interrelationships will be established, as the new acquisition will support existing parts of the business.
- Redundancy of management and employees and reduction in force are not likely although some key people in the target may leave or be replaced. Retention of key people is important.
- Differences in organizational culture, identity, and management practices between the acquirer and the target will not be an issue unless there are certain aspects of the target firm the acquirer cannot live with.
- Differences in strategy and brand names will have to be resolved.

Enter a New Line of Business

In this case, the objective is to enter businesses where the acquirer has little or no previous experience. Typically, opportunities exist to grow revenues, add distribution, add new products and services, acquire new technologies, and acquire new management talent with different perspectives.

This strategy was used by conglomerates during the 1960s and 1970s. The objective was to diversify away from a company's core business due to limits to growth in the core business, antitrust challenges, and the desire to find opportunities with uncorrelated cashflows. The latter strategy was designed to lower the business's risk and thus cost of capital. Many conglomerates, however, never delivered value to shareholders. Unfortunately, it proved easier for investors to diversify their own personal investment portfolios than for companies to do so. There are a few exceptions, such as Berkshire Hathaway and General Electric, which have made numerous successful acquisitions.

The potential sources of synergy in this strategic objective thus include:

- Lower fixed costs through the elimination of a few redundant functions, e.g., corporate staff, information technology, sales staff
- Lower cost of capital for a combined firm by reducing firm risk through diversification

- Intangibles such as a broader pool of available management talent and business know-how

This means that:

- No functions or activities will be consolidated, with the exception of cash management, treasury functions, and financial statements. Typically, the acquired company will:
    1. Either operate as a division of the acquirer, whereby the senior management of the target will report into the acquirer's structure
    2. Or be a wholly-owned subsidiary whereby the acquirer controls the target through board representation
- Operations will be neither consolidated nor standardized because there are no sources of operational synergy (e.g., operational cost reductions or cross-selling opportunities).
- High levels of consolidation and standardization may take place in subsequent acquisitions in the new line of business if the initial acquisition is a platform for further market concentration, e.g., as in the case of General Electric and Tyco International.
- Redundancy of management and employees are not likely, although some key people in the target may leave or be replaced. Retention of key people is important since the acquirer rarely has its own people to transfer to the target.
- Differences in organizational culture, identity, and management practices between the acquirer and the target will not be an issue unless there are certain aspects of the target firm the acquirer cannot live with. Differences between the senior management teams may be an issue.
- Differences in strategy and brand names will not likely be an issue.

Table 2-3 summarizes the five types of strategic objectives and the synergies possible within each type. Each box presents the level of synergistic benefits for each strategic objective. Table 2-4 shows the level and type of integration that each objective is likely to require. Each box in this table presents the level of integration required.

WHEN MULTIPLE STRATEGIC OBJECTIVES ARE BEING PURSUED

The discussion of strategic objectives above is somewhat simplified in that more than one objective may be present in a particular merger or acquisition. Much of this will depend upon the scale and nature of the merger or acquisition. In the case of a small acquisition, a single objective and limited synergies may be all that are sought. In a mega-merger such

Table 2-3   Linking Strategic Objectives and Synergies

	Strategic Objective				
Type of Synergy	Consolidate within a Geographic Area	Extend or Add New Product or Service	Enter a New Geographic Market	Vertically Integrate	Enter a New Line of Business
Cost	High	Low	Low	Moderate	Low
Revenue	Low	High	High	Low	None
Market Power	High	Moderate	Low	High	None
Intangible	Moderate	Moderate	Moderate	Low	Low

Table 2-4   Strategic Objectives and Impact on Integration

	Level and Type of Integration		
Strategic Objective	**Consolidation**	**Standardization**	**Coordination**
Consolidate within a Geographic Area	High	High	High
Extend or Add New Product or Service	Moderate	Moderate	High
Enter a New Geographic Market	Low	Low to High	Low to High
Vertically Integrate	Low	Low	High
Enter a New Line of Business	Low	Low	Low

as in the case of Daimler-Benz and Chrysler, or AOL and Time Warner, multiple objectives and synergies are critical to the success of the deal. Obviously, in the latter case the nature and depth of the integration will be far more complicated and difficult to manage.

For example, in the acquisition of Chrysler by Daimler-Benz, multiple objectives and sources of synergy were hoped for. Objectives included market consolidation, geographic expansion, and extension of new products and technologies. Synergies included fixed- and variable-cost reduction, cross-selling of products, increased market power, and intangibles. The synergies from the deal five years out were expected to be $3 billion, with $1.4 billion in cost savings in the first year. This would be derived from several sources. First, savings would include reductions in general and administrative overhead, lower raw material cost (both companies combined purchase roughly $60 billion in materials from outside suppliers), lower advertising overhead, and more efficient utilization of R&D.

Second, it was envisioned that economies of scale could be achieved in components such as engines, transmissions, and car platforms, all of which consumers do not directly associate with the brand of their cars. Third, some opportunities for cross-selling were also envisioned since over 90 percent of Chrysler's sales came from the United States and over 60 percent of Daimler's sales came from Europe. Moreover, neither company had product offerings in the same segments (i.e., price points and car types). Fourth, sharing of technological know-how could be achieved. Daimler would bring airbag technology, ABS braking systems, an electronic stabilization program, and fuel cell development, among other technologies. It would also bring quality and durability know-how. Chrysler would contribute computer design technology that reduced development time and costs, and lean manufacturing that reduced development and manufacturing times and costs. On paper, this was another "marriage made in heaven." From a financial perspective, the deal was viewed as a great deal for Daimler. It purchased an undervalued company in Chrysler (U.S. auto stocks were depressed) using its own stock, which was flying high prior to the merger.

Although nice in theory, the success of these strategies, synergies, and improvement in profits and cashflow would depend upon whether they could be implemented in practice. As a worst-case scenario, Daimler had to preserve the stand-alone value of Chrysler. At best, it needed to secure synergies to improve the overall capabilities of both firms. Initially the deal proved to be a good deal for Daimler shareholders, especially with respect to EPS. Over time, this has been questioned. The preservation of Chrysler and the achievement of many synergies have been more challenging. The many cultural conflicts and problems between the management of both companies have been well documented.

RECENT PERFORMANCE HISTORY OF THE TARGET

It is vital to get a fix on the recent financial performance history (e.g., the last three years) of a target and the causes of that performance (e.g., management decisions, operating measures, market trends) before you can understand the nature of the integration effort. Such an assessment will enable you to determine the depth (e.g., replace management, change operating procedures, introduce new technology) and speed of interventions required by the acquirer in the target firm to ensure that projected earnings and cashflows materialize as predicted. These interventions are essential regardless of the synergies being sought.

If the target has been performing well, and is projected to continue to do so, little intervention may be required. If, however, the target is in need of a dramatic turnaround, significant intervention will be required.

PUTTING IT ALL TOGETHER

In this chapter the importance of valuation, pricing, and synergy in driving the integration process and the relationship among these elements in creating value was examined. These relationships are depicted in Figure 2-2. Throughout the remainder of this book, I address the activities that need to be managed during the transaction, transition, and integration stages to ensure that integration is effectively managed, value is preserved, and synergies are realized. When applicable, I describe how the activities may need to be managed differently depending upon the strategic and financial objectives outlined above.

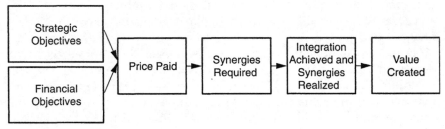

Figure 2-2   Key Relationships in Value Creation

3

LAYING THE GROUNDWORK: MANAGING THE TRANSACTION STAGE

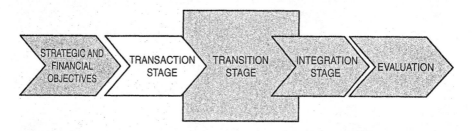

STRATEGIC AND FINANCIAL OBJECTIVES › TRANSACTION STAGE › TRANSITION STAGE › INTEGRATION STAGE › EVALUATION

Integration should begin long before the closing. In fact, it should begin during the transaction stage when negotiations are taking place, due diligence is being conducted, and valuations are being performed. Since information is the lifeblood of sound decisions, gathering the right information at this stage can be invaluable. The objective of due diligence is to acquire factual information that helps the buyer understand:

1. The assets and liabilities of the target, both on and off the balance sheet
2. The sources of revenues, costs, and profits
3. Those factors that will either facilitate or hinder the successful integration of the target

From this information, decisions need to be made concerning whether to walk away from a deal, what price to pay for a target, and what issues need to be managed to ensure successful integration. Typically, due diligence focuses on items 1 and 2 above, with a heavy concentration on issues that can be quantified. They are often the domain of the legal and financial organizations and have been discussed in depth elsewhere.[1] Rarely are the "soft issues" that affect integration deeply examined. Rarely do they serve as "deal killers" when they should. Often, however, they do determine after the closing whether integration succeeded; if earnings, cashflows, and synergies were achieved; and whether value was created. The soft issues are often the top reasons why synergies are not achieved.

This chapter and Chapter 4 will focus on four integration objectives and activities that are paramount during the transaction stage. These are presented in Table 3-1.

In this chapter three primary activities are discussed. The first activity focuses on organizing for information gathering. The second addresses an often neglected but pivotal area of analysis, cultural assessment. The third concentrates on the behaviors of those individuals who come in contact with the target organization and negotiate deals. This early contact sets the stage for the ensuing relationship that forms between the acquirer and the target. The last activity, which is the focus of Chapter 4, deals with an area that has often determined the success of a merger or an acquisition, assessment of key target people.

ORGANIZING FOR INFORMATION GATHERING AND ANALYSIS (DUE DILIGENCE)

Efficiently and quickly gathering and analyzing useful information about a target as early as possible, but prior to the closing, is essential to the integration process. In particular, learning about similarities and differences between the acquirer and a target and their implications is pivotal. Therefore, an organized, systematic process for doing so must be created.

Table 3-1 Transaction Stage

Objectives
1. Gather and analyze information to learn as much as possible about a target
2. Negotiate the right price
3. Create a constructive environment for successful integration, and preserve the value of both the acquirer and the target
4. Anticipate roadblocks that need to be managed for effective integration

Activities
1. Organize for information gathering and analysis
2. Assess the culture of the target
3. Guide the behaviors and attitudes of negotiators, due diligence teams, and deal makers
4. Assess key target people

This includes (1) choosing someone to lead this effort and (2) creating and developing able and ready due diligence teams.

Companies vary on the sophistication of the due diligence effort, often depending upon their acquisition experience, the volume of deals they do, and their involvement with outside experts. An organized effort can be very important, especially when time or access to a target is limited.

The importance of an organized effort is exemplified in the due diligence efforts of a major U.S. telecommunications company that took a stake in a privatized European telephone company. The company was given one-week access to a data room to examine information that was made available. The company was not an experienced acquirer and had to quickly identify and assemble the resources it needed. Since there were multiple businesses interested in the European operation, the selling company had the power in the deal and controlled the due diligence process. To complete the activity effectively and efficiently, the U.S. company needed to:

- Identify the due diligence skill sets needed.
- Choose a team leader.
- Identify the people who possessed the skills sets.
- Brief the people on the target and country, on the local culture, and on the business environment.
- Provide people with the checklists and tools to conduct analyses.
- Ensure that the team members worked together.

Several elements ensure a successful due diligence effort. These include choosing a champion, creating a team of experts, and making the right assessments. Each of these is discussed in more detail below.

Choosing a Champion: Leading the Effort

One of the major challenges during due diligence, and throughout the integration effort, is fragmentation.[2] Many experts are involved in gathering and analyzing information. They may come from different functional areas, corporate staff, business units, and geographic areas. In their quest to quickly finish their jobs, there is a risk that there is little communication and coordination among them. Sometimes there may be competition among them as they seek to control the process. This can be problematic since among due diligence team members there is a need to share information. Sharing helps identify consistencies and inconsistencies in information and conclusions. This is the objective of due diligence. Moreover, it is essential that the information gathered and conclusions reached during due diligence are passed on to those who are responsible for integration planning and implementation. Often, this does not happen, and essential insights gained early in the M&A process are lost.

To avoid fragmentation it is best to assign a "champion" (e.g., an executive) with ongoing responsibility for overseeing and leading the M&A process through the transaction, transition, and integration stages.

Since not all M&As are alike, the role of the champion needs to vary. In the case of a mega-merger it is likely to be a CEO or a direct report that will have responsibility for the overall merger. It is not uncommon for the chief financial officer to assume this role. For a company that is acquiring multiple smaller companies, for example as part of a roll-up, the champion will have responsibility for the overall M&A process, involving multiple acquisitions. Depending upon the number of deals being transacted, different individuals, who report to the champion, may have responsibility for each deal.

The Champion ensures that:

1. A leader of the due diligence team is chosen for each acquisition, where multiple deals are being done.
2. A core due diligence team is available and able at any time to execute the activities necessary during the transaction stage.
3. Transition and integration teams are ready and available during the transition stage (see the discussion on integration transition structure in Chapter 6).
4. Continuity and communication among due diligence, transition, and integration teams takes place.

Creating and Building the Due Diligence Team

Based on the experience of a number of successful acquirers, I have identified 10 steps that characterize a well-functioning due diligence team.

1. Identify and recruit a limited number of the acquirer's people who are most knowledgeable in areas of the business to be analyzed and who have good project management skills to serve as project leaders.

On the basis of breadth of knowledge, skills required, and availability, a dedicated pool of people should be drawn from both inside and outside the organization. This does not mean that these people will be permanently assigned to due diligence activities, but that they are part of a network of people who are ready when needed. How often they are utilized will be a function of the level of M&A activity.

This pool includes people with financial, legal, sales, marketing, operational, R&D, and human resources skills, among others. The pool should involve more than one person for each area investigated in case one person is not enough or is not available. Temporary replacements for these individuals in their normal job should be identified if due diligence activities demand too much of their time. The decision to include people should be balanced with the need to maintain the secrecy of M&A negotiations and deals.

Where needed, outside experts and consultants should be utilized. In a recent study of international deals, a colleague and I found that outside experts were critical to success in acquisitions when a company was making an acquisition in a new country.[3]

2. **Train the team members to:**
   a. Work together effectively and efficiently (through the use of team building).
   b. Identify the specific issues to be investigated and the questions they need to ask (i.e., develop and use a due diligence checklist).
   c. Identify the type of information they need and the source of that information.
   d. Secure the information.
   e. Operate in a sensitive and confidential situation.
   f. Present their findings to decision makers in an interpretable format.

3. **Assemble the team quickly when a potential target becomes serious.** Team members will be responsible for particular areas of investigation and, depending upon the size of the acquisition and the magnitude of issues to be examined, may serve as project leaders who manage subteams of other people. For example, an assessment of a target's human resources practices may require a team of experts who understand compensation, benefits, leadership development, performance management, and legal compliance.

4. **Use dedicated project leaders and team members throughout the duration of the due diligence effort, even though the tendency is not to do so. If necessary, team members may be used on an as-needed basis.**

5. **Co-locate the team in a secure facility when feasible and desirable, either in corporate headquarters or offsite if proximity to a target is critical.**

6. **Brief (to the extent confidentiality allows) the team and leader on as many of the strategic and financial considerations surrounding the acquisition as possible.** This provides them with the needed background to intelligently identify and examine the issues critical to integration.

7. **Organize the following after the briefing:**
   a. Develop and circulate a directory of all team members and how they can be reached at any time since communication among members is critical to validating information secured.
   b. Choose a standard software package for reports (e.g., Microsoft Word), presentations (e.g., PowerPoint), and data analysis (e.g., Excel) to ensure a smooth integration of information gathered.
   c. Organize and manage communications among team members.
   d. Make a presentation of team findings to deal makers and negotiators.

 e. Centrally locate and maintain an indexed library of critical documents, reports, and presentations at the team's work site to ensure quick and easy access.
 f. Schedule meetings among team members.
 g. Use a project management framework for the team to:
  i. Identify deliverables.
  ii. Clarify working parameters.
  iii. Define activities to be performed.
  iv. Set time frames and milestones.
  v. Assign accountability for major activities.
  vi. Define resources (e.g., people, financial) needed to support the activity.
  vii. Monitor progress and take corrective actions.

8. Develop a strategy as a team for how to approach the target. It is critical to remember that once an acquirer's personnel "enter" the target, a signal is sent as to the acquirer's culture and attitude. Invariably, the target's management and employees will react (either positively or negatively) to this. Due diligence team members should be as unobtrusive and respectful of target people as possible while ensuring that necessary information is collected.

9. Meet as a team as needed—but no less than once a week—to report findings, share and validate insights, and deal with any interrelationships among team members.

10. Keep a select number of people from the team together through the transition stage to ensure continuity of knowledge and relationships with a target's people. This is a crucial element in successful integration.

ASSESSING THE CULTURE OF THE TARGET

Abitibi Consolidated Sales Corporation, the U.S. subsidiary of Abitibi-Price of Canada, understands the important of cultural analysis during the transaction and transition stages. This largest producer of newsprint in the world attempts to gather cultural information from a target as soon as it can when making an acquisition. At the early stages of an acquisition, the company will simply attempt to observe a target from afar, noting cultural artifacts such as how the employees dress and answer the phone. As the company progresses into due diligence, it will attempt a full cultural assessment, including interviews with and surveys of target employees. In its merger with Stone-Consolidated, Abitibi Consolidated got the 20 people in both companies considered critical to the success of the merger together in an off-site meeting to analyze and discuss their cultures and aspirations for the new organization.

Before Compaq acquired both Digital Equipment and Tandem Corporations, its HR teams analyzed the cultures of both companies from afar. This gave Compaq key insights into the challenges it would face and the interventions to employ to successfully merge the combined companies. It also allowed Compaq to move quickly once the deals closed.

Southwest Airlines undertook a comprehensive cultural due diligence prior to its acquisition of Morris Air, a smaller entrepreneurial firm. Using cultural information, Southwest carefully managed the integration, which resulted in a profitable outcome. In contrast, USAir's lack of cultural assessment and awareness and its autocratic methods in its acquisition of Piedmont Aviation caused years of cultural warfare.

Despite some solid examples of success in cultural due diligence, the cultural fit between an acquirer and a target is one of the most neglected areas of analysis prior to the closing of a deal. Often culture is considered too soft and fuzzy. It does not have the precision of financial analyses or the excitement of potential synergies. Moreover, it is typically within the domain of the human resources organization, which is often not invited into the M&A process before the closing—perhaps with the exception of conducting analyses of benefits and compensation costs.

Although many definitions of culture exist, most experts agree that it characterizes the basic values, beliefs, and assumptions that members of an organization hold.[4] In many organizations, especially small and successful ones, culture can be very powerful in shaping how people think and behave and has been shown to have a direct impact on an organization's growth and profitability.[5]

In essence, cultural analysis is pivotal for two reasons. First, cultural differences may be so extreme that they can impede successful integration, thwart the achievement of synergies, and thereby lead to poor financial results.[6] When faced with an acquisition, a target's managers and employees become much more aware of their culture, especially if it is different from that of the acquirer. In such cases, the potential for "culture clashes" and dysfunctional conflict between the acquirer and the target increases greatly.

Second, understanding cultural differences early in the acquisition process serves to identify critical issues that will need to be managed to ensure a successful integration. Rather than wait for these issues to emerge after the closing, warranting a crisis management response, early understanding can ensure that such issues are managed from day one. In Chapter 8 interventions for facilitating cultural integration are examined.

The assessment of cultural differences is somewhat complex, with a variety of methodologies available for doing so. In this section I elaborate upon some of them and demonstrate how they can be used to facilitate the integration process.

The primary responsibility for assessing culture should lie with a human resources or organizational development expert or outside consultant knowledgeable of this area. This person should become a member of the due diligence team. With input from others, this person conducts the assessments, interprets the results, and determines the implications of the results.

There are several important steps in assessing the impact of culture on a merger or an acquisition. These include determining:

1. How important culture is to a particular acquisition
2. How similar and different the buyer's and target's cultures are
3. What impact such similarities and differences might have on the success of integration and synergy realization
4. What interventions should be employed during integration to capitalize on similarities and deal with differences

To that end, the remainder of this section is dedicated to making such assessments and increasing the probability of integration success. The relationship among the steps is presented in Figure 3-1 and discussed below.

Step 1   Determine the Importance of Culture

Although cultures may be different, some differences may not be important. To determine importance three questions need to be asked:

1. To what extent is the target going to be integrated? If little or no integration is planned based on the financial and strategic objectives presented in Chapter 2, then the impact of cultural differences is less likely to be an impediment. Impact will be felt the most in areas and activities that are being integrated and by executives after a deal is closed. Regardless of the strategic objectives underlying an acquisition, executives of a target will have to report somewhere into the acquirer's organization and conform to certain ways of doing things.
2. To what extent are interventions in the target planned? Similar to the question above, if no interventions such as productivity improvements are planned, then the impact of cultural differences is likely to

Figure 3-1 Steps in Assessing the Target's Culture

be minimal. To the extent that the performance of the target is inadequate, intervention will likely increase and cultural differences will have greater impact. For example, a buyer may decide to put a greater focus on accountability in the target than has existed in the past.

3. How tolerant is the acquirer of cultural differences? Regardless of strategic considerations, the acquirer simply needs to ask itself the extent to which it will allow a target to be different. Such differences may be critical to the success of an acquisition, especially if it is in new lines of businesses. Nowhere is this more important than when a large company acquires an entrepreneurial company or enters into a new country or region. Moreover, a target may bring valuable new ways of thinking to the acquirer.

Step 2 Assess Culture

There are two key components to cultural assessment. First, the acquirer should assess its own culture. In some companies this has already been done. Second, the acquirer should examine the culture of the target, preferably using the same approaches to measurement as it used in its own company.[7]

Cultural assessment of an acquisition can be a complex process and greatly depends upon access to a target. Also, more than one level of culture may be operating in a company, especially if the company is a large multidivisional one. Cultures may vary by divisions, functions, and geographic areas (especially in the case of international deals).[8] During due diligence, access and the depth of the assessment may be very limited, thus making it very difficult to make all these types of assessments, and the buyer may have to settle for a more generalized view of the target's culture.

If this initial assessment reveals no "deal killer," then deeper assessments to understand how to manage integration may be conducted during the transition, and if necessary the integration, stage. In the following sections (1) the dimensions of culture to be examined and (2) the methods available to assess culture are addressed.

Dimensions of Culture

The list below characterizes the dimensions of culture I have employed in my research and consulting work.[9] It is useful to assess how the target management behaves with respect to each dimension.

1. Centralized versus decentralized decision making
2. Speed in making decisions (slow versus quick)
3. Time horizon for decisions (short term versus long term)
4. Level of teamwork
5. Management of conflict (degree of openness and confrontation)
6. Risk orientation and entrepreneurial behavior

7. Process versus results orientation
8. Performance orientation (measurement orientation and goal achievement)
9. Focus on responsibility and accountability
10. Degree of horizontal cooperation and coordination (across functions, business units, and product lines)
11. Level of politics
12. Focus on rules and policies
13. Nature of communication (openness and honesty; speed; vehicles— written versus face-to-face, meetings)
14. Openness to change

Methods Available to Assess Culture

Assessment of culture is rather complex. There are direct and indirect methods requiring differing levels of contact and access to information with a target firm. These include secondary sources of information (i.e., little or no contact with a target) and primary sources (i.e., direct contact with a target). Each method is described below.

Secondary Sources of Information

By using these sources, a rough understanding of the target's culture can be pieced together without direct contact. Such sources of information include:

1. Internet
2. Newspaper, journal articles, and other periodicals
3. Speeches given by management
4. Interviews with your own employees who have worked for or closely with the target
5. Interviews with knowledgeable and trusted business brokers, consultants, and other industry participants (e.g., large customers, suppliers, other customers)

When secrecy of negotiations is important, the fourth and fifth sources may be problems since they could violate secrecy or disclosure agreements with a target. The first three, however, bear little risk of disclosure.

The dimensions of culture presented above should be used as a guide for assessment. When interviews are conducted, people should be asked to "describe how (the target) runs its business." They can also be asked to comment on each dimension as a probe (e.g., "Can you tell me about the level of cooperation among functional areas in getting work done?"). However, keep in mind that since most respondents will have observed the target as an outsider, or may have limited memory, such an assessment may be superficial.

As an example, a Catholic health-care system was interested in selling some of its hospitals to a publicly traded hospital management company (HMC). The hospitals in question no longer fit within the geographic scope of the seller's system. Before selling, the seller wanted to understand HMC's culture and what would likely happen to the hospitals after the deal was closed.

HMC had grown rapidly over 10 years by aggressively making acquisitions and engaging in joint ventures. The Catholic system's management had serious concerns, however, about whether the values and ethics of its hospitals would be compromised once they were sold to HMC. In anticipation of negotiations, it decided to quietly conduct an assessment of HMC. Since the seller did not want HMC to know about it, secondary sources were used. Appendix 3-1 contains the assessment that was conducted.

Through the use of an Internet search (based on information that included SEC documents, trade journals, newspapers, and the like) and select interviews with other hospitals that had dealt with HMC, the assessment was conducted. Since HMC was fairly high profile, such information was relatively easy to gather and a solid story could be pieced together. On the basis of this assessment, the Catholic system's management decided not to undertake the sale and looked for another alternative.

Primary Sources of Information
Primary sources permit a more detailed understanding of a target's culture to be pieced together. This approach, however, requires direct contact with the acquirer. Such sources of information include:

1. Observation of the target's behaviors during acquisition meetings and negotiations. This source is the easiest source to use. Primarily, it requires that managers from the acquirer who come in contact with a target keep notes on the cultural dimensions presented earlier. With some training, managers can keep notes on what they observe. Although their observations would not be based on a systematic assessment, it would provide additional data points for validation.

2. Examination of company documents and other artifacts (e.g., organizational charts, human resources policies, meeting minutes, company core values statements). This source requires more direct information from the company, but little interaction with employees. This, again, may be critical when a target's management does not want its employees to be contacted. Depending upon what information is gleaned, the depth of analysis can vary. Statements of values and culture articulate what a company's intentions are. They may reflect actual behaviors or not. More detailed documents on actual human resources policies such as measurement and reward systems, training and development programs, career management systems, and budgetary processes may be more revealing. The extent to which statements and practices coincide, the higher the probability that the assessment is valid. Observation of actual behaviors and company artifacts may be even more powerful. Some companies have even employed anthropologists and sociologists to assess cultures.

For example, Ciba Geigy's U.S. corporate staff, in anticipation of its merger with Sandoz, prepared a simple cultural assessment of its partner. When the organizational charts and management practices of the two companies were analyzed, it was apparent that there were two very different views on centralization and decentralization. Ciba had highly centralized staff activities located in New York. Sandoz, on the other hand, believed that staff activities should be decentralized and contained within divisions. Prior to the closing of the merger, the top-management positions of the soon-to-be new company, Novartis, were announced. As expected, most of the key positions went to Sandoz people. Based on the assessments, it was apparent that the new organization would likely be decentralized. And, indeed, it was.

Prior to the closing of its merger, Chevron and Texaco shared with each other numerous documents concerning each company's cultures and ways of operating. Chevron, in particular, shared a document "The Chevron Way" that "sums up who we are, what we do, what we believe in, and what our goals are for the future." The document clearly articulated the company's vision and values and thus how it was trying to behave. As in any case, the extent to which those visions and values were embraced and manifested in the behaviors of people is unknown and requires a deeper level of analysis.

3. Interviews and focus groups with target managers and employees, and surveys and questionnaires. The final two sources require the greatest contact with people, but may reveal the greatest amount of information about a target. In addition, they allow a broader and more systematic exposure to the organization. Therefore, the acquirer can assess the extent to which there is a "single" culture across the target organization. In small organizations, where the leaders are more likely to embody the culture, access to members of the senior management team may be sufficient to learn about the culture. In large companies characterized by multiple divisions spread across the globe, assessment may be more challenging. There are likely to be several cultures, with perhaps a higher set of national and corporate cultural attributes. In such cases, integration will probably vary as well as the cultural issues.

Focus Group and Interview Guidelines. When conducting interviews and focus groups the following protocol is recommended:

> "We want to learn more about how (the target) runs its business and would like to use your experience to help us understand that. There are no 'right' or 'wrong' answers. This is not a judgmental exercise. We would appreciate it if you would be as candid

as possible. We will not share your specific answers with anyone or identify who you are. The more realistic the information we receive, the more likely that the integration will go smoothly. I am going to ask a few questions and would like your insights on them.

"Describe how (your company) operates..."

You can let people talk for a couple of minutes and then ask them to comment on each dimension as a probe:

"Can you tell me about the level of cooperation among functional areas in getting work done?" etc.

"Perhaps you can identify and tell me something about some people who would be considered heroes in the company and why.

"Are there any aspects of the organization and the way it operates that people take particular pride in? Are there any aspects that are critical to the success of the company?"

You can give them some examples: events such as company picnics, awards received, awards given to employees, logos, songs. Depending upon the cooperation among the people, you may ask:

"Are there any aspects of the organization and the way it operates that people would like to change?"

In some cases, the acquirer may not have much access until an acquisition agreement is signed (i.e., the transition stage) or even until after closing. When this is the case, a detailed cultural assessment will have little impact on the decision to consummate the deal and pricing, but will play heavily in the integration. In general, when limited cultural information is available, the acquirer must assess how much risk it is willing to take in moving forward and consummating the deal.

To assess culture in this context, focus groups or interviews with representative people throughout the organization can be employed. People should be chosen from different divisions, geographic locations, and functions to ensure a representative picture and to capture differences across the corporation.

The final source of cultural information is a survey or questionnaire. Surveys and questionnaires can be distributed to managers and employees throughout the target. They can even be accessed online. They provide a numerical score and allow the acquirer to systematically examine the nature of the target's culture and the extent to which there is a "single" culture across the organization. Moreover, they can identify the importance of each dimension. There are numerous commercially available instruments on the market that basically address the dimensions above.

It is recommended, to the extent that time, access, and costs allow, that different approaches (e.g., questionnaires and interviews) to conduct the cultural assessment be used. Multiple approaches help minimize bias and provide validation. When there is convergence among more than one source, there is greater confidence in the conclusion. When there is a lack of convergence, discussions to understand why this is the case should be undertaken.

Step 3   Assess Cultural Fit Between an Acquirer and Target

Based on the cultural profile, document and discuss any gaps. This will provide insights into similarities that can be leveraged and built upon, and potential sources of clash that may need to be managed. Also, attempt to isolate those dimensions that the target feels strongly about or are important to its success. You can assess importance in two ways: (1) by rank-ordering each dimension or (2) by rating each dimension on a five-point scale (1—not very important to 5—very important).

As an example using the dimensions of culture presented above, I asked the senior managers of both an acquiring and acquired company to assess their own cultures. The buyer was a large corporation, whereas the seller was a smaller entrepreneurial firm that offered new products and possible cross-selling and joint new-product development opportunities. More importantly, the valuation and subsequent purchase price were based on the buyer's ability to capture the synergies. Interviews and a survey instrument were employed to assess both companies' cultures. The initial plan was for the acquired company to be integrated into a major division of the buyer. Both companies were internationalized, with multiple divisions and geographic locations around the world. Included in this process was the CEO of the selling firm and his staff, the division president of the buyer and his staff, country managers, and selective other personnel from both organizations, including those involved in sales and new-product development. This analysis was conducted during the transaction stage to get a sense of whether these companies could work together and what the integration challenges would be like after the closing. Both parties agreed to this analysis after a letter of intent had been signed and the parties were well on their way to drafting a definitive acquisition agreement. Neither party had contractually agreed to do the deal yet.

The results of the survey are presented in Table 3-2. The table is a map of the extent of differences for each dimension. Keep in mind that the results were a composite of the responses of a large number of people and that there were variations in perceptions even among people from the

Table 3-2 Cultural Profiles

	Always	Often	Elements of Both	Often	Always	
	1	2	3	4	5	
Centralized decisions		x			y	Decentralized decisions
Fast decision making		y		x		Slow decision making
Short-term focus		x	y			Long-term focus
Individual orientation		x,y				Team orientation
Confrontation of conflict			x,y			Avoidance of conflict
High-risk tolerance		x			y	Low-risk tolerance
Focus on results		x	y			Focus on process
People held accountable		x,y				People not held accountable
Horizontal cooperation		y			x	Silo oriented
High trust among people		y		x		Highly political
Bureaucratic		x			y	Entrepreneurial
Open and honest communications	y		x			Guarded communications
Fast communications		y		x		Slow communications
Direct face-to-face communications			y	x		Indirect communications
Resistant to change		x	y			Open to change

Statistically significant differences

x = Target
y = Acquirer

same organization. These differences were in large part a function of the fact that across members of each organization there were variations in perceptions and in the culture itself. To determine whether differences between the acquirer and the target were greater than between members of the same organization, statistical tests were conducted.[10] The tests confirmed that in a number of cases the differences between the organizations were indeed significant. These are indicated in the boxed in areas in Table 3-2. By using these results, the impact of differences could be examined. Table 3-3 presents the average rankings of the importance of each dimension. To assess importance, respondents were asked to rank-order each dimension according to the impact it had on the success of the company.

Although interview and archival data were collected they are not presented here for sake of brevity. For the most part these data confirmed the survey results and provided many illustrations of how the culture manifested itself. The multiple approaches of cultural assessment strengthened the validity of the findings.

Steps 4 and 5   Identify the Impact of Cultural Gaps and Develop and Execute Strategies

The next steps in the process are to use the information in the cultural profile to assess the impact that the differences have and the strategies that need to be considered to manage such differences. Of importance here is to gauge the need to capture synergies (based on the valuation and pricing), the degree of cultural differences, and the nature and depth of inte-

Table 3-3 Average Rank Order of Cultural Dimensions

	Acquirer	Target	
Centralized decisions	1	1	Decentralized decisions
Fast decision making	9	3	Slow decision making
Short-term focus	3	13	Long-term focus
Individual orientation	4	5	Team orientation
Confrontation of conflict	7	15	Avoidance of conflict
High-risk tolerance	10	4	Low-risk tolerance
Focus on results	5	11	Focus on process
People held accountable	2	12	People not held accountable
Horizontal cooperation	11	6	Silo oriented
High trust among people	12	7	Highly political
Bureaucratic	6	2	Entrepreneurial
Open and honest communications	13	8	Guarded communications
Fast communications	14	9	Slow communications
Direct face-to-face communications	15	14	Indirect communications
Resistant to change	8	10	Open to change

gration required. It is also critical to determine the importance attached to the various dimensions and the level of resistance to change by either of the firms involved. Such strategies may include terminating the deal, adjusting synergy expectations and valuations, or working with the target to manage gaps. The latter will depend upon levels of access to and cooperation with the target. It may be the case that resolution of gaps has to wait until after an acquisition agreement is signed or until the deal is closed. At that point, however, it may be too late. Based on the steps conducted above, a table similar to Table 3-4 can be constructed. The table allows the acquirer to systematically examine the impact of differences on each dimension and choose a strategy for dealing with it.

In the example presented above, it was clear that there were a significant number of cultural issues that could prevent the deal from succeeding. After the profiling, this became quite apparent to the buyer. Although the acquirer's division president was prone to discount the results due to the strategic attractiveness of the deal, he chose to explore the implications of the deal further. Specifically, he put several options for consideration on the table. These included:

1. Walk away from the deal.
2. Lower the synergy expectations, valuation, and purchase price.
3. Decide whether he could live with the differences and whether they would preclude a successful integration and achievement of synergies. For example, an independent and autonomous division for the target was considered.
4. Integrate the target slowly.
5. Change the buyer to become more compatible with the target and vice versa.

After numerous discussions with his management team, option 2 was his first choice. Unfortunately, the seller would not drop the price low enough to justify the deal. After agonizing over options 3 to 5, the buyer chose to walk away. Although the target was a good potential strategic fit, he came to realize that the cultural problems would prevent a successful integration and achievement of the synergies that were the true source of value underlying the deal.

GUIDE THE BEHAVIORS AND ATTITUDES OF NEGOTIATORS, DUE DILIGENCE TEAMS, AND DEAL MAKERS

The negotiation process is another area in which the acquirer has the opportunity to interact with the target. It is critical for negotiators to realize that such interactions set the stage for the integration process. During

Table 3-4 Culture Assessment

Cultural Dimension	Culture of Target	Culture of Acquirer	Gap between Cultures	Importance of Dimension	Impact of Cultural Gaps on Deal or Integration	Strategies
Centralization of Decision Making	Highly decentralized	Highly centralized	Great	1	• Significant potential conflict • Trying to change culture of target will harm its performance	• Leave target culture alone • Change culture of acquirer • Change culture of target • Do not do the deal • Adjust synergy expectations and valuations

the negotiation process the target's management begins to learn about the acquirer's culture and what is in store for the target after the deal is closed. Therefore, it is essential that deal makers and negotiators attend to their negotiating style.

Further, negotiations with a target often entail more than just the purchase price, especially with respect to small firms. Early concerns with such issues as target managers' roles in the future, retention of employees, and compensation and benefits packages, among other issues, will be on the table. As such, deal makers and negotiators should:

- Quickly learn major integration concerns of the parties selling the business
- Examine what issues need to be resolved to do the deal
- Assess the subsequent effects any agreements might have on synergies, cashflow, earnings, and subsequent integration efforts

To this end, close communication between negotiators and the due diligence team is essential, as will be future communications with those responsible for integration.

Appendix 3-1 Secondary Sources of Culture*

The preliminary study reported below was undertaken to help Catholic Healthcare System (CHS) develop a basic understanding of the culture (i.e., core values and management practices) and agenda of HMC. The study is based on a comprehensive search and analysis of public sources of information (e.g., journals, annual reports, news clippings) available on HMC, select interviews with hospital administrators currently or recently involved in joint-venture negotiations with HMC, and several reports by stock analysts. The interviews, however, were not comprehensive, but were with personal contacts who requested anonymity. As such, many of the conclusions drawn herein are speculative and limited and should be interpreted as such.

The report is divided into two parts. Part one discusses HMC's culture and agenda and part two addresses some thoughts I have on how to deal with them.

HMC'S CULTURE AND AGENDA

"Capitalist," pragmatic, and profit driven are the best ways to describe HMC's culture. The organization is led by James Smith, who in 1990 decided to aggressively change the paradigm for doing business in the health-care industry. In fact he has a paperweight on his desk that states "If you are not the lead dog, the view never changes." After an unsuccessful attempt to take over DEF in 1985, Smith, a health-care merger and acquisition attorney, and Oklahoma financier Robert Jones, formed HMC and bought two hospitals. With the support of a young management team and Smith's leadership, they have aggressively acquired close to 200 for-profit and not-for-profit hospitals over the past seven years to form HMC with approximately $10 billion in annual revenues. From an initial investment of $250,000, Smith, who is 40, is now worth $200 million. From all indications he continues to move aggressively and is well capitalized to do so. HMC has stated that it may operate as many as 500 hospitals within the next 10 years. It appears that Smith is committed to building a health-care empire. Based on his background, it seems that "empire" as opposed to "health care" is the key term here. Although it is speculation,

---

* The names of the companies involved, essential statistics, and geographic information have been changed to protect anonymity. The essence of the analysis and the conclusions reached have remained the same.

I suspect he would have been very happy to do what he is doing in any other industry if the same opportunity arose. As such, it does not appear that he has a driving philosophic commitment to providing "high-quality" health care. This is not to suggest that quality is unimportant, since it may be an important source of competitive advantage. It is just to suggest that low cost, profit, and growth may be more important.

It is very clear that HMC is being driven from an investor perspective, with financial results and stock price being of paramount importance. This suggests, consistent with my experience with other publicly traded companies and an examination of HMC's annual and other reports, that Smith and HMC likely have earnings per share growth and return on equity as their primary goals. Although it is speculation, I suspect that these goals would clearly take precedence over indigent care and "high-quality" health care if "push came to shove." To these ends, I further suspect that Smith, like most CEOs of similar-type companies, spends most of his time "on the outside," with the investment community, legislators and regulators, and major payers. As such, operational control is likely delegated to key senior managers, especially at the regional level. Smith appears to manage regions from a distance using financial indicators and does not seem to get involved in operations unless regional managers do not perform according to the indicators. Currently, investors believe in HMC's long-term strategy for the industry and its short-term performance. However, HMC may face numerous organizational challenges in the near future as it integrates the recently acquired B and D systems. Integration may be challenging given Smith's earlier unwelcome takeover attempt of DEF in 1985. Moreover, it is not clear how deep HMC's management talent is and how long it can organizationally sustain such rapid growth.

Smith's strategy for HMC is quite clear. Recently, he stated that "Our business is no different than a factory. We're building a nationwide network based on providing high-quality care at the most reasonable rate." Robert Jones recently described HMC as the Wal-Mart of health care. Again, comments such as these suggest that the primary focus will be on efficiency and profit. HMC's strategy (clearly demonstrated in Georgia where it dominates the market), not unlike others, is to create a highly efficient system with strong national supply purchasing power, regional economies of scale, and better facility utilization. It is are utilizing information technology wherever possible to facilitate efficiencies and effectiveness. Also key to HMC's strategy is to continue to grow its network of referring physicians.

In addition to hospital acquisitions and joint ventures, HMC is also acquiring and joint venturing with outpatient surgery centers and discussing joint ventures with nursing homes. In general, it prefers ownership to alliances and ventures and has aggressively targeted not-for-profits. Perhaps joint ventures may be useful to HMC in laying the groundwork for future acquisitions or for building relationships with physicians it can leverage in the future. It is important to note in the sample of joint ventures I examined that HMC had at least 50 percent ownership and equivalent board representation and management control. The implications of this position are quite important. It is unlikely that after the closing of a venture deal CHS would have much leverage over HMC beyond enforcing the venture agreement, or be able to muster a majority of board members to change the way the target hospitals are being run.

It does not appear that HMC has a particular agenda for meeting the needs of the poor and indigent. In a number of speeches, Smith has claimed, however, that HMC does a better job at that than do not-for-profits when one takes into consideration corporate income taxes and that not-for-profits have an unfair playing field. There has been some speculation that HMC will aim for better-insured customers, while Catholic not-for-profits will focus on the indigent. Noting that universal access is coming, HMC recently said, "I have no problem with their (Catholic canon of ethics). Their mission was to take care of charity patients. That mission is past."

However, in a recent acquisition of a DOC hospital, St John's, in Fort Lauderdale, Florida, HMC agreed to a certain amount of charity care and retained the hospice program. It does appear to be pragmatic enough to do what it takes to strike a deal. But, I think "pragmatic" versus "philosophic" is the key word in describing HMC's approach to charitable care. In Florida last year it did make $200,000 in charitable donations, with $80,000 going to local AIDS groups.

HMC has also been quite tough in its dealings. In fact, some have described Smith as a bounty hunter. According to a *Wall Street Journal* article, "HMC has employed big money, tough tactics and relentless pressure to become Georgia's largest provider of health care." In Atlanta, the state capital, it paid 26 lobbyists to push for tight restrictions on tax exemptions for not-for-profit hospitals, which are primary competitors and acquisition targets. To motivate management of one hospital to sell, HMC bought land near the hospital and allegedly threatened to build an outpatient surgery center to perform 70 percent of the operations performed by the hospital. To gain a contract with Jones County in Georgia, HMC slashed prices and released a study showing that the tax breaks given to competing Barnes Memorial Hospital and other not-for-profits were worth more than the charity care HMC provided. HMC won the contract. The Barnes Memorial situation led to a great deal of mud-slinging, but both sides claimed the other started it. In another case, HMC, soon after the owner of a local health-care company in Fort Myers, Florida, died, swooped in to purchase the business from her estate.

Three not-for-profit hospital administrators who are negotiating joint ventures and were interviewed said that HMC has behaved legally, professionally, and ethically thus far. They also noted, however, that HMC's managers are "staunch capitalists." In order to enhance its credibility and image of providing state-of-the-art health care, HMC is presently in various stages of negotiations with at least 17 academic health centers nationwide. Earlier this year a large medical school organization entered into negotiations with HMC to establish an extensive health-care network. In spite of the organization's history of entrepreneurial ventures, while providing indigent health care, it recently broke off negotiations with HMC. Hospital administrators cited a "clash of cultures" between the organizations as the main reason. The organization felt that HMC was too aggressive to consummate the deal, too capitalistic, and too rigid over who would be in charge. Another hospital administrator in Atlanta, who generally finds HMC more ethical than some hospital chains, notes that when presented with a difference in operating philosophy, "HMC may give lip service, but it is clear that they are in charge."

It appears to me, based on conversations I have had with a number of people in the industry, that HMC may be positioning long term for an HMO environment where covered lives may be the key to financial performance. As such, it may be positioning through acquisitions, alliances, and other means to maximize the number of persons enrolled in its managed-care plans. To support this, HMC has been very aggressive in building tight alliances with referring physicians by offering them equity interests in their local HMC subsidiary. Further, such interests are contingent upon the physicians signing noncompete clauses preventing them from investing in other health-care ventures. Moreover, a 1992 FAHCA (Florida) study of patient admissions by physician-owners at HMC's Jones Hospital, a 236-bed Miami institution, found Medicare patients that they referred there stayed an average of 8.48 days, while those sent to competing institutions averaged 13.5 days. While the Florida agency said the numbers were inconclusive, it points to possible profiteering, with more complicated, less profitable patients being steered to other hospitals.

DEALING WITH HMC

At this point I can only speculate, since I have no inside knowledge of HMC. It appears that HMC's core values, culture, and agenda are quite different from those of CHS, especially with respect to indigent and quality health care, i.e., basic core values. As such, I suspect that CHS will have great difficulty reaching a successful agreement with HMC.

There appear to be a number of risks from continuing negotiations and engaging in a venture with HMC. First, CHS must consider any reputational damage among its external stakeholders and employees and any co-optation of its mission. These are major core issues. I suggest that CHS ask itself whether "it could sleep at night" if it were involved with HMC. For example, if CHS partners with HMC, what impact would such a relationship have on potential affiliations with other Catholic hospitals? Would it appear that CHS "sold out"?

If CHS decides to continue joint-venture negotiations with HMC, it should do so *very carefully* and ask some tough questions. It is apparent that HMC is committed to growing rapidly and is aggressive in doing so, and wants to do a deal for the target. I suspect it would prefer to buy the target and not have to deal with CHS as a partner. However, HMC is so hungry to grow that it would settle for a venture, perhaps as an interim step. As such, a great deal of caution is warranted. HMC's agenda and goals are clear. Moreover, it is very pragmatic and may initially make concessions with respect to such issues as indigent care to do a deal. The real issue, however, is what life for the target will be like after the deal is closed.

From my experience with mergers, acquisitions, and joint ventures, not all issues can be specified in the written agreement, although as many as possible should be. In the end, however, many issues will have to be resolved outside the formal agreement. *Thus, CHS needs to feel confident that it can trust and work with the specific people and organization it will be involved with at HMC.* Since HMC is very large and regionally decentralized, it appears that the people and specific culture and agenda in Colorado (the location of the target) should be the focal point of further thought and analysis. Keep in mind, however, that the Colorado region will still likely reflect the basic core values, culture, and agenda of the overall corporation. Further analyses should focus on such day-to-day operating management issues as primary measures of organizational success; orientation toward indigent care and community service; tolerance of the canon of ethics; focus on employee empowerment and teams; performance management and reward systems; administration/medical staff relations; orientation toward quality-care approaches to conflict management and problem solving; philosophy of employee and management development; management control systems; and approaches toward promotion, staffing, and termination. Moreover, general perceptions of operating management's honesty, integrity, fairness, and credibility should be examined. To directly learn about these issues, interviews with local HMC managers and employees and other joint-venture partners, employee surveys and focus groups, facility inspections, and examinations of key records and documentation should be employed.

If CHS decides to continue negotiations, the governance structure of the venture and a definition of what "operating control" means should be thoroughly examined. These include management and board control; roles, responsibilities, and composition of the management team and board; bailout provisions for CHS; and mechanisms for making decisions and resolving disputes and conflicts.

Although it may be easy to halt discussions at this time because HMC appears to be "different," it may be worthwhile to continue negotiations and analyses. First, the venture may provide CHS with a good opportunity to learn more about HMC and how it operates. CHS may face HMC down the road as a competitor. Moreover, CHS may learn more efficient practices for operating a hospital. Second, if CHS divests itself of the target, its mission in Colorado will cease. This joint venture may be the only hope of preserving the mission.

Whatever course CHS pursues, it should do so objectively and with solid data and information. Failure to do so will likely result in a grave mistake.

4

ASSESSING KEY TARGET PEOPLE

With few exceptions, the selection and retention of key people during a merger or an acquisition is critical to the success of a deal.[1] Even in cases where there is significant redundancy, certain people will be essential. These may be people who are needed for the long term or long enough to ensure that the transition and integration process is successfully completed. Most companies are always in need of talented people, and a merger or an acquisition is an excellent opportunity to secure them. As such, an acquirer's ability to identify people key to the success of the merger or acquisition, and to assess whether they can effectively contribute and are willing to stay, is of utmost importance.

The sooner such assessments can be made, the better. Until people are named to key positions, the "me" question will preoccupy many people's minds. Good people are likely to update their resumes and start looking for new jobs. The net outcome is not likely to be positive, resulting in possible value leakage. Although it would be desirable to assess everyone in a target or merging organization, at this stage it is not possible. It would require too much time, access, and too many resources. Focusing on key people at this point is sufficient. During the transition and integration stages, these assessments will become essential.

This chapter presents several key steps required to determine the staffing of key positions. It also provides examples of tools for assessing people and making staffing decisions. Such decisions, however, are not easy to make. They require assessment of people in both the target and acquirer.

The person with the primary responsibility for assessing key managers and employees will be someone from human resources (HR), with the input of relevant line managers (i.e., to provide inputs on functional competencies) and outside consultants. This HR "point" person should be a member of the due diligence team and subsequently a member of the staffing integration team (see Chapter 6). The level of HR person involved will depend on the level of the positions being assessed.

A key to the success of an acquisition is having a sufficient number of people with needed talent, skills, competencies, style, and motivation. As such, the acquirer must:

1. Assess staffing needs to manage through the transition and afterward to run the business.
2. Assess the capability of the target and other sources to meet these needs.
3. Assess staffing time frames.
4. Develop strategies for closing any gaps in staffing needs.

Much the same as with assessing culture, the challenge in assessment is going to be the level of access to a target. It is recommended that both primary and secondary sources (see the previous chapter) again be considered.

STEPS IN THE ASSESSMENT OF KEY TARGET PEOPLE

The relationship among the steps are presented in Figure 4-1 and discussed below.

Step 1 Assess Staffing Needs

This requires that a rough pro forma of the consolidated postclosing organization be developed to determine the:

1. Basic organization structure
2. Key positions
   a. Number of positions
   b. Roles and responsibilities for each position (i.e., position description)
   c. Talent, skills, competencies, style, and motivation needed for each position (if profiles have already been developed, use them)[2]
   d. Target staffing costs (salaries and benefits) the acquirer is willing to sustain and what the actual costs are likely to be

Figure 4-1   Assessing Key Target People

Financial and strategic objectives play a key role in this assessment. For example, where levels of consolidation and redundancy are high, there is not likely to be a shortage of people, although there may be a shortage of qualified people. Where there is geographic expansion and growth and where redundancies are few, acquired people may be critical to success, especially if there is a shortage of talent in the local market.

Step 2 Examine Staffing Capability

Next, examine staffing capability in both the target and the acquirer. It is recommended that such assessment be undertaken with the three highest levels of management and with other key people (including high potentials). Key questions to address include:

1. Who are the key people in the target? These may include people with:
   a. Technical knowledge (e.g., research and development and new-product development, marketing) that cannot be easily replaced
   b. Important relationships with key customers, employees, government officials, and other stakeholders
2. To what extent will target people "fit" within the acquirer's organization? If they do not fit, can the acquirer live with such mismatches, and how can they manage them?
3. How likely are key target people to remain with the acquirer and be motivated during the transition stage and after closing?
4. Does the target have capable successors to key managers and personnel? Are they likely to remain?
5. Does the acquirer have sufficient replacements if target people are not retained?
6. Can sufficient replacements be hired in the marketplace if target people do not stay?
7. How long will it take to find replacements, and how long will it take for them to be performing on the job?
8. How much will it cost to meet the staffing requirements?

Step 3 Assess Staffing Time Frame

Third, determine for how long key people are needed. Some people will be needed only for the duration of the transition but will have no future with the company, whereas others will be retained as long-term employees. This distinction is important because many companies fail to consider transitional needs.

Step 4 Identify and Execute Staffing Strategies

Finally, based on the staffing needs identified in the pro forma organization, and the staffing capabilities and time frame, identify any potential short-term and long-term gaps in key positions. Then develop a staffing strategy.

The strategy should focus on:

1. Retaining key target people (more will be said about strategies for retaining target people in Chapter 7)
2. Identifying possible successors in the target
3. Identifying the acquirer's replacements
4. Preparing to recruit replacements in the marketplace
5. Terminating the deal if critical people cannot be retained or replaced

Using the information you've gained from the steps conducted above, you can construct a staffing assessment table like the one shown in Table 4-1. After the table is constructed, the pros and cons of each strategy should be examined.

ASSESSING KEY PEOPLE

Four major questions are useful in assessing people:

1. Have the key people performed effectively in the past?
2. Do the key people have the talent, skills, competencies, style, and motivation to manage in the new organization?
3. What is the likelihood the key people will fit and succeed in this new environment?
4. What actions, if any, can be taken to ensure that key people will succeed?

Answering these questions is more an art than a science. No single source of information can provide answers to these questions. Moreover, each source has certain limits to validity. As such, to answer these questions companies must rely on a variety of approaches and tools.

As is the case in cultural assessment, there is no single or easy way to assess managerial capabilities or intentions. Also, since such assessments are more personal than are cultural assessments, they are likely to engender reactive responses. Great care must be taken during such assessment. It is suggested that primary and secondary sources be utilized with consideration of the following:

Target Company Documents

Various company documents can be examined. Such documents, however, may reflect past accomplishments and not accurately reflect future potential. In addition, depending upon the sophistication of the target, many companies may not ever have prepared such documents. Key documents to look for include:

Personnel records. These records identify staff, how they can be contacted, what their roles and responsibilities are, what development

Table 4-1 Staffing Assessment

Key Position	Number of People Needed	Target Candidates	External Candidates (Including the acquirer)	Readiness for the Position	Likelihood Person Will Take the Position If Offered	Retention or Recruitment Strategy	Cost of Strategy	Pros and Cons of Person

activities they have participated in, and what their salaries and benefits are.

Business plans and personal goals. These provide insights on results achieved by key managers.

Performance appraisals. These provide insights on how people have performed on key competencies and behaviors. Be careful, however, since many companies' appraisals are not very accurate or comparable across companies.

Succession plans. These identify successors to all key positions.

Development plans for high-potential managers. These identify any high-potential managers, their stages of development, development activities completed, and development needs remaining.

Interviews

Incumbents. Interviews should focus on what the key players have accomplished and how they have done so. Be careful not to reveal too much information about the acquirer's criteria for judging people, since these may elicit "socially desirable" responses. Any interview techniques that human resources has developed for interviewing prospective employees might be very useful.

Seller or senior management. Such interviews should focus on basic insights about who the key people are, how important their retention is, and what the downside risks are if they should depart. These insights should be tempered by the fact that the target management is interested in selling the company and might be interested in looking after its people.

360 degree interviews. To the extent possible, such interviews should focus on soliciting independent information on key managers from peers, subordinates, superiors, and other relevent parties (e.g., customers, suppliers).

Leadership Style and Psychological Assessments

There are numerous tools and testing companies available for assessing managers' psychological makeup and leadership style. These assessments may be useful in determining the extent to which people fit with the acquirer. Again, any tools human resources has developed for assessing prospective employees might be very useful here.

Resumes. Resumes may provide insights on people's work experience, including the:
- Number of jobs and positions they have held
- Frequency and changes in employment
- Types of companies and industries they have worked for and their tenure
- Major accomplishments
- Future goals and aspirations

Talent, Skills, Competencies, Style, and Motivation[3]

In putting a new organization together, the right mix of talent, skills, competencies, and styles is critical. Determining what kind of people will allow a merged organization to achieve its financial and strategic objectives is paramount in the process. Does the company want a by-the-book or a creative CFO? Does it want an entrepreneur who takes risks or a loyal and conventional manager? Does it want to put its key people in an environment where they will be strongest or where they will be continually frustrated? Does it want all to fit a cookie-cutter image, or does it want diversity in style, approach, and expertise?

Even when the right mix has been decided, the challenges are not over. Assurances are needed that the styles of the players on the new team will complement each other. Does the company know in advance how a new team member is likely to relate to the rest of the team and to the demands of the work environment? Would it help to know what really motivates key people or to be forewarned about what is most likely to cause them stress? Could executives benefit by knowing how to discuss individual differences so their teams could work more effectively? Most merger executives and managers say yes, and yet these are the issues that are often overlooked and in the end can make or break a merger or an acquisition.

Knowing what kind of talents, skills, competencies, and styles are available and how each "player" is likely to best succeed still isn't the end of the people side of due diligence. The next step is integrating the players in such a way that creates a well-coordinated team. More is said about this in Chapter 8. If the styles of the team fit together nicely, the sailing should be pretty smooth. If they don't, much more thought has to be given to whether that "newcomer" from the acquired or merged company who appears to have a totally different approach or style from that of the existing players is a challenge worth taking on. Given the way mergers have gone over the last several years, putting the wrong people in place for the sake of goodwill can be a costly mistake.

In this section, near mistakes and the successes that resulted from the people side of due diligence are explored. A "shortcut" process that can improve the accuracy of selection and accelerate the assimilation of new players into a team is laid out, and vignettes of how this process has worked in three merger situations is described.

The "Shortcut": An Up-front Assessment Tool

The shortcut proposed is no panacea, but aids significantly in determining whether people have the right combination of talent, skills, competencies, styles, and motivation to succeed in the newly created environment. In effect, the shortcut reduces the time needed to get both an individual and a team into place and in a productive mode once selection decisions are made and integration is under way. Instead of spending 6 to 18 months learning what motivates people's best performance and how they lead, make decisions, work with peers, adapt to change, or handle stress, the shortcut provides reliable indicators about talent and fit from the beginning. It enables executives and managers to identify, in advance, where managing the team will be nearly seamless and where trouble might begin.

A tool that facilitates us in this process is called the Birkman Method. It is a highly validated and reliable instrument used by over 5,000 organizations worldwide and has 50 years of research supporting it. Most organizations use it to assess the strengths and differences among individuals and to facilitate productive relationships. My colleagues and I use it not only for its team-building power, but for its strong predictive capability. From this predictive dimension, we are able to lay out a spreadsheet of the organization's talent and individual job strengths. Those who assess people during due diligence can thus zero in more quickly on missing talents, skills, and competencies, and confirm whether the desired candidate(s) appear to have the requisite styles and motivations. The assessors can also estimate whether the value of the talents, skills, and competencies brought by particular candidates is worth the costs of managing potentially significant differences.

Our process is a useful shortcut that supports the more complex and traditional way of determining the fit of new team members that rely on such measures as:

- Performance reports and past development plans
- Seniority
- Placement request forms
- Information gathered from board members, from peers, from subordinates
- Preestablished ratios set by the HR group for the desired mix of acquired and acquiring staff
- Information garnered from interviews

These are all useful methods for acquiring the data needed, but often, as noted above, they are not available. Moreover, the traditional methods only give part of the picture. They do not give us the insights needed to create the best mix of all the people available.

We go beyond these commonly used measures by adding our shortcut as a compensatory step. By that we mean that the assessment reports generated from our process support other data and do not stand alone in decision making about the selection of candidates. In every instance, this shortcut is used in conjunction with all the other sources of information available to the acquirer or merger partner. In fact, Birkman reports help us structure the way we look at and use the other traditional information. With insights from the assessment, we can dig deeper in interviews for areas of talents, skills, and competencies as well as look for comments in performance appraisals that support the indications of style or approach.

The tool's predictive assessment capability emanates from computer-generated reports completed by candidates for positions in the new organization. A computerized questionnaire to assess people takes only about 45 minutes to complete and can be easily accessed online. The resulting spreadsheets allow us to explain a team's profile, an individual's fit to specific job functions, and the motivations, behaviors, and reactions each person brings to the job. At a glance, integration leaders have available the kinds of data they need to make decisions about the selection of key target talent and about the fit of that talent to the existing team and the company's environment.

A walk through the five-step "talent fit" method, along with some due diligence lessons learned, demonstrate the power of this assessment process. I will draw from the following examples:

- An insurance company where the designated CEO-in-waiting really did not have what was needed to take the company to a new level of growth
- Two banks that moved to such different rhythms that all the senior management of one had to leave the dance floor to make room for those who could move to a faster beat
- A large energy company where the merger created simply more of the same

Five-Step Talent-Fit Decision Process
From the earliest stage of due diligence, we follow these assessment steps:

Step 1 Assess whether the targeted individual has the requisite talents, skills, competencies, and style to do the job. We look at:

- Whether this person really could do what needs to be done
- How well he or she compares with others who have significant tenure in the kind of position and environment this job represents
- What approach we could expect this individual to take in getting the job done
- How the person would see problems and attempt to solve them

Step 2 Assess the environments and relationships that motivate the targeted individual's "best" performance. At this point we want to know to the greatest extent possible whether the predominant relationships among the team and in the overall environment will bring out the best or cause stress in a newcomer. For example, we look at the fit of a candidate's profile to the overall "climate" of the work environment and to the typical interpersonal relationships in the new company. Where would this candidate thrive—would it be in an environment that is fast-paced or thoughtful, continuously changing or focused, competitive or collaborative, self-starting or highly directive, frank and straightforward or characterized by subtle and diplomatic communication, highly pragmatic or intuitive and feeling-oriented, risk taking or risk averse, conventional or individualistic? When it looks like the match of the team environment to the motivational needs of the candidate is not there, we dig deeper to determine what would have to happen for this candidate to perform well. In this step of the people side of due diligence, we have insights into how a person will do a job. We can use this information to conduct probing interviews and to glean past successes or failures from the candidate's professional experience.

Step 3 Assess the target individual's interest in the functional area proposed for him or her. If offered the position, would this individual really want to do it?

Step 4 Compare the fit of the targeted newcomer to the existing management team. Are there more similarities than differences in style? If there are strong differences, are there areas that might be considered irreconcilable?

Step 5 Determine whether to eliminate the targeted newcomer from consideration or to offer him or her a spot on the team. If the latter, determine whether special effort is needed to assimilate the newcomer into the existing team. Is the cost of taking this talent into the team minimal or excessive?

Talent Spreadsheet
The starting point is a talent spreadsheet, or what the Birkman Method calls "Organizational Strengths." It highlights the potential strengths and gaps of talent represented by members of a team or work unit. It also gives insights into the way members of the team manage and get things done. By knowing the mix of talents on the team, a leader can determine what strategies and tactics will create the greatest chance of success in managing that team.

What we look for first are the predominant management styles and the specific talents brought to the organization. At a glance, we can see the surfeits and deficits of a team. The talent spreadsheet in Table 4-2, from an insurance company we have renamed "Healthy Life," provides a detailed example of the kind of information we can have at our fingertips.

The spreadsheet consists of career functions and categories that, when interpreted, depict talent and style. Each category is ranked on a scale of 1 to 10 (with 10 being the highest fit to a talent or style category). In looking at the predominant strength of Healthy Life's top-management team, we see above the far left column of numbers that the tallest bar connotes strength in planning. The CEO, sales VP, EVP, and VP corporate planning and policy all bring a strong talent for innovation and vision to the team (scores of 7 to 10). In terms of other strengths at Healthy Life, the sales VP and the general counsel contribute talent in the realm of communicating and persuading. The VPs of operations and customer service, as well as the company's EVP, share a talent for expediting; while the CFO, the VP of corporate planning and policy, and the EVP show they have strong potential to

Table 4-2 Healthy Life's Talent Spreadsheet / Organizational Strengths

	Planning	Communicating	Expediting	Administrating	Knowledge Specialist	Directive Management	Delegative Management	Artistic Careers	Educational Careers	Social Service / Counseling	Employee Relations / Training	Medical Professions	Direct Tangible Sales	Direct Intangible Sales	Consultative Tangible Sales	Consultative Intangible Sales	Legal	Crafts / Technical	Police, Fire, and Security	Petrochemical	Engineering / Technical	Science / Technology	General Administrative	Numerical Administrative	Administrative Professionals	Banking and Finance	Accounting
Averages	7	6	5	6	4	4	7	7	7	6	6	5	6	7	6	5	5	5	5	5	6	7	6	6	5	5	4
CEO	7	5	4	8	2	2	8	8	8	9	6	6	5	4	5	6	4	3	3	4	8	8	6	4	4	3	1
VP sales	8	8	5	7	1	7	9	8	9	9	8	7	9	2	9	5	4	4	5	7	7	7	7	4	5	3	3
VP operations	3	4	4	2	10	4	5	2	2	3	5	4	5	9	8	9	9	10	4	5	5	7	7	2	2	1	1
General counsel	6	8	3	5	4	5	5	6	8	7	6	8	8	8	7	4	5	4	4	5	6	2	1	3	5	6	6
EVP	9	6	7	9	3	1	9	9	9	9	5	5	4	8	6	7	6	8	8	4	7	9	9	7	5	4	4
VP customer service	6	6	5	5	4	4	7	5	6	6	6	7	7	6	8	3	7	8	7	8	7	4	4	5	6	6	6
CFO	6	6	9	9	2	8	5	8	7	4	6	6	6	3	6	8	1	1	1	2	1	4	10	9	9	9	9
VP corp. plng. / policy	7	4	7	9	2	3	9	6	6	8	4	3	3	2	3	8	5	3	4	3	5	8	9	6	3	6	3
Dirk*	1	1	8	4	10	3	2	1	1	2	1	1	2	1	1	8	6	9	9	8	1	3	8	5	9	9	9

*Designated CEO-in-waiting

contribute in the administrative area. At a glance, we see that only planning is an overall corporate strength (meaning in the 7–10 "very strong" range). This is a company with innovative talent but no particularly strong implementation or sales "signature theme."

The situation faced by Healthy Life was as follows:

- Nontraditional competition was fierce.
- Signing up new customers was the only way to win.
- The company had just bought out a rival competitor.
- One of the conditions proposed in the acquisition discussions was that instead of naming co-CEOs, the current CEO of the acquired company would step into the role of EVP for 18 months and then take over as CEO when Healthy Life's current CEO was slated to retire. The current EVP would take a package and exit. Twelve months down the road, a new EVP would be identified.

We looked at the gaps between what was needed and what talents, skills, competencies, and style existed within the merging organizations. First, competition suggested that a strong "sales approach" was called for.

The board of directors was concerned that the demonstrated operational talent of the acquired CEO, Dirk Jones (name changed), duplicated strength the company already had, particularly in its current VP of operations. The board members felt new strength in relationship management both inside and outside the company was needed in their future CEO if the company was going to be competitive. It was the board that insisted on mapping talent to the new company's intended strategy.

Let's take a look at the talents Dirk brought to the newly created Healthy Life from the acquired company. He had a track record as an "expeditor," having come up the ladder from operations. His expeditor summary score was 8. He had 1's in planning and communicating and a 5 in administrating. His managerial style indicated he probably was very directive (10), and he scored in the 8's and 9's on technical, engineering, and administrative specializations. Extremely bright and well liked by the acquiring CEO, Dirk had moved up to the top in his former company very quickly because he was organized and precise and could deliver on time.

The concern was whether he had the strength to take Healthy Life to the next level by bringing in new business. If he did not, would the cost to the company be too great? Was there enough time to test out his approach before two other giants in the insurance industry combined? Were Dirk's strengths already present in the acquiring company's current VP of operations? In fact, it looked to a few board members as if the current VP had a stronger record in operations management than Dirk did. Did they need carbon copies of the same skill and talent set?

Career Predictors

Moving on from the talent spreadsheet, we focused on a report that dug into indicators that predict a match with those who have tenure in specific job categories and functions. This report, called interchangeably "Career Predictors" or the "Interview Guide," is not a measure of skills but a benchmark of how a person thinks compared with others who:

- Are typical of those with tenure in specific occupations
- Have been successful in specific ways of analyzing problems and creating solutions
- Share similar managerial style and responsibilities and the ability to adapt to stress, responsibilities, and organizational politics

The report tells us whether the candidate can match those who have significant track records in doing the job in question. In analyzing this report, we took into account the context of the merger, the organizational culture of the new company or team, and the positions to be filled. Higher scores on this report indicate more motivation and interest for traditional job responsibilities, functions, and managerial style. Lower scores indicate a nonconventional, often entrepreneurial, hands-on or risk-taking approach. Extensive research has shown that the degree of interest in something and motivation to work is linked to performance effectiveness.

As with all elements of our process, we use the "Career Predictors" report with other information about a candidate's education, past experience, and performance. It is an extremely useful tool for structuring an interview because it allows the interviewer to focus in on those talents, skills, competencies, and styles typically associated with particular roles and functions. What it does not tell us is whether the candidate will take on that job or role, or how the candidate would do it. That will be discussed later in the chapter.

First we looked at Dirk's scores in categories that related to occupations of a creative or social relationship nature (e.g., arts, education, social service, sales, and law; see Table 4-3). Every one of his scores on a scale of 1 to 10 were 1, indicating weak interest in being involved in those specific career areas or in using a particular style associated with careers requiring relationship skills. As we moved into production and administrative career categories, Dirk's scores moved up. His managerial style matched those of directive managers with significant tenure. While he may need extra incentive to work hard, his scores definitely matched those who adapt easily to the chain of command and who are loyal and committed to the goals of their organizations. In the area of adaptability to stressful situations and in social responsibility his scores were above average. We could now be fairly certain that Dirk had real strength of character and, if CEO, would take a conventional approach to managing the company.

What we discovered was that while Dirk's profile matched those of managers who are strong technical managers as well as good corporate citizens, he didn't match up with the requirement for Healthy Life's growth. Looking at the rest of the senior managers, we saw that only the VP sales and the general counsel had a match in business development

Table 4-3   Career Predictors (the "Interview Guide")

	Arts	Education	Social Services	Sales	Consultative Sales	Legal	Production	Enforcement	Engineering	Office Admin.	Admin./Prof.	Fiscal	Knowledge Spec.	Directive Mgmt.	Delegative Mgmt.	Work Motivation	Self-Development	Corporate Adapt.	Social Adapt.	Social Respons.	Public Contact	Global Contact	Conceptual
CEO	7	5	6	5	8	10	5	7	3	5	4	2	8	2	2	2	9	2	8	2	10	10	7
VP sales	9	1	4	9	9	8	2	4	4	7	4	3	7	1	5	5	8	7	8	6	10	7	4
VP operations	3	3	2	3	8	5	8	10	7	2	2	4	2	10	4	4	6	2	4	4	3	6	8
General counsel	2	4	6	10	9	7	2	5	5	4	3	3	5	4	4	4	8	7	5	6	6	8	3
EVP	8	4	8	3	5	8	7	2	3	5	9	2	9	3	4	4	9	10	9	6	8	4	9
VP customer service	4	1	4	7	6	3	4	7	6	4	5	5	5	4	5	5	7	6	5	4	6	3	4
CFO	6	9	8	4	1	8	5	2	2	9	10	10	9	2	7	7	10	6	8	7	2	8	10
VP corp. plng. / policy	10	9	4	1	1	8	6	3	2	9	9	3	9	2	2	2	10	2	7	6	6	8	9
Averages	6	5	5	5	6	7	5	5	4	6	6	4	7	4	4	4	8	5	7	5	6	7	7
Dirk	1	1	1	1	1	1	9	3	9	8	8	8	4	10	3	3	6	10	7	7	1	1	6

predictors, and the VP sales had a stronger blend of managerial and administrative strengths than did the general counsel. The VP sales, however, was not yet ready in terms of "seasoning" to take on the CEO role.

Perceptual Filters

At this point we examined the information from which we could glean clues about the ways in which Dirk might typically look at problems and invent solutions. Going back to the talent spreadsheet, a "perceptual filters" report was generated in order to get a quick picture of how he might be expected to approach work.

When we approach a work situation or when we are engaged in an interaction, our perception of what is going on is our individual reality. We get to that reality through the "perceptual filters" we use—those expectations and assumptions we bring to the table. When we begin to take the time to acknowledge that other people don't necessarily see things the way we do, a shift can occur. The degree to which we show tolerance and understanding of other approaches and views—of those "filters" through which other people see issues and approach problems—the greater the chance that each style can contribute something useful to the whole.

If we apply this concept to leading an organization, it is apparent that when leaders have an understanding of how people relate to vision, mission, and goals and to the structure of the organization and its culture, there is a much better chance they will be able to develop more integrated and accepted solutions to business issues. They can take valuable insights from those who are engaged in planning and operations and blend them with ideas coming from the marketing and administrative sides of the house. The key here is to develop and look for the ability to "understand" or "appreciate." Leaders do not have to accept every perspective, but by listening to the ideas that come through filters different from their own, an appreciation of the value offered by diverse perspectives is developed. When this occurs, they have a much better opportunity to build the integrated and supportive team needed to carry the merged organization forward!

Returning to our integration in the insurance company, Healthy Life, let us look at where Dirk came out in this filtering process. He very squarely placed in the operations and technical filter category. That meant he most often assumed that problems related to business growth could generally be related to technology, to a lack of insistence on results, or to just too much emotion interfering with "the facts." He would most probably expect solutions to come quickly through either his own or the immediate direct involvement and technical expertise of others. His dominant approach would undoubtedly be one of "Let's get on with it and get this project done." With such a focus on "results now," we could likely predict a tendency to ignore the subtle social and relationship issues that are important in both developing business and motivating others.

In Figure 4-2, we see that other filters are portrayed by the functions planning, marketing and sales, and finance and administration. Those who see things predominantly through a planning filter tend to view things in terms of the future. They focus more on long-range benefits and implications. They are most likely to assume that problems result from oversimplification, from a lack of analysis, from an inability to see the big picture, from the tunnel vision of others, or simply from a lack of appreciation for the originality of one's creative approach. A person who sees things through a planning filter would be expected to reach a solution by synthesizing all available information and by using holistic reasoning and long-range thinking. A planning filter approach tends to be strategic. When people lead through a marketing and sales filter, they get results through communication, persuasion, motivation, and enthusiasm. Those operating through a finance and administration filter focus on detail, control, consistency, and systems that have worked in the past.

We are now brought back to the observation we made in the beginning of our analysis of Dirk's style. He appears fundamentally a technical thinker who would exclusively use this filter's style in approaching issues in Healthy Life. For us this is a red flag, because the job called for at least equal strength in seeing and acting on issues from a "get-out-there-and-sell" communicating and persuading perspective. Healthy Life's current CEO, overwhelmingly planning-oriented but with a high

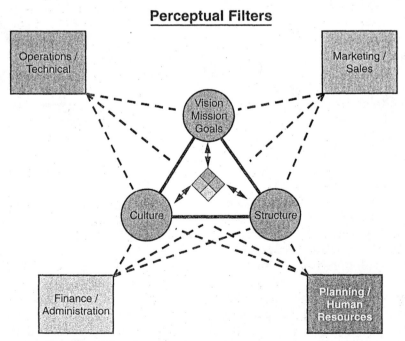

Perceptual Filters

Figure 4-2   Perceptual Filters

need to have things done his way, was preoccupied with innovative new products and services. At this point, he just wanted to keep the place running, and he wanted the integration to move fast. He was sure the customers would be lining up to enroll in the creative new plans the company was poised to announce.

He saw that by bringing Dirk in as his EVP, he (the CEO) could make sure operations ran smoothly and products and services got off the drawing board and to the customers. He would let the future take care of itself. In this case, the future stemmed from a long past that the CEO had with Dirk's father. They had been college roommates and best golfing buddies over the last 35 years. He had known Dirk since he was a baby and had watched him grow into a responsible, action-oriented adult. When Dirk was recruited by a top insurance company out of his MBA program, Healthy Life's CEO was pleased for him. He knew Dirk would get onto a fast track through the company's management development program—but he hadn't estimated Dirk's rise to be so fast. He hadn't even had time to bring him into his own company! He had always said that one day he'd have Dirk on his team. He just never thought it would have come through an acquisition!

Even though he acknowledged that Dirk's social style was introverted, his solution would be to put a development plan together that would include sending Dirk to an Ivy League advanced executive management program. He estimated that would provide Dirk with a solid theoretical update of what it takes to lead a growing company. While interacting with other CEOs, Dirk would also have the opportunity to learn how important the social aspects of leadership really were. For Healthy Life's current CEO, it was a matter of putting information in and analyzing it, then taking actions around what had been learned. A second part of the CEO's plan was to take Dirk under his wing to "acclimatize" him to the required social routine that had proved successful for him during his tenure as Healthy Life's CEO. Despite his penchant for creativity, the current CEO had a real streak of impatience.

Assessing the Motivational "Drivers"

The talent spreadsheet, the career predictors, and the perceptual filters gave us insights into types of individual talents, matches with various occupations, the presence of certain traits, and the approaches and the styles Healthy Life's senior team (including Dirk) would bring to the job. These reports didn't tell us, however, the team's most productive ways of getting results. Like the board of directors, we wanted to go more deeply into how Dirk would exercise his talents. We knew the current CEO wanted to put Dirk in as his replacement. Already, we had seen enough signposts that warned us this could be a big mistake. While the CEO had brought us into the company, we had committed to the board to use every tool in our arsenal to identify the pros and cons of this choice. So we prepared for our next level of analysis.

We took Step 2 of our talent-fit method and turned to what distinguishes this tool from other assessment instruments. We wanted to understand what really motivated Dirk—what were the drivers in his personality that would describe to us how he'd achieve results for this company. We reviewed Dirk's specific motivational needs and most productive styles of achieving results in a vast range of personality areas—from communicating, to being sociable, to organizing, to competing, to directing, to using energy and emotion, to handling change, to making decisions. The report we used, dubbed the "Components," refers to the "strengths and needs" of one's personality. This report goes beyond a person's usual behaviors—those that others can observe and identify—to the hidden, underlying needs and values that are the reasons we tend to act productively or unproductively. The data also indicate what specific environment or interaction will likely trigger the type of performance desired in a particular role or job. Here we find the keys to *how* people use their talents, carry out career responsibilities, and personify desired styles of behavior and decision making.

We wanted to hone in on the areas that connoted leadership strength—strong communication style and an inclination to take risks, to be assertive, to delegate, to be involved with others, and to adapt easily to change or to stressful conditions.

Strengths and Needs
In this report (Table 4-4), personality elements are rated on a scale of 1 to 99. Low scores indicate one type of behavior; high scores, another. Scores of 50 are the median—a blend of high- and low-scoring tendencies.

In Dirk's case, we saw that he was motivated to work alone or with just a few individuals (low scores on "Acceptance"). This was the opposite of all other members of Healthy Life's senior management, whose scores were well above the 50 range and represented sociable, gregarious, team-oriented behavior. Dirk's penchant for working alone was reinforced by a style of communication ("Esteem") that was "to the point," if not terse. His communication scores indicated little motivation to engage in social conversation or chit-chat or just tune in to where other people were. In other words, it would not be common or comfortable for him to walk around and talk to people. Indicators of his approach to planning gave us clues that he would be very detailed and precise. He was probably a manager who liked to work to a plan and wouldn't necessarily be prone to either delegation or spontaneity.

Next we looked at how he gave and received direction. Against the backdrop of the talent spreadsheet and the "Career Predictors" reports we reviewed above, which had painted a picture of him as operationally and administratively oriented, we erroneously expected him to behave in a "chain-of-command" way. Instead, we were surprised by indicators that suggested he was probably the type of person who slid quietly into a leadership challenge when one presented itself. Where there was a vacuum in leadership, he was not afraid to take on that role; albeit, the role in which he was most comfortable was one of technical leadership.

Table 4-4   Strengths and Needs Report

Dirk	Esteem	Acceptance	Structure	Authority	Advantage	Activity	Challenge	Empathy	Change	Freedom	Thought
	13/19	5/5	95/49	49/6+	10/10	49/35	95/95	46/20+	67/32+	58/36+	31/31+

89

His style of giving direction ("Authority"—average) indicated he was directive but in a slightly suggestive, nonauthoritarian way. This meant that most of the time he would leave people alone to be "self-directive" and that when he needed to, he would be there to direct the operation. For himself, he would flourish in an environment in which he was allowed to be self-directive but in which there were agreeable, pleasant relationships. He would have a tendency to avoid confrontation at all costs, except when he was not allowed to set his own course or when his judgment about a situation was questioned. When that occurred, we could expect to see a very different side of Dirk. Under stress (most likely when people were telling him what to do), he was likely to argue, become domineering, and exercise strong and direct authority.

Dirk's profile reflected an exceedingly strong achievement motivation. In fact, he was no doubt an "overachiever"—his performance records had proved that. His scores, however, indicated he did best when he had encouragement from others who could cheer him on. He needed lots of feedback to tell him how he was doing. We factored that in with the previous indication that he liked to work alone and was not easily prone to seek out others. On the one hand, this meant he probably wouldn't be stressed by "loneliness at the top," but we questioned how he might get his need for encouragement met if he tended to avoid being with people. We wondered if he could enjoy the role the board expected of the CEO, and if he did not, how long he would be able to sustain his drive to achieve.

Finally, we delved into Dirk's orientation to competition. It appeared Dirk mainly liked competing against himself (high "Challenge"). Other indicators ("Advantage," "Activity," "Empathy") showed he was more interested in opportunities to help other people than to compete against them. His motivation to negotiate or sell appeared negligible. All indications showed he would prefer a more thoughtful environment to one that was fast-paced, and he would not be prone to take an aggressive stance on issues. We further saw that his low "Advantage" scores, coupled with a low need for freedom (independence), meant he would probably shy away from taking risks. Additionally, his need for a steady income and for stability seemed stronger than any need he might have for influence.

As we checked off our leadership criteria, we saw that his strongest motivations were to achieve, but to get his "best achievement behavior" he needed the support of a low-key, noncompetitive, reflective, and stable environment where he could work alone and be his own boss. At this point, we didn't feel we had a match with either what the board wanted or what the competition demanded.

Interests
We were now ready to move the analysis of Dirk's profile to Step 3 (Table 4-5). Would he want the CEO job for which he was targeted? We know from research done on interests, that people are most likely to enjoy and succeed in areas in which they have a strong interest. Thus, we started with the number one need in Healthy Life—persuasive interest. We discovered

Table 4-5   Interests

	Persuasive	Social Services	Scientific	Mechanical	Outdoor	Numerical	Clerical	Artistic	Literary	Musical
CEO	88	22	89	38	10	36	68	80	95	49
VP sales	63	40	89	24	36	17	40	98	83	96
VP operations	63	17	79	72	43	52	30	57	83	75
General counsel	84	73	51	38	91	17	10	17	65	75
EVP	28	40	79	50	43	45	30	69	95	98
VP customer service	28	28	79	55	70	45	30	99	54	87
CFO	5	79	11	31	60	99	55	41	10	99
VP corp. plng. / policy	7	17	67	55	36	52	46	99	95	87
Averages	46	40	68	45	49	45	39	70	73	83
Dirk	5	3	79	98	89	81	30	57	32	10

that only the current CEO and the general counsel had above-average persuasive interests. Dirk's score on a scale of 1–99 was a 5—way below the cutoff that could signal interest in the arena of selling ideas, concepts, or products. While only the general counsel and the CFO had above-average interests in relating to public issues or getting personally involved in being a champion for a cause, Dirk's score was 3. A low score like a 3 is not at all a strong indicator that he'd personally put himself into promoting.

Those interests that were above average in Dirk's profile clustered around scientific, mechanical, outdoor, and numerical activities. This told us he was probably drawn to technical, task-oriented, operational endeavors. All his scores in areas that signal strength in "relational" activities were below average, indicating it would be a stretch for Dirk to put himself in environments that required fortitude for socializing and influencing. Coincidentally, none of the other officers on Healthy Life's senior team appeared to have the complete mix of interest ingredients that would compel them to seek out opportunities to persuade or convince others.

We felt at this point we had enough information to make a recommendation on whether this target candidate, Dirk, was the right choice to become Healthy Life's next CEO. We packaged Steps 1 to 3 of our shortcut assessment together with Dirk's personnel history and interviews with peers, subordinates, and his board members, and presented our findings to Healthy Life's CEO and board. This information confirmed the board's hunch—what the organization would have in Dirk appeared to be a technically very competent manager, quite well suited for an operational leadership job. His profile did not indicate a strong underlying motivation or natural talent to lead the company in the increasingly competitive service arena. For that matter, other than the general counsel, no other member of the acquiring management team had what the board wanted in its next CEO. (*Note*: The general counsel was not a viable candidate because family issues prevented him from taking on the social obligations that went with the CEO job.)

We spent quite a lot of time with Dirk, reviewing his talents and motivations. In the end, he decided he really had never felt comfortable in his role as CEO of the acquired company when he was pushed into that job two years earlier. He was put there because he had done a great job in operations. It seemed to him that he was wearing a suit that did not fit him well. In addition, he really didn't like having to manage all the diverse issues that came up—from personnel, to finance, to customer relations. He wanted to have fun in his job, and so far, being CEO wasn't fun for him.

We explored what his dream job would be. It was to head the operations of a smaller and more technical, scientific, engineering-related company. We put him in touch with a headhunter who specialized in the petro-chemical industry and in less than a month he had his dream job in a firm that was noted for its ability to deliver projects to customers. In addition to a good hiring package, the company was in a location that pleased both him and his family.

The board began a search for the current CEO's replacement, and after about six months the ideal candidate emerged. Her career experience was in banking, but she had all the relationship and leadership skills Healthy Life needed. She began working with the outgoing CEO and took over the reins of the company a year later. The integration of the two companies went smoothly in almost every respect, and the transition to new leadership was almost seamless. We had followed most of the five steps in our process and learned an important lesson or two. First, we learned to look beneath the top manager's desires for a certain individual to become his or her successor. There had to be some strong reason that Healthy Life's CEO wanted to put forth a candidate who from the earliest appeared to have neither the right mix of talent nor the necessary motivation for the challenge. Next, we learned that it pays to ask the candidate in question what he or she really wants out of his or her career—because it just might be something other than what top management had in mind!

The Case of Two Banks

This next example is one of a real clash of social and cultural styles. Here we focus on Step 4 of our talent-fit method by comparing the differences between an upstart entreprenuerial youngster and the refined stability of the granddaddy of regional banks.

In this merger of two banks (the names have been modified), we find an upstart acquiring an inveterate and respected institution. New Summit Bank was a young, 10-year-old bank with both progressive and aggressive vision and leadership. It was situated in a region of growing and dominant technology development. To better serve the younger affluent customer base coming into the area, the bank needed more branches. It chose as its acquisition partner, Golden Shores National Bank, a stable, historic, and conventional community bank with roots in the region for over 90 years. A prime consideration was that Golden Shores had more than 50 branches within the commuting radius of the technology corridor.

The corporate profiles of the two banks were very different (Tables 4-6 and 4-7). New Summit had real strength in strategizing for the future and creating a variety of products that appealed to younger, more technologically and consumption-oriented clients. It used the latest in technology and was noted for its internal focus on results. It was generally an efficient, friendly, fun place to work, where staff was on a first-name basis.

Golden Shores had an established and aging clientele. People banked there because their grandparents and parents had accounts with the bank. Its officers were leaders in traditional community organizations such as the Rotary Club and Chamber of Commerce. Its hallmark was the "upper-crust" polish it exuded along with the formal courtesy it extended to its customers. The offices were opulent and colonial in style. Products were geared to individuals who physically visited the bank. The bank's reputation was for meticulous accounting and personalized customer service.

When we looked at the talent spreadsheet of each bank in the context of the four major talent requirements (planning, communicating, expediting, and administrating), we saw that New Summit had almost equal strength in the first three requirements of planning, communicating, and expediting; the fourth, administrating, was below average. Conversely, Golden Shores came up very strong in administrating, made an average showing in communicating and expediting, and fell below average in planning talent. The intention of the merger was to expand the reach of New Summit through the network of Golden Shores' branches while emphasizing new products and new, more efficient, technology-linked banking services.

In essence, the deal was for "real estate." While due diligence had confirmed there would be a clash between the "visionary, sales, and delivery" leadership talent of New Summit and the "control mindset" of Golden Shores, New Summit's CEO did not want a backlash from Golden

Table 4-6 New Summit Bank—Talent Spreadsheet / Organizational Strengths

	Planning	Communicating	Expediting	Administrating	Knowledge Specialist	Directive Management	Delegative Management	Artistic Careers	Educational Careers	Social Service / Counseling	Employee Relations / Training	Medical Professions	Direct Tangible Sales	Direct Intangible Sales	Consultative Tangible Sales	Consultative Intangible Sales	Legal	Crafts / Technical	Police, Fire, and Security	Petrochemical	Engineering / Technology	Science	General Administrative	Numerical Administrative	Administrative Professionals	Banking and Finance Accounting
Averages	7	6	4	7	4	4	7	6	7	7	8	6	6	7	5	5	5	5	5	6	7	6	5	7	5	4
CEO	8	7	5	7	5	4	8	8	9	9	9	8	8	9	7	7	7	8	7	7	8	6	5	6	5	4
EVP bus. development	8	9	2	8	2	7	9	2	4	9	9	7	9	9	6	6	8	2	4	5	7	5	2	5	5	2
VP commercial sales	9	8	6	9	3	5	9	9	9	9	9	8	8	8	7	7	4	4	4	4	5	8	7	8	6	3
VP lending	9	6	5	10	2	1	10	9	10	9	10	6	6	5	5	5	5	6	5	7	8	7	5	9	3	2
VP operations and CIO	5	4	3	6	7	2	6	3	5	4	7	4	3	5	3	5	9	9	9	8	9	4	4	3	1	1
VP customer service	8	6	2	10	2	2	8	8	8	8	9	6	6	5	7	3	4	3	4	5	6	9	9	10	8	6
CFO	1	3	7	1	10	8	1	1	1	1	1	3	2	5	2	3	6	6	7	7	7	2	4	10	7	10
General counsel	6	5	5	7	2	6	5	5	6	6	6	6	5	6	7	7	2	3	2	3	4	5	2	6	6	7

Table 4-7 Golden Shores National Bank—Talent Spreadsheet / Organizational Strengths

	Planning	Communicating	Expediting	Administrating	Knowledge Specialist	Directive Management	Delegative Management	Artistic Careers	Educational Careers	Social Service / Counseling	Employee Relations / Training	Medical Professions	Direct Tangible Sales	Direct Intangible Sales	Consultative Tangible Sales	Consultative Intangible Sales	Legal	Crafts / Technical	Police, Fire, and Security	Petrochemical	Engineering / Technology	Science	General Administrative	Numerical Administrative	Administrative Professionals	Banking and Finance	Accounting
Averages	4	5	7	5	6	6	4	5	5	5	4	6	5	5	5	6	4	5	5	4	4	5	5	6	6	7	6
CHM &CEO	4	3	5	2	7	10	1	3	5	7	2	9	9	8	7	7	3	4	3	5	2	1	4	4	4	8	6
President	3	6	6	3	9	5	1	2	4	5	1	9	6	7	5	4	5	7	5	6	5	1	1	3	4	4	7
VP operations	1	6	8	2	7	7	1	1	1	2	1	5	3	3	3	2	5	6	6	7	6	2	2	2	3	8	9
VP lending	7	4	7	5	5	10	5	8	8	9	7	9	9	9	8	7	4	6	3	3	3	5	6	8	8	8	9
VP customer service	7	4	7	10	4	1	7	8	7	6	2	2	1	1	3	9	5	2	4	3	4	10	9	10	8	5	2
VP fin./admin.	3	6	8	8	6	3	3	3	2	3	5	4	5	5	3	1	6	6	7	5	6	8	8	8	6	6	7
General counsel	6	3	9	7	1	5	7	7	6	6	6	6	5	3	6	10	3	2	2	2	2	10	10	9	9	8	8

Shores' established community customer base. His fear was that he would be known as the punk upstart who conquered the revered uncle, and publicity could hurt for awhile. He had to find a way to work through the differences in style. Our process provided him with a neutral tool to demonstrate to both the chairman and the president of Golden Shores that their senior-most leadership would not be comfortable with the aggressive approach embraced by New Summit's leadership. His goal was for them to see that the combined organization could benefit from the talent strength of both. At a glance they could see the talent "gap" in administration and New Summit and this "missing element" very much in evidence in Golden Shores' talent spreadsheet. Literally, all it took was a look at the comparative talent spreadsheets of these two organizations.

Although Golden Shores had the talent that New Summit lacked, the tenure of the officers overseeing administration, legal, and customer service was nearing its end, with each of these three officers 6 to 36 months away from retirement. The talent was there, but soon these three officers would be gone. This was enough for the leaders of Golden Shores to follow New Summit's logic. The numbers spoke the reality. New Summit's CEO felt that if each of these officers had hired in their own image, he would find similar "control strengths" in their direct reports. He also hoped these strengths would be combined with youth, with vision, and with a sense of urgency.

Together the two CEOs searched down the ranks of *Golden Shores* for individuals in administration and in customer service who were motivated by both competition and personal accountability and who could be expected to adapt most easily to the dominant leadership style of the new company. Though not so obvious at first glance, they found their new leaders—one and two layers, respectively, beneath the existing rank of top officers. It would take some straight talk to convince the staff being leapfrogged that their subordinates had what the new company needed and that these appointments were in the best interests of the entire company.

Next, given the ages and the motivational interests of the other three top Golden Shores officers, it was clear that they lacked, for the most part, the traits that favored adaptation to the aggressive atmosphere of the new company's senior management team. The decision among the leaders of both banks was (1) to create severance packages for the existing Golden Shores leadership team and (2) to immediately put the two newly identified Golden Shores leaders (administration and customer service) to work on the new company's integration teams. The chairman and CEO of Golden Shores decided to depart completely from the banking industry, while his president retired and accepted a seat on the new company's board.

With the addition of Golden Shores' talent to the new company's customer service organization, an immediate campaign was launched to reach out to Golden Shores' existing base of customers to:

- Explain the exciting new products available to them
- Assure them they would not become a number in a faceless computer

- Assure them that the same personalized service they had enjoyed at Golden Shores would become a trademark of the new company

The administrative talent tapped from Golden Shores took over, as the new VP of finance and administration replaced New Summit's VP, who was somewhat short on both vision and communication skills. Though not easy from an ego standpoint, this integration was completed more efficiently and smoothly than most of its kind. While information from our process was certainly not the only data used in the assessment decisions, it made the job much less contentious than other situations where mostly subjective or outdated performance information was used.

The key lesson learned in this case is that the integration effort can be facilitated by quickly assessing and choosing key people. The trick is to move and communicate quickly. That means explaining why certain people have been tapped for leadership roles and why certain systems and processes are being jettisoned or adopted. So long as both the "incoming" and "acquiring" staff understand the reasons behind the moves, there is a much better chance they'll accept changes in leadership, get on board, and work to integrate and be integrated into the newly created environment.

Speed cannot be overemphasized. The faster people are put in place and systems are changed, the better. The merger that decides not to put pressure on the "acquired team," and basically lets things sit to work themselves out, is the one that ultimately fails. This one went very fast—due to the entrepreneurial, action-oriented style of New Summit's CEO and the diplomatic style of Golden Shores' chairman and CEO.

Impact of the Organizational Life Cycle on Talent Needed
This last merger vignette is one in which two extremely large companies merged in order to stay alive in the face of recently merged competition. From a short-term financial perspective, the merger made sense. What was difficult to see, from our perspective, was that by coming together, they really didn't create anything new.

There didn't seem to be that important "value added" that would steal the competitive advantage from this new company's closest challengers. In the long term, we thought the financial gains would be eroded by competitors with newer and more efficient products and services. In this case, we entered with an analysis of where each organization was in its own life cycle so the organizations could see what they might be facing down the road.

Where a company is in its organizational life cycle (Figure 4-3) gives one a sense of what kinds of talents are needed at a particular time in history. When an organization is new and young, it needs structure and stability. When it is old and somewhat immovable, it needs to reinvent itself with new ideas, new flexibility, and new approaches to the marketplace.

The life cycle can be linked to the talent spreadsheets, like the ones we looked at in the cases of the insurance company, Healthy Life, and the two

Organizational Life Cycle

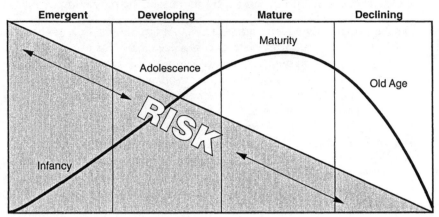

Figure 4-3   Life-Cycle Stages

banks, New Summit and Golden Shores. The typical life cycle for any organization looks like a bell curve. It begins as a start-up (or an emergent organization), and then moves into growth (or a developing organization), followed by maturity, and finally into decline.

At each of these stages, certain driving talents are required. During the emergence or infancy of an organization, the key talent required is innovation and strategic vision. Recalling from our talent spreadsheet that innovation and strategic vision are characterized by "planning," we call this start-up or infancy the "planning" phase of an organization's life cycle. It is here where ideas abound about products and markets.

As the company develops, it needs the talent to persuade its markets and promote its product. This can be referred to as its "marketing and sales" phase. It is where marketing and sales grow both in depth and in breadth. In maturity, the talent need is for implementation, delivery, and focused direction. Here, an organization establishes stronger production methods and processes, and it focuses on delivery targets. At this point, an organization is centered in its "operating phase."

As it heads into the declining or aging years, a company's talent is focused primarily on details and systems—keeping business going as usual. This is the "controlling" period of organizational life. Most organizations like to think they possess the requisite talent at each phase in their development. The fact of the matter is that if you look closely and scrutinize where the money is being allocated and where senior management targets most of its attention, there really is a predominant focus in each stage.

Take the case of a 100-year-old power company. Known for a century as a leader in power generation, renamed here as International Power and Energy Company (IPEC), it honed its skills to perfection in production and delivery. As the world changed, the company maintained its R&D by doing cutting-edge research on alternative sources of energy. But this futuristic preoccupation was just one pocket in a huge, lumbering organization where the top leadership continued to focus its talent on what it had always done best—build power-generating plants, produce, and deliver. It was squarely in the maturity stage of the organizational life cycle. Along came the Internet and deregulation, and companies that had been considered upstarts began to offer products and services that cut into the margins of the traditional power suppliers.

Although successful in acquiring other regional companies that enabled it to expand its reach (doing what it had done so well), IPEC was stymied by the mergers of other similar organizations. Eventually it was acquired by a well-established, but younger, power company that needed IPEC's international presence. A talent spreadsheet of the acquiring company (Midlands Power Company) shows that its predominant talents lie in vision and in sales. In essence it appears to be nearing the end of its "adolescence" as the "expediting" bar inches up in scale to the "planning" and "communicating" bars. Figures 4-4 and 4-5 present the talent spreadsheets of Midlands and IPEC and of the merged companies, respectively. The merged company spreadsheet shows the resultant mix of talents reminiscent of IPEC's original configuration.

Combined, the company brings nearly twice as much strength in expediting as it does in planning and communicating. Administration is the weakest of all the talent areas. Could this mean more of the same? By combining a mature organization with an aging adolescent, have we created a near carbon copy of what IPEC was at the time of its acquisition? Our concern is whether it has enough of a futuristic focus to enable the combined company to beat the creative competition in the long haul.

Talent Spreadsheet - Acquiring Company
(Midlands Power Company)

Talent Spreadsheet - Acquired Company
(International Power and Energy Co.)

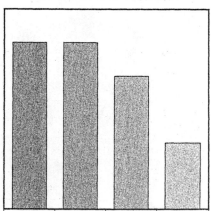
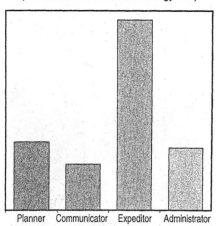

Figure 4-4   Talent Spreadsheet of Acquiring and Acquired Companies

To compete with the upstarts, who have brought changes to the way energy is marketed, this newly combined energy conglomerate will have to dare to bring in people who don't fit the mold of their predominantly operational leadership. We have shown them through the talent spreadsheets and historical precedents that they must step up to the challenge and bring in those who are far more visionary in outlook and ability. For the new company it means having the courage to take risks and not stick to what was done well in the past. If the planning and communicating strengths of the combined organization were on a par with its expeditor strengths, we would feel much more confident about the new company's ability to bring added value to the marketplace. Without this value added to galvanize the spirit and drive of the new organization, other possibilities could occur.

One scenario has to do with whether the more freewheeling adolescent acquiring company has what it takes to withstand the conventions and precedents adhered to by the IPEC contingent. Using the life-cycle diagram, the talent spreadsheets, the "Career Predictors," and the components, we were able to explore the opportunities and the pitfalls in selection and help the acquiring company make more appropriate choices in its key people. Our role in due diligence was to provide the merging organizations all the insights we could bring about what they have, what they lack, what the talents, skills, competencies, and style of the key players are, and how they may expect them to interact in productive times and in stress.

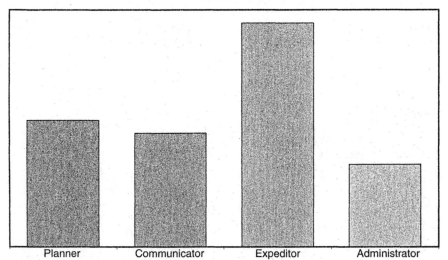

Figure 4-5   Talent Spreadsheet of Combined Companies

A FINAL NOTE

I have attempted to illustrate in this chapter and Chapter 3 several important elements of the integration process that need to be considered during the transaction stage and their potential impact on the success of the integration process and the accomplishment of strategic and financial objectives. Inability to manage these elements during this stage should not deter the acquiring and merging companies from doing it at later stages of the integration process. The earlier the better, but better late than never!

5

PREPARING STAKEHOLDER COMMUNICATIONS AND VALUE PRESERVATION

Communicate, communicate, communicate! Almost every experienced executive who has managed integration and every expert who writes on the topic agree that you cannot communicate enough during this process. Most people, whether it is employees, customers, distributors, or investors, do not like uncertainty, especially if it is prolonged and involves issues that are likely to have a direct bearing on them.

It is a basic premise that most people have a need to make sense out of the world they live in so that they can adjust, plan, and take action. However, the process of making sense requires information and people who are resourceful and creative and will do what it takes to "figure things out." This will happen whether executives keep people informed of what is going on or not. In the absence of formal communications, people will turn to the rumor mill and other sources of less accurate information. They will also fill in additional details based on inferences and assumptions drawn from their previous experiences, from information publicized in the media, and from the experiences of others. People will also use their imaginations. The problem here is that all these sources are outside the control of executives and contain both accurate and inaccurate information.

The implications are clear. Failure to manage the communication process creates an uncontrolled and random process of making sense inside and outside the organization, which can lead to ideas and actions that are detrimental to both people and the merger integration itself. These include inaccurate perceptions, lost trust in management, morale and productivity problems, safety problems, poor customer service, and defection of key people and customers. It may also lead to the loss of the support of key stakeholders at a time when that support is needed the most.

However, regardless of how well executives communicate during a merger or an acquisition, uncertainty will never be completely eliminated. The objective is to minimize as much uncertainty as possible, especially with regard to issues that directly impact people and organizations.

The decision about when to begin the communication process is not an easy one to make. It requires a balance between the need for secrecy (e.g., to respect the target management's desires to keep the deal quiet, to prevent other buyers from entering the bidding process, or to fulfill legal or regulatory requirements) and the activity of the rumor mill. As such, it makes the most sense to consider communicating early (e.g., when discussions with a target have commenced) rather than later (e.g., with a formal announcement of the deal). The key, however, is to try and beat the timing of the rumor mill whenever possible. The impact of late communications and uncertainty was clearly felt in the acquisition of Digital Equipment by Compaq Computer. Compaq's senior management waited until after the acquisition closed before communicating with people. Tired of the uncertainty, a number of Digital vice presidents resigned from Compaq within a year after the merger and days before their severance agreement expired. On the other hand, companies such as Computer Associates and Cisco make communications with targets a high priority. They utilize rapid action teams that visit acquired employees within days to brief them on merger and acquisition plans.[1]

Acquiring executives should make communication a key discussion point with the target or a merger partner during the drafting of a letter of intent or memorandum of agreement. Although an acquirer does not have control over a target, the acquirer should strongly encourage the target management to initiate a communication process within its own firm. Again, this may affect the state of the target when the acquirer gains control. It also sends a signal about the acquirer's values and culture.

When dealing with a unionized work force, a partnership with the union should be attempted. If the union is cooperative, it may be worthwhile to use the union to help communicate with employees. Failure to include the union may lead to the creation of an enemy when one did not exist before. If the union is hostile, then the acquirer management may have to bypass it and wage a public relations battle.

In general, there is one major recommendation most successful acquirers give: Overcommunicate and overinform! The next section describes some basic, sensible steps to take to achieve effective communication.

KEYS TO EFFECTIVE COMMUNICATION

Consider these eight key elements when establishing a communication process:

1. Establish a communication philosophy.
2. Be timely and relevant.
3. "Walk the talk."
4. Be careful of secret meetings.
5. Understand what people want to hear.
6. Choose effective communication media.
7. Identify and communicate with all key stakeholders.
8. Develop and execute a communication plan.

Establish a Communication Philosophy

Before developing a communication plan, it is useful to determine the basic philosophy underlying it. The philosophy represents the core values driving the plan and guides managers in executing it. The acquiring and acquired companies need to begin this process by examining any core values they have articulated to run their own organization and any guiding principles they established to drive the integration (see Chapter 6) so that they can ensure that the communication process is consistent with them. However, regardless of the company's core values, several elements are essential to the success of any communication process.

Honesty Is the Best Policy

Honesty may sound a bit naïve when we consider the political gyrations that take place within and among organizations. However, not only is it morally the right thing to do, but it actually works! Why is this the case? There is a simple truism that applies to the communication process: "The truth happens whether it came from your mouth or not."

If the objective of an executive is to manipulate employees and other stakeholders in the short run, dishonesty is likely to work. Reassuring people that everything is fine and that "no one is likely to lose their job due to the merger" or "nothing will change as a result of the integration" may seem calming and perhaps comfort people in the short run. This assumes that they will believe these statements. However, the minute there is a loss of jobs or things do change, which is inevitable, people will clearly remember the reassuring statement that was made and assume that management deceived them. If all people are let go, such as in a plant shutdown, then we might not have to worry about the implications. No one will be left. Perhaps there will be some lawsuits and complaints. However, if there are people who remain, the situation becomes far more complicated. This is even more critical if the primary assets of the company are intangible and invested in people. Certainly customers, investors, and shareholders will also remember if they were misled.

For example, I was involved in the sale of a company in California. The purchase price being asked was far in excess of the value of the tangible assets reported on the balance sheet. The company, which made fans to cool chips in personal computers, owned very little property and equipment. The only real tangible assets were tied up in inventory and receivables, and they were not a significant part of the asking price. So what explained the value of this company? Most of the value was inherent in top-notch design engineers and relationships with customers and distributors. If these intangibles "walked out the door" or were significantly demotivated, the company would be worth very little. Knowing this led us to conclude that communications would be a key part of employee, customer, and distributor retention and of value preservation. It worked. The company had no defections. The stakeholders appreciated the company's diligence in keeping them informed during the deal.

A colleague and I tried to empirically determine whether honest communication really makes a difference to employees.[2] We conducted a study in two similar light manufacturing plants of a division of a *Fortune* 500 company preparing to be merged. The study was conducted prior to the merger. In one plant 126 employees were provided with an enriched "merger preview." The preview focused on giving employees frequent, relevant, and honest information about the merger through detailed newsletters, telephone hotlines, weekly meetings between employees and supervisors who were continually briefed by senior management, and meetings between individual employees and the plant manager whenever personal decisions had been made. Information communicated included background on the merger and information on layoffs and severance benefits, transfers, compensation and benefits, and integration plans for the combined firm. In the other plant there were no formal communications provided to the 146 employees other than an initial letter from the CEO explaining the rationale for the merger. This type of communication had been typical in the company.

We were interested in determining whether the communications had an impact on a variety of outcome measures related to the retention and well-being of the firm's intellectual capital. These outcomes included stress; perceived uncertainty; job satisfaction; organizational commitment; company's trustworthiness, honesty, and caring; intention to remain within the organization; and employee performance, absenteeism, and turnover. As shown in Figure 5-1, we collected data both before and after the merger announcement and before and after the merger preview was implemented. After the announcement of the merger there was a significant increase in stress, perceived uncertainty, and absenteeism. There were significant declines in job satisfaction; organizational commitment; company's trustworthiness, honesty, and caring; and intention to remain

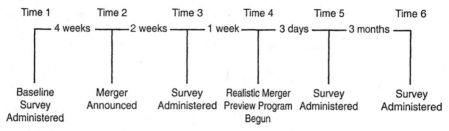

Figure 5-1 Time Line of Major Events

within the organization. Indeed the announcement of the merger did have a significant and negative impact.

The key question now was whether the merger preview would help ameliorate these negative outcomes. There was a significant difference between the plant receiving the merger preview and the one that did not. Specifically, the preview plant reported significantly lower perceived uncertainty, higher job satisfaction and performance, and greater commitment to and trust in the company and management. The merger preview appeared to stabilize the level of dysfunctional outcomes, and this effect continued over time. Figures 5-2 through 5-4 illustrate these effects for several outcomes. Of importance is that none of the merger preview outcomes were as strong in comparison to those prior to the merger, demonstrating the impact that such an event can have. It also suggests that communication cannot eliminate these outcomes—it can only hope to improve them. Indeed, honest and frequent communication does work!

Critical to the success of a merger or an acquisition is the ability to build a new organization. This requires that the best people be retained and motivated. Clearly manipulation does not work in this situation. Whether people remain motivated and stay will depend upon the credibility of those leading them. Often during integration, executives will need to ask people to trust them as the many complicated decisions are being worked out and are not quite ready to be communicated. The credibility quotient of these executives will be measured by the gap between what they say and do and what ultimately happens. The greater the gap, the lower the credibility. The lower the credibility, the less the likelihood they will successfully be able to lead.

As the preceding discussion suggests, executives are often going to have to ask people to trust them and to wait for answers. Thus, going into the integration they must draw upon their relationships with people. The critical issue is whether they are credible prior to the integration.

What does all this mean in practice? While people can always be honest, they cannot always be open; i.e., they cannot always tell others all the details of what is going on. As such, it is best to use the following three approaches in communicating:

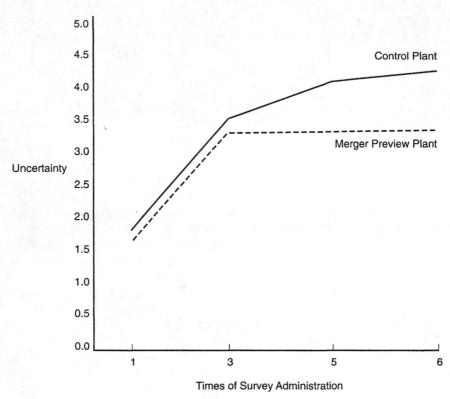

Figure 5-2 **Longitudinal Effects of Merger and Realistic Merger Preview on Uncertainty**

1. "If I can tell you, I will."
2. "If I do not know the answers, I will try and find them."
3. "If I cannot tell you, I will explain why."

I have found these responses to be quite effective. For example, I was assisting in the sale of one publicly traded company to another. The rumors concerning the buyer were rampant and in fact quite accurate. Moreover, the buyer was a direct competitor whom the employees were not thrilled to work for. Employees of the target kept asking management to confirm the rumors. Since the sale had not been made public, the company's executives could not confirm it. They were bound by SEC insider trading rules and obligated to announce the sale publicly before releasing a widespread communication within the company. To stem the rumor mill, they openly communicated that they could not comment due to SEC rules and explained the rules in simple terms to the employees. Although the employees thought such rules made little sense, they appreciated management's efforts. Soon after, the sale was then made public. As this

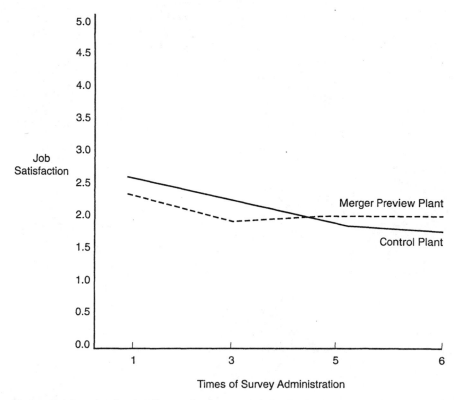

Figure 5-3 Longitudinal Effects of Merger and Realistic Merger Preview on Job Satisfaction

example illustrates, at some point you must be able to give tangible answers. Too many "I don't knows" will lead people to conclude that executives are withholding information or are ineffective. Neither bodes well for their credibility.

Further, executives must avoid giving unrealistic information. If they have either good or bad news, they need to deliver it. The best approach is to be realistic. People are capable of dealing with and responding to all types of news. Sometimes executives like to put a positive spin on communications. Either they are trying to manipulate interpretations of the facts, or they are trying to insulate people from the realities of a negative situation. Both are mistakes. My experience suggests that it is best to give people the facts so that they can have time to deal with them and plan how they will move forward. It is also best to avoid offering speculation instead of solid information. People often interpret speculation as information and will react in what may not, in the long run, be in their best interests or those of the company.

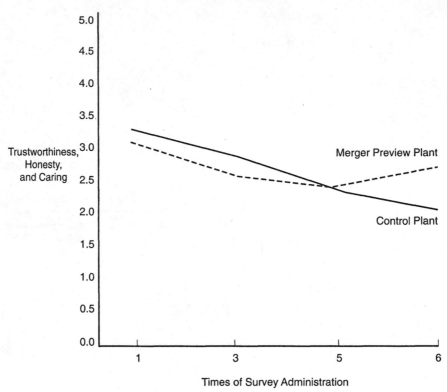

Figure 5-4 Longitudinal Effects of Merger and Realistic Merger Preview on Perceived Trustworthiness, Honesty, and Caring of the Company

Be Timely and Relevant

It is essential to provide information to people about issues that they are concerned with as early as possible, but no later than immediately following the formal announcement of the acquisition. Naturally, most employees want to know about what is happening to their departments and to them. Customers want to know how the deal will affect the service they receive, whether the company will be around, and the like. Until they do know, they will remain restless and maybe even defect.

"Walk the Talk"

Executives must be prepared to back up what they say (the credibility gap). If they make a commitment they cannot keep, they will be measured against it. If they speculate about something that will happen and it does not, they will also be measured against that. Trust and loyalty develop over time when there is consistency in word and action. Behaviors must conform to stated company philosophy, values, and policies.

Be Careful of Secret Meetings

Rarely is a meeting to discuss a delicate issue a secret, and it is prudent to begin such a meeting with that assumption. Secretaries often arrange such meetings, and it is human nature to share information. Employees notice that their manager or multiple managers are gone on a particular day and assume they must be up to something. Even meetings that take place at remote locations and times are difficult to hide. I have talked with numerous salespeople who have encountered executives meeting in secrecy in airport airline clubs. I even encountered an employee who learned about a clandestine meeting held by the executives of his company late one Saturday night. The company was rumored to be up for sale. On his way home from a party, he drove by corporate headquarters. He noticed a number of executives' cars parked in front of the executive office building. By Monday morning the rumors were running rampant and were quite creative.

In general it is safe to assume that someone knows the meeting is taking place. Therefore, it is wise to ensure that at such meetings the last item on the agenda should be communication. Specifically it is important to:

1. Develop a clear message. Avoid ambiguous messages.
2. Ensure that there is consensus among those participating in the meeting. Everyone needs to be "singing from the same sheet of music." I have found that employees from different work units communicate with each other and compare notes, especially through e-mail. If managers and executives deliver different messages or different interpretations of the same message, inconsistency of interpretation within the organization is likely. Not only will this fuel the rumor mill, but it will undermine the credibility of management.
3. Decide whether to communicate proactively or reactively. At a minimum, those attending the meeting should be prepared for "elevator talk"; i.e., what should I say if I am approached by someone? This is a moment of truth when employees will be waiting for an unambiguous, unflinching response. Anything short of that will send a mixed message.

Understand What People Want to Hear

I learned about what is important to people while traveling with a CEO of a merged company. It was just after the closing and we were visiting all the operations of the acquired company. He was in the process of visiting 15 locations in 20 days. He was conducting cafeteria-style meetings to explain the vision behind the new company and to announce organizational changes that had been made. In particular, the top two levels of the combined organization had been named, but many positions below these levels were still in the process of being decided. It was early in the trip, and the

CEO asked me if I would sit among the employees and give him my reaction to his presentation after he was finished. After being introduced to the audience as the consultant assisting with the integration, I took a seat. During the "vision" presentation, an employee on my left nudged me and asked me if I knew whether he had a job or not. I told him I did not know. Then he asked me if I would deliver a message to the CEO. I agreed. He asked me to tell the CEO: "If I have a job, this is the best vision I have ever heard and will support it. If I do not have a job, I could care less." On that day it became clear to me what people are really interested in hearing about. This is not to argue that people are not dedicated to their jobs or care about their companies. It is to illustrate that until the "me" issues are taken care of, it is very difficult for people to embrace a merger.

If the issues that management presents during merger presentations and the issues people want to hear about are examined, you get two very different stories. Table 5-1 provides examples of these two perspectives. Although executives do not always know the answers to "me" questions, it is important to realize that the sooner they answer these questions, the sooner people will be able to move on and start the process of building the new organization.

Choose Effective Communication Media

Once the communication philosophy and the message are established, the media need to be determined. The most effective way to communicate daily with employees is through face-to-face communications with supervisors and managers.[3] The best way to communicate major changes is through *dialogue* with senior managers in town hall–type meetings. This

Table 5-1 What People Want to Hear About

What executives think are important	What employees think are important
• Vision for the merged organization • Strategic benefits of the merger • Reasons for changes and transitions • Changes in the company name • Changes in organizational structure and management • Changes in product lines, etc	• Will I have a job? • What will the company *and I* gain/lose from it? • How can I be successful in the new environment? • Changes in benefits and compensation • Changes in job and role • Changes in perks • Greater or fewer career opportunities • Provisions for layoffs • Severance benefits • Internal transfers ("voluntary") • Outplacement services • Changes in company systems, policies, etc.

means two-way communications! The same approach often works with key stakeholders. They would like to have a dialogue with key executives and managers concerning changes that will significantly impact them. Other media that can be used to communicate include:

1. Rumor mill. Create employee communications committees within your organization to improve information channels. Such committees should be made up of a cross section of informal leaders.
2. Videotapes, memos, Intranet sites, or e-mail for hard-to-reach groups.
3. Normal company newsletter.
4. Transition/integration newsletter.
5. Bulletin boards.
6. Intranet and Internet sites.
7. Telephone hotlines.
8. Internal publications of press releases.
9. Brochures.
10. Training sessions.
11. Employee assistance program representatives.

It is best to examine the media that employees are most likely to respond to and consider valid sources of information within the acquirer and the target. Rather than guessing what works, it is more useful to assess options directly and use the media that are most likely to have the desired effect. I have conducted several studies with companies to determine the usefulness of their media in the eyes of employees. Particular focus has been given to the availability of information, the believability of information, and the usefulness of information. In addition to the 11 items noted above, I have also examined outside sources such as customers, suppliers, local media, and friends. The results are usually eye-opening and often challenge assumptions that executives have about various media. In one study it was clear that the president of the company was the most useful and believable source of information. In another, the president lacked credibility. However, his executive vice president was highly respected. Whom would you send out to visit with the troops?

It is also important to provide all employees who interact with key stakeholders (e.g., joint-venture partners) with information so that they can effectively respond to questions about the status of the integration. Otherwise employees will be perceived as ineffective and out of the communication loop.

Identify and Communicate with All Key Stakeholders

Although the discussion above has primarily focused on employees, it is important that an acquirer communicate with other key stakeholders as well. Key stakeholders are those that might be affected by integration, or perceive that they will be, and can have a direct bearing on the success of an acquirer, a target, or the integration. Typical stakeholders include:

1. Customers
2. Distributors
3. Financial analysts and consultants
4. Trade and business press
5. Government agencies
6. Communities in company locations
7. Shareholders
8. Unions
9. Joint-venture and alliance partners

This list of stakeholders may grow or shrink, depending upon the companies and situation involved. In general, much like employees, these stakeholders will be concerned with how a merger or an acquisition will affect them or the groups and individuals they represent. For example, a union has the capability of striking or restricting organizational changes that can be undertaken. For a military contractor, the Department of Defense can have a significant impact on new contracts and the preservation of existing ones. In an international context a government may have a significant impact on changes created by the merger of two oil companies. Financial analysts' assessments of the status of integration can also have an impact on an acquirer's stock price. And the list goes on!

Develop and Execute a Communication Plan

Regardless of the stakeholders, an organized communication plan is essential. It ensures that the right communications are provided to the right stakeholders at the right time.

Table 5-2 illustrates the basic elements required in any sound communication plan. The plan must identify:

1. The objective behind the communication
2. The message to be communicated
3. The target audience (stakeholder) of the message
4. The most effective media (including people) to employ in influencing the stakeholder
5. The timing of the communication

Table 5-3 illustrates a more detailed employee communication plan that was used by an acquirer in the process of making multiple acquisitions. The plan was designed for employees and managers of acquired companies, during the transaction, transition, and integration stages:

Table 5-2 Basic Communication Plan

Who says	What To	Whom Using Which	Media Pursuing Which	Objective	When

- To help them understand:
  - Why their company was bought
  - How it would be integrated with the acquirer
  - Changes that were being made and implemented
  - How changes would affect them

- So that they would:
  - Remain with the company
  - Support the changes
  - Maintain levels of performance

- Using "believable" media that allowed people to:
  - Get information when they needed it
  - Engage in two-way communications
  - Resolve issues in a timely manner

Although the format of the plan presented in Table 5-2 is somewhat different, it still addresses the elements presented in Table 5-3. A more detailed stakeholder communication plan that was developed for a large acquisition is presented in Appendix 5-1.

Ensure Coordination and Consistency

The management and coordination of communications is as important as the plan itself. All communications must be coordinated to ensure consistency among media and over time. When inconsistent information is delivered across multiple media or over time, it sends a message to employees and stakeholders that the executives of the companies involved in the merger or acquisition either are totally disorganized or are manipulating them. Neither is useful.

Single-point coordination and communication guidelines can help avert inconsistency. I have found that a communication integration team

Table 5-3 Employee Communication Plan

Stage	Communication Messages	Media
Transition Stage (Following the Formal Announcement of the Acquisition)	• History of the acquirer • Vision for business unit • Why target was chosen and strategy of combined organization • Need to focus on customers and day-to-day operations • Process that will be used to integrate the acquisition • Need for intercultural cooperation • Key decisions that have been or will be made	• Initial visit to target by the acquirer's business unit executives with possible support of target firm's president • Immediate follow-up through written or electronic media
Transition and Integration Stages	• Status of integration process • Changes being made and impact on strategic objectives • Impact of changes on people and how they will be managed • Integration successes achieved during the communicaton period • Orientation to the acquirer for newly acquired people	• Major changes announced by the acquirer's business unit executives during site visits or videos • Follow-up through written or electronic media • More routine changes through written or electronic media • Personal impacts and changes through face-to-face communications with direct managers

can be of great help. This team, working with other teams as part of the integration process, becomes the central clearinghouse for messages to release to employees and other stakeholders. The ultimate responsibility, however, for what messages are communicated lies with the leaders of the integration process. The team advises on messages, media, and timing and serves as the watchdog for consistency. This team should include those involved in employee communications, media relations, and public relations. The team needs to continually interact with other integration teams to understand the many issues requiring communications and their status. (More will be said about the integration transition structure in Chapter 6.)

Develop a Workable Communication Process

In addition to coordination, it's vital to have a process in place for ensuring that communications reach people and that issues are resolved on a day-to-day basis, especially during the transition stage. Too often, those sending communications have a sense of relief once a message has been sent. They can now check that item off their long list of activities that need to be performed as part of their plan. Unfortunately, once the message is sent, the work only begins. Was the message received and understood? Was the issue resolved? If not, then the entire communication process has been a waste of time.

A workable process requires an understanding of the organization and people involved and some creativity in developing an approach that ensures that messages went through and issues were resolved.

For example, I consulted with a company that was making several small to medium-sized acquisitions a month. Backroom activities were to be centralized by the acquirer. Many of the target's field activities were to remain geographically decentralized but standardized to best practices within three months after the closing. There were many activities to manage and many issues and questions that would arise. The level of activity within the acquirer was frenetic, and the opportunity for issues to fall between the cracks was great. The acquirer also had a shortage of integration staff. One area of concern was communication. Target employees did not always know whom to contact when they had questions or needed to get issues resolved. To manage the problem, a simple but consistent and workable communication process was developed. Several key roles were created: a transition team communication leader who attended all meetings of the transition teams and a key communication contact located in each field or branch location of each acquired company.[4] The role of the new positions are described as follows:

Transition Communication Leader (TCL)
This person would:

- Attend all weekly transition team meetings.
- Frequently interact and communicate with other members of the transition team.
- Prepare weekly (or more frequently as needed) communication updates for the acquisitions, presented in either the company newsletter, a special integration newsletter, or faxes and e-mails.
- Manage the execution of the transition communication plan.
- Be a central point for tracking, escalating, and resolving problems and issues coming from the acquisitions. This would include:
  - Compiling weekly tracking reports.

- Notifying transition team members of issues impacting their area.
- Reporting on issue resolution and channeling issues to functional area executives (i.e., sales, operations) or transition team members for resolution.
- Coordinate all communications with transition team leaders.

This process would ensure that:

- All integration communications are coordinated.
- There is a close connection between integration decisions and activities and communications.
- Someone is dedicated to, and responsible and accountable for, managing and implementing integration communications.
- All important issues and problems coming from the acquisitions are tracked and documented, and reports are submitted to senior management to keep them informed.
- Solutions needed by the acquisitions are provided in a timely manner.

The TCL would:

- Report directly to, and clear all messages and media with, the senior leadership team.
- Review all messages with the integration champion and other transition team members to ensure accuracy and consistency.
- Respond to all problems and issues that come from the key contact person by:
  - Either directly answering them.
  - Or routing them to relevant transition team members or other relevant parties.

Key Communication Contact (KCC)
For each acquisition, an acquired manager, based at the acquired company, would be appointed as a key communication contact person. This person would ensure that clear lines of communication exist between the acquired firm and the TCL.
The KCC would:

- Work with branch managers and regional managers to try and resolve their problems directly.
- Work with the TCL to ensure that critical problems and issues that cannot be resolved locally are brought to senior management's attention and are addressed.
- Ensure that all issues and problems that are encountered, as well as solutions that have been implemented, are documented and sent to the TCL, and be responsible and accountable for ensuring communications are disseminated to the relevant acquired organization's personnel.

Once the roles were created the next issue would be how the communication process would work. Within each acquisition there were several branch operations and thus branch managers. Below is a process that we employed to effectively facilitate the communications between the branches and the ICL. (See Figure 5-5 for a diagram of the process.)

Branch managers would contact the KCC directly with questions, problems, and issues. The KCC would first try to resolve the issue at the local level. If the problem was resolved, the KCC would submit a completed Issue Tracking Form (see Table 5-4) with the solution to the TCL. Then the KCC would communicate the resolution directly to the branch personnel who submitted the request. The tracking of locally resolved issues was essential for the TCL to maintain a complete understanding of the progress and obstacles in the integration project.

If the issue could not be resolved locally, the Issue Tracking Form was completed and sent to the TCL. The TCL would then review the issue and assign it to the appropriate transition team member or whoever was deemed best able to resolve the issue. The issue would then be added to the Issue Tracking Report and assigned a priority code of red, green, or yellow.

- Green was assigned to routine issues that the TCL believed would be resolved by the next reporting period.
- Yellow was assigned to those issues where the time frame was long, the cost was high, or the impact would be widely felt.

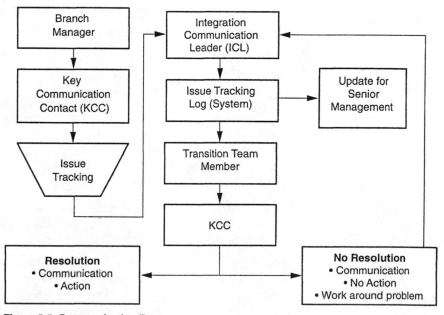

Figure 5-5 Communication Process

Table 5-4 Issue Tracking Form

Submitted by _____	Phone Number _____
Location _____	Date Issue Submitted _____
Branch Submitting _____	Key Contact at Branch _____

What is the issue we need to resolve?

Was the issue resolved at the local level? And if so, how and when?

Who in the branch/functional area experienced the problem?

Was the issue raised by a customer or in the presence of a customer? If yes, please explain.

Does the issue impact other employees in the branch? If yes, please explain.

What other areas are impacted by this issue?

In what format should the resolution be communicated?
Newsletter
E-Mail
Memo
Fax
Phone
Other

Could customer communication be required?	Y or N
Could customer communication be desired?	Y or N
Is there a customer impact?	Y or N
Could training be required?	Y or N
Is follow-up needed?	Y or N

- Red was used for issues or problems that were considered general roadblocks to the progress of the assimilation project.

All issues coded red would appear on a daily progress report submitted by the TCL and the transition champion. A red issue remained on the daily report until it was resolved or the status justified a green code.

The Tracking Process
The TCL would track all assigned issues along with their priority code in a weekly report submitted to the transition champion. The transition team and others with specific issues or problems to resolve were responsible for

submitting a progress report to the TCL by Thursday of each week. This update was critical for the issue tracking and resolution process. The resolution would be submitted to the TCL, who would then communicate with the KCC. Staying "in the loop" allowed the TCL to accurately report progress to the integration champion.

If no resolution could be reached by the transition team or others assigned to the issue or problem, the TCL escalated the issue by first contacting the appropriate vice president.

Due to the overwhelming number of inquiries being fielded by the integration team, an effort was made to filter all questions from the branch personnel through the managers in the branches. Therefore, the only branch personnel who should be contacting the KCCs were general managers, operations managers, service managers, and installation managers.

Although this filtering process may have been perceived as cumbersome by branch personnel, the process was necessary for a number of reasons.

- Limiting the number of calls to a manageable level allowed the KCCs to field questions and communicate solutions in a timely manner.
- The filtering process required the managers in the branches to review all operational problems or issues occurring in their branches and to understand the solutions.
- The managers had the opportunity to review the issues for impact on other employees in the branch and decide if other branch personnel needed to be briefed on or involved in the issue.

The KCCs and the TCL needed to review each issue and eventual resolution for applicability throughout the company. The KCCs would review issues escalated to them from the branches for impact on other branches. In other words, should the problem and resolution be communicated to all other branches in the KCC's market? Such decisions should also be approved by the regional manager. In a like manner, the TCL needed to review problems and resolutions for applicability and impact to all branches in both the acquired companies and the acquirer's system.

The KCCs would complete an Issues Tracking Form for all problems that were raised by branch personnel. The TCL would input the information from these forms into a log that could be used to produce the weekly tracking reports. When contacting the branch personnel with the resolution to the question raised, the KCC could fax, e-mail, or phone the employee with the information. The TCL would follow up with a phone call for those resolutions that were judged to be complex, or that deviated greatly from the branches' current procedures. All branch personnel would be provided within 24 hours of their request with a report on the status of the issue. The branch personnel submitting the request would be updated weekly until the issue was resolved. These updates were delivered by fax, e-mail, or telephone. The final resolution would be added to the weekly tracking report. The example presented above illustrates the importance of proactively communicating and resolving target company issues in a timely manner.

HANDLING EMPLOYEE TRAUMA

Regardless of how well executives communicate with employees during integration, many employees may still have difficulty dealing with uncertainty and the actual events unfolding around them. As Figures 5-2 through 5-4 illustrate, many measures of employee well-being do not come back to "normal," even with a sound communication process. Therefore, executives must be prepared to deal with the trauma that employees might have. Keep in mind that trauma may vary depending upon the situation and the people involved. Where significant changes such as job loss, relocations, and new work processes are likely, trauma will be greater. Where the integration process drags out and the period of uncertainty is lengthened, trauma will also be greater.

Finally, not all people handle difficult situations similarly. Their psychological makeup and broader personal situation can have a dramatic impact. Clearly, it is not possible to control how people will react, but it is possible to understand, anticipate, and take some actions to help deal with people's reactions. In this section some insights on how to do so will be presented.

Set an Example

The behavior of executives and managers during a merger has a significant impact on the behavior of employees throughout an organization. It sets the tone for people and communicates what is acceptable and what is not. This is so, regardless of what managers say. During a merger or acquisition, people's emotions are likely to be higher than normal, as people are concerned, and even worried, about what is going to happen to them. As noted above, they are looking for every bit of information they can find to figure out what is going on. This includes watching managers' behavior and reactions, sometimes with the precision of a microscope. They attend to the words, voice tone, and body language. Often employees attach meanings to these, even when they are virtually meaningless or irrelevant to their own situation. The following is a case in point.

The vice president of an information technology group in a large company was responsible for consolidating his operation with that of an acquirer. His operation was to be shut down. Several people were to be retained and transferred to the acquirer's operations, and a number of people were to be let go. Decisions concerning individuals to be retained were pending.

During one weekend the VP was facing serious personal family problems and was quite upset. (The problems had nothing to do with the merger.) He came to work on Monday preoccupied and stressed. He had not slept much of the weekend. As he walked to his office to begin the day, a programmer passed by him and greeted him. Wrapped up in his own problems, the VP did not acknowledge her. In fact, later, he did not really remember having met her. An hour later the programmer was in the personnel office distraught that she was losing her job. She was convinced that the VP avoided her because he was afraid to tell her the bad news. She was upset that he did not look at her or even wish her good morning.

This example is typical of how many people behave during such times. Now, was the VP entitled to be in a bad mood? Absolutely, he is human. Was it prudent for him to demonstrate it? That is an interesting question. People are entitled to behave any way they want, but when they are in a perceived position of power, their behavior, intended or not, can have a dramatic effect on people. Be sensitive and be careful. People are quite creative in attaching meaning to and correlating things that are not related.

Kubler-Ross's Five-Stage Model[5]

A number of years ago a well-known psychologist, Elisabeth Kubler-Ross, developed a model for how people cope with traumatic events. The model depicts five stages. Each stage is part of a transition process that people typically go through. It is important to note that not everyone goes through all the stages, and the duration of each stage may vary. Simply put, some people are able to deal with the event and move on quickly, whereas others are not. Regardless, the framework gives you some understanding of where people are in the process and why. It helps you better deal with them. The stages are discussed below.

Disbelief and Denial

Stage 1 is characterized by a failure of people to recognize and accept what is happening. In a sense it is a defensive reaction that helps people insulate themselves from an uncertain and unpleasant situation. Essentially, people do not believe the events are happening. This is typified by reactions such as "There is no way that this merger will take place," or "They would be crazy to make changes to our organization—we have been very successful." These comments are often made when there is evidence to suggest otherwise.

The best thing a manager can do in this situation is to continue to present people with factual information about what is happening. Often, pleas to people to face reality do not work. It is more than just an intellectual exercise. For some, it just takes time to face up to the truth. Others are able to adjust quickly.

Anger
This is an extremely dysfunctional stage where people come to understand the reality. Rather than constructively accept the events and move on, they react emotionally. They may keep their anger inside or may lash out. This can range from grumbling, to open confrontation, to violence. Often, people will blame others for what is happening. Typical comments include "How can the idiots in management agree to this deal," or "This deal is likely to ruin our company." This stage can be dangerous, depending upon the individuals involved. It is best for you to get professional advice. Employee assistance program representatives or the human resources organization may be of help.

Bargaining
In stage 3, reality is beginning to set in, but people have not quite come to fully accept it. They still believe there is an opportunity to reverse decisions and outcomes, even if it is not possible. They may try to negotiate. If they are part of a layoff, they may try to bargain to get their name off the "list." They may even plead and explain why theirs is a special case. They still are holding onto a probability when, in fact, the reality is a certainty. The key for managers is to maintain their position and continue to provide accurate information. You may feel pressure to give people encouraging signs, but do so only if your encouragement is based in truth.

Depression
In this stage, reality has set in, and people may feel helpless because events are out of their control. They may feel they have no option. This may lead to a sense of hopelessness and thus depression. Depressed people show all sorts of dysfunctional behaviors, including lethargy and lack of caring.[6] They may retreat from the situation and either fail to come to work or not produce when at work. In this stage it is best to help someone seek professional assistance. It is clearly beyond the scope of managerial competencies unless the manager is certified in counseling, psychology, or psychiatry.

Acceptance
Clearly this stage is the most healthy and productive. This is the point where people accept what is happening and are ready to move on and deal with the situation. Recognizing, creating, and acting upon alternatives is the key here. This is an excellent time in which you, as an executive or manager, can help people do this. This may include transfering people to other operations or helping them avail themselves of company-sponsored outplacement and job search activities.

Regardless of the stage in which people find themselves, it is crucial to remind yourself that there are limits to your own capabilities in assisting employees traumatized by a transition. The most dangerous thing managers can do is to "play psychologist." The most productive thing they can do is to help people identify resources available to help them.

How People Cope with Change and Transition[7]

It is obvious just by watching people that they do not all have the same psychological makeup and that they do not all react to change the same way. It is important that managers recognize why people react differently to the same situation. It may provide managers with insights on how best to deal with people. The key point to understand is that not everyone will react the same way. Someone's opportunity is someone else's threat. Four key elements affect how people react: situation, self, supports, and strategies. Each is described below.

Situation

There are aspects of each person's situation that affect the way he or she reacts. Often, managers are unaware of these, and the work environment is just one aspect. For example, a 25-year-old with no family and no mortgage may view a merger-related relocation across the country as a great opportunity. It is a chance to live somewhere new and develop career opportunities. For someone who is 50, with elderly parents and with children in high school and college, relocation may be a dreaded threat. Although the opportunity to relocate may objectively be the same, the reaction will be entirely different. Some aspects of the situation to consider include:

1. Does the person see the transition as positive, negative, expected, unexpected, desired, or dreaded?
2. Did the transition come at the worst or best possible time?
3. Is it surrounded by other stresses?
4. Is it voluntary or imposed?
5. Is this the transition's beginning, middle, or nearly the end?

Self

Clearly, aspects of each person's psychological makeup contribute greatly to the person's reaction to an event. Experience in having made a significant transition is extremely important. People who have gone through such an experience are more likely to understand how the transition unfolds and what it feels like. More importantly, experience helps people realize they can successfully get through a new transition. I have observed that people who have been through a merger or major acquisition are far more equipped to deal with one the second time around. Also key to understanding people's reaction is whether they see that they have options. If they believe that there are no options other than the status quo, they will feel trapped and dependent. These are most likely to elicit strong reactions. Some aspects of the person to consider include:

1. What is the person's previous experience in making similar transitions?
2. Does the person believe there are options?
3. Is the person basically optimistic and able to deal with uncertainty and ambiguity?
4. Does the person have high self-esteem?

Supports
Support systems help people cope with transitions. Two in particular, social and financial support, help explain people's reactions. As many of us have found, we often lose perspective of a situation, especially when under stress. Having others to talk with allows us to vent and to have the assumptions we make about events challenged and brought back to reality. When people have no social supports, they can easily exaggerate the negative aspects of a situation and develop stronger reactions. Financial support provides people with a cushion to help them withstand a loss of employment. It also takes away the potential threat of job loss, since people's perceived dependency on the job is reduced.

Strategies
How individuals perceive a situation and the capabilities they have for dealing with it also explains their reactions. When people feel they have no control of events and don't have an accurate understanding of how the events are unfolding and the impact the events are likely to have, they are more prone to react strongly. That is why advanced and honest communication is essential. It gives people sufficient time to plan realistic strategies for how they will manage their personal situation. Some aspects of the strategies to consider include:

1. Does the person have the ability to change the situation?
2. Is the person's interpretation of the situation in need of change?
3. Does the person know how to manage stress?

How Managers Can Help
Given that people are likely to react differently during integration, what can managers do to help? First and foremost is to realize they are not psychologists. It is not the intent of this section to train psychologists, but to develop a sensitivity to and an understanding of how people deal with transitions. As such, it is suggested that managers do not attempt to provide personal psychological counseling. If they do so, they may be stepping beyond their knowledge base and hurt people rather than help them. Moreover, they may be putting themselves in jeopardy, since one often does not know how a person will react to advice.

Managers should counsel work performance issues. They should assist people in getting the proper help they need. When such situations arise, contact an employee assistance program representative or someone in human resources. Often they understand the best approach for getting someone help. Moreover, it is helpful to them in discerning whether a pattern is developing in the organization that requires a more systemic approach.

There are a number of general initiatives that can be taken to help employees. First, human resource departments are likely to have stress reduction and change sensitization workshops available. These can range from brown-bag lunch sessions to all-day sessions. These meetings provide people with basic skills for managing through a transition.

Second, meetings with employees to share and solve common concerns are quite helpful. Avoid general "bitch" sessions, because they only lead to venting. Sessions that are solution-oriented help people move forward and focus on things within their "sphere of influence," i.e., things they can control. Third, help people understand what their real work options are and how they can best take advantage of them. Choices here may include job transfers, resume writing, interviewing skills, job search, and the like. Managers should also provide whatever insights they can, but should direct people to get professional help when they do not have the knowledge or skills themselves. The human resources department may have programs or books on the topic.

MANAGE CUSTOMER RETENTION

Customer retention is central to ensuring the financial success of a merger or an acquisition. It is critical to set clear and achievable retention goals emphasizing quality (value) of customers retained as well as the overall retention figure. In other words, retention of all customers may not be important, such as the desired loss of unprofitable customers. To establish a reasonable retention goal, the target's customer base will need to be segmented into categories with known profitability levels. The categories can be the target's established segments if the profitability of their segments has been tracked. If not, the customer base will need to be segmented using the acquirer's standards. Once a retention goal is set, a retention plan should be developed.

A retention plan should be implemented immediately after approval by the transition team leader and the champion. The retention plan should include the following components:

- Communicate with customers, as discussed above.
- Use employee incentive plans.

- Use employee and point-of-contact tools.
- Create a customer retention SWAT team.

Use Employee Incentive Plans

Encourage customer retention among target employees by introducing upbeat incentive programs focused on retention of target customers. Provide awards and recognition for those employees who have direct contact with customers. Provide retention tools to support point-of-contact retention efforts. These could include:

- Calling lists with points on how to make effective retention courtesy calls
- Monthly retention tracking reports to show ranking of employees or locations
- Customer account recovery process (questions to ask before customer closes out relationship)
- Thank-you notes to sign and send to customers

Create a Customer Retention SWAT Team

This team (probably placed with the customer service unit) would be staffed with experienced telephone personnel who will handle outbound retention calls to high-value customers and inbound calls from employees and high-value customers. It is recommended that this group be empowered to extend special offers to target customers.

A FINAL COMMENT

Communication and value preservation are clearly major challenges throughout all stages of the integration process. For many executives it seems like a perpetual uphill battle. Issues are always changing, uncertainty continues to mount, and people want to know what is going on and how it will affect them. Effective leaders must rise to the challenge and continue to communicate with all stakeholders even when they feel overwhelmed. Failure to do so is likely to lead to value leakage and unrealized synergies.

Appendix 5-1 Merger Stakeholder Communication Plan

Below is a stakeholder communication plan (see Table A5-1) that was employed in an acquisition. The acquirer manufactured products for the defense industry and acquired a company that would help diversify it toward a balance between defense and commercial customers and products. The plan identifies communication objectives, stakeholders, messages, media, and stages in the integration process when certain messages should be delivered.

Communication Objectives

1. Promote positive attitudes toward new company through timely education of stakeholders about all aspects of merger.
2. Introduce the new management team and organization:
   a. Background and personality
   b. Organizational structure
   c. Commitment of management team
3. Communicate management's:
   a. Philosophy on industry
   b. Vision for success
   c. Business strategy
   d. Viability of new company
4. Minimize speculation and anxiety due to changes taking place.

Stakeholders (Target Audiences)

1. Employees
2. Customers
3. Distributors
4. Financial analysts/consultants
5. Trade and business press
6. Government agencies
7. Communities in company locations
8. Shareholders

General Messages

1. This is a "new" company rather than an extension of either ABC or XYZ.

Table A5-1 Communication Plan

	Transaction (Pre-Announcement)	Formal Announcement	Transition/Integration (Post-Announcement)
Customers	Managed letters Telephone hotline Key customer visits Internet messages Trade show guidelines	New customer newsletter Advertising and promotions	Direct mail on changes
Distributors	Trade show guidelines Management letters key distributor visits	New distributor newsletter Advertising	Direct mail
Press and Communities	Press materials Expand news bureau Announce milestones through briefings	Press/analyst tour Wire photos News releases Meetings with community leaders	New company profiles
Shareholders	1st-quarter report October annual meeting	Personal letter	February analysts' meeting
Government Agencies	DOD briefings Personal letters Visits with key agencies and people Crisis plan Attend critical meetings	Advertising Press coverage	
Employees	Newsletter inserts Site visits Executive memoes, e-mails Video interviews Telephone hotline Intranet messages	Newsletter/transition newsletter Celebration Management and supervisor briefings	Social gatherings Company meetings Leadership training

2. We are not conquering XYZ but building a stronger transformed company:
   a. The integration of employees from both organizations offers a truly unique opportunity to strengthen and restructure.
   b. The new company is committed to drawing on the best talents from both ABC and XYZ.
   c. The new company is committed to the ongoing welfare of ABC and XYZ employees.
3. This acquisition was part of a planned, ongoing company strategy.
4. XYZ is an ideal fit for ABC in terms of products and markets:
   a. Minimal duplication—areas of overlap between the firms are few
   b. Complementary product offerings in similar markets
   c. Broader international presence
   d. Greater commercial market emphasis resulting in faster growth—if we can successfully manage the integration
   e. Enhanced military offerings for ABC through complementary products from XYZ
5. The new company will be:
   a. The only major manufacturer driven by niche marketing growing faster than either previous entity
   b. Innovative in developing niche products and technology for market segments:
      i. Custom applications complemented by standard product lines
      ii. Able to serve broader markets with these products
      iii. Better able to serve military, industrial, and commercial markets
6. The new company will be committed to niche marketing because:
   a. There are greater opportunities for profits.
   b. The new "balance" of served markets fosters greater stability.
   c. It has historic expertise and specialized capability in niche marketing.
   d. These markets have a greater barrier to entry.
   e. The new company has critical mass required to do so in the 1990s and beyond.
7. The new company is committed to economies of scale driven by market opportunities.
8. The combined companies will guarantee a long-term domestic source of U.S. military technology.
9. The new company will merge the ABC and XYZ entities with maximum speed.

General Approach

1. Take advantage of brand name/corporate names and logos while working toward integration.

2. Combine ABC and XYZ logos in advertising treatments.
3. Centralize all product introductions.
4. Focus on a tag line that speaks to consolidation:
   a. "The vision of one"
   b. "The power of one"
5. Utilize one corporate typeface and colors.
6. Focus media spending on short blitz versus slow build.
7. Develop communications plans for all external and internal announcements.
8. Employees will be notified first on important news prior to releasing it to the press.

Initial Activities

1. Form central communication committee:
   a. Membership from both ABC and XYZ
2. Weekly input to and from Merger Integration Office (MIO):
   a. Long lead time notice of impending action
3. Establish approval process for communications actions: Recommendation of steps:
   a. Legal review
   b. XYZ concurrence
   c. Final approval (MIO leader, CEO)

STAKEHOLDERS AND COMMUNICATION MEDIA CUSTOMERS

1. "Executive briefs" outlining key issues:
   a. Personal briefings for key customers
   b. Personalized letters for other customers
2. Toll-free hotline number:
   a. Answered by customer service
   b. Provide specific questions and answers
3. Newsletter:
   a. Quarterly in first year
   b. Launched at announcement
   c. Series of stories on acquisition and integration
4. Site visits for key customers
5. Direct mailings:
   a. Theme-oriented publications
   b. Office or home keepsake
   c. Tied to advertising message

6. Advertising:
   a. Image-oriented
   b. Product-oriented
   c. Corporate guidebook for logo, typeface, colors
7. Media coverage:
   a. Reprint mailings
8. Customer briefing center update
9. Trade shows:
   a. Audit current shows
   b. Utilize new-sector theme
   c. Look like billion dollar company through:
      i. New presence/new booth
      ii. New corporate guidelines for:
         (1) Graphics
         (2) Message
         (3) Shows attended
   d. Question and answer sheet for booth staff on tough questions
   e. Eliminate controversy and conflict in messages between ABC and XYZ booths
   f. Gifts denoting new company

Press and Communities
1. Formal briefings
2. Meetings with influential industry consultant (i.e., Dataquest)
3. Personal meetings with company spokesperson
4. Preparation and mailing of press materials:
   a. Photos
   b. Bios
   c. Organizational chart
   d. New company press contact and number
   e. Feature on the future of the company
   f. New company capabilities brochure
5. Press tour (domestic and international):
   a. Trade
   b. Business and financial
   c. Industry analysts
6. General business publicity:
   a. Radio tapes
   b. Teleconferences
   c. Wire service photos
7. Expand existing news bureau:
   a. Identify and train spokespeople
   b. Clarify who talks to whom
   c. Decide how to handle incoming press calls

8. News releases:
    a. News of transition team
    b. Announcements:
        i. Business and trade
        ii. Photo opportunity
    c. New appointments
    d. Reorganizations
    e. Products:
        i. New introductions
        ii. Distributor assignments
    f. New company thrust and focus
9. Meeting with community leaders:
    a. Reassure community leaders of continued support (grants, charity, participation)
    b. Develop crisis plan in event of layoffs or facilities close

Distributors
1. Message development on new distributor strategy
2. Communicate through:
    a. Personal briefings
    b. Personal letters
    c. News stories in their publications

Shareholders
1. Special section in *FYI Magazine* (for shareholders)
2. First- and second-quarter report
3. Personalized letter from management at announcement
4. February financial analyst meeting:
    a. Invite industry analysts
5. Special financial analyst briefings:
    a. At announcement
6. Announcement at October annual meeting
7. Coverage in annual report
8. Corporate/image advertising

Government Agencies
1. Contingency plan:
    a. Department of Defense (DOD) briefing:
        i. Between ABC and XYZ
    b. Editorial boards with government books
    c. Crisis plan:
        i. Question and answer preparation
        ii. Releases

  iii. Press calls
  iv. DOD calls
   v. Position paper (ABC commitment)
  vi. White paper (issue-oriented to fewer government suppliers is better)
 vii. Legislative mailing
viii. Speakers bureau
   (1) Need for on-share suppliers in industry
   (2) Personal letters from ABC management
   (3) Special conferences:
      a. Attend quarterly meetings

Employees
1. ABC/XYZ newsletter and e-mail and Intranet insert—"The power of one update":
   a. Transition to single employee newsletter
   b. E-mail
   c. Intranet site
2. Visits to operations of ABC and XYZ by both CEOs:
   a. Internal version of company presentation
   b. Question and answer session
   c. Follow-up video distribution
3. Executive e-mail and Intranet briefings:
   a. Key breaking events
   b. Announcements
4. Video conferences by CEOs via satellite and Intranet when needed and where possible
5. Merger hotline
6. Company meetings:
   a. Use regular meetings for question and answers
   b. Arrange special meetings when needed
7. Theme promotion:
   a. Buttons, posters, banners
8. Leadership training programs
9. Social gatherings:
   a. Picnics
   b. Open house

6

PREPARING FOR INTEGRATION: MANAGING THE TRANSITION STAGE

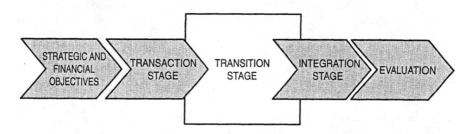

Now that the decision to do the deal has been made, the next interesting challenge emerges—figuring out whether and how to integrate the companies. How should these decisions be made, and who should be involved? Although these are seemingly simple questions, they are quite complex to answer in practice. There are numerous decisions to be made and people involved. Without a structured decision-making process, integration is likely to be chaotic and political, with many issues and decisions falling between the cracks.

The integration transition process typically begins after a formal merger or acquisition agreement has been signed, and should be completed prior to the closing. The extent to which integration plans can be developed earlier provides organizations the needed momentum to capture important changes identified during the transition process.

Unfortunately, thorough preplanning is not always possible. Sometimes, as in the case of a hostile takeover, there is a lack of cooperation prior to the closing, and planning can only take place after there is a change of control of the companies. Sometimes, as in the case of a merger between direct competitors, the parties are restricted in what they can talk about and jointly plan due to potential antitrust issues. Often the lawyers involved will guide this effort. Regardless of the timing, the need for a well-managed transition process remains a critical element in the success of any integration effort.

The basic objective of the integration process is to take two previously independent organizations and merge them together in some fashion. This requires that a process for managing the transition from "two to one" be created. The nature of this process will vary depending upon the:

1. Amount of concurrent acquisition activity being undertaken by the acquirer
2. Relative size and complexity of the organizations involved
3. Nature of the integration that is planned

The more the concurrent acquisition activity, plus the greater the relative size and complexity, plus the greater the depth of the integration, the more the process needs to be formalized, replicable, and staffed with dedicated resources. Simply put, a firm making an occasional small acquisition with little integration is less likely to need a full-time staff dedicated to this activity. It does need, however, a well-managed process and an ad hoc team of people who can easily be mobilized to lead and assist the integration.

On the other hand, a firm that is actively rolling up a fragmented market will be able to justify a full-time staff and need a more sophisticated, well-managed process to handle the integration activity. A mega-merger will also require a well-managed, dedicated integration process due to the sheer enormity of the work to be done.

STRATEGIC AND FINANCIAL OBJECTIVES AS THE DRIVER

As noted in Chapter 2, strategic and financial objectives and subsequent synergies should be the major drivers of the M&A integration process. It is most desirable if these have been thought out prior to doing the deal or at least during due diligence, but often they are not. In such cases, they must be addressed during the integration stage. Unless these elements are understood, it is extremely difficult to effectively set priorities, drive the integration process, and create value for investors. Sound decisions both with respect to organizational structures, systems, and process and with respect to people to retain will be impossible to make.

With smaller acquisitions the financial and strategic objectives may have been well thought out prior to the deal, especially if a buyer is clearly seeking targets that fit a particular strategic need (e.g., products, geographic entry). In such cases the transition process focuses specifically on how to integrate the target into the new organization.

In a large merger it may take more time before a clear strategy is developed. The merger may have been agreed to based on a vague vision, with many details of the strategy to be determined during the transition and possibly not until after the closing. It has been argued, for example, that some of the oil industry and automotive mergers were done for defensive reasons and that the strategies behind them were not thought out in much detail. General synergies, usually in terms of cost reductions, were identified early in the deal, only to be captured in detail during the transition and integration stages.

With the strategic and financial objectives as drivers, there are several key integration objectives to be accomplished and activities to be managed during transition. These are presented in Table 6-1 and discussed in the remainder of this chapter.

CREATE AN INTEGRATION TRANSITION STRUCTURE

GTE and Bell Atlantic created a transition integration structure to form Verizon.[1] To manage the many complex details involved in combining these two complex companies, they created the Merger Planning Office. It was jointly led by GTE's executive vice president of strategic development and planning and Bell Atlantic's executive vice president of strategy and corporate development. The office, which was staffed by a number of full-time staff members, was responsible for managing the overall integration planning process. This included key activities, timetables, financial results, synergy capture, and issue tracking and resolution.

The merger integration process involved three phases: (1) gathering and analyzing data on how the companies might fit together, (2) developing staffing and business plans, and (3) implementating the plans. For the data gathering and analysis phase, eight integration teams that focused on specific areas in both companies were created. These teams examined each company's practices, looking for synergies and best practices. Integration teams focused on areas such as:

1. Consumer and small business
2. Large business, federal, wholesale business, data/Internet working, technology and infrastructure management

Table 6-1   Transition Stage

Objectives
1. Complete unfinished analyses.
2. Create a cooperative integration environment.
3. Plan the integration.

Activities
1. Create an integration transition structure.
2. Articulate integration guiding principles.
3. Decide what to integrate and how to do it.
4. Develop an integration project plan to drive implementation.

3. Domestic wireless
4. Telecom network and operations
5. International and directories
6. Legal, regulatory, and government affairs
7. Human resources
8. Finance and headquarters support

Based on the recommendations obtained from phase 1, phase 2 began. This phase started six months prior to the closing and focused on the finalization of business strategy, organizational design, and the naming of the top leadership of Verizon.

Smithkline and Beecham began its transition integration structure by creating the Merger Management Committee (MMC), which consisted of an equal number of executives from each company. The MMC then created seven planning groups (i.e., integration teams) to identify the synergies and business opportunities that the combined organization could attain. Seven teams were formed for:

- Information, financial, and accounting systems
- Corporate headquarters
- Pharmaceuticals organization
- Pharmaceuticals manufacturing
- Pharmaceuticals R&D; marketing and sales
- Animal health
- Over-the-counter/consumer products

The seven teams were charged with developing strategies for their areas and creating five-year plans. Another group was formed to coordinate the work of all the other groups and to interface with the MMC. This group ensured that all tasks necessary for integration were identified and carried out and priorities were set; work was reviewed by the MMC in order of importance. A computerized master plan was employed to ensure that the work was properly monitored.

Based on due diligence and preliminary projections of the new company's performance, Fleet and BankBoston identified $600 million in cost savings through consolidation and $350 million through divestiture. They wanted to achieve these results in 18 months.

To accomplish these results, a Merger Integration Office staffed by both Fleet and BankBoston managers with expertise in mergers, organizational structure and dynamics, strategic planning, and risk management, among others, was created. The managers developed objectives, a process, and a timetable for accomplishing merger goals. They formed 66 integration teams of employees from both banks working within the business or staff areas to be merged. The integration teams were given support from 10 full-time cross-functional teams of employees from both banks. The 10 teams focused on communications, divestiture, facilities, finance, human resources, legal, marketing, revenue, risk management, and systems and operations.

The examples above characterize what other companies have done to manage the integration process. The key lessons drawn from their experiences are that to facilitate the integration process a transition structure should be created to ensure that:

1. The strategic and financial objectives underlying the acquisition drive the integration.
2. A comprehensive and effective integration plan is developed and executed.
3. Collaboration among and commitment of those needed to make the integration a success is garnered.

How elaborate the transition structure should be depends again upon the nature of the M&A activity. Regardless of the approach, some basic elements are common to all structures:

1. An individulal or a team needs to be accountable for ensuring that the integration and the necessary level of coordination among various people and groups are successfully accomplished.
2. Financial and strategic objectives must drive the effort.
3. All functional and support areas, lines of business, and geographic operations from both organizations need to be examined to determine whether and how they should be integrated.
4. An acceptable approach to making integration decisions must be agreed to.
5. A project-based implementation plan to ensure that all activities essential to a successful integration should be defined and executed.
6. Sufficient commitment among key individuals, groups, and other stakeholders to the implementation of the plan must be realized.

A general transition structure that has been effectively used by successful acquirers is discussed below and illustrated in Figure 6-1. The structure is built on a series of cascading teams with increasing levels of detailed responsibility for integration analyses and recommendations. The figure shows what the structure looks like for a single merger versus a company making multiple acquisitions as part of an industry roll-up.

Merger Integration Office or Integration Champion

A merger integration office (MIO) or integration champion (IC) has primary responsibility for leading the integration effort. In a merger this is likely to be jointly led by senior managers from both organizations (e.g.,

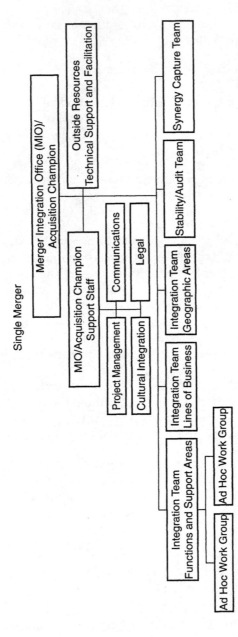

Single Merger

Merger Integration Office (MIO)/
Acquisition Champion

Outside Resources
Technical Support and Facilitation

MIO/Acquisition Champion
Support Staff

Communications

Legal

Project Management

Cultural Integration

Integration Team
Lines of Business

Integration Team
Geographic Areas

Stability/Audit Team

Synergy Capture Team

Integration Team
Functions and Support Areas

Ad Hoc Work Group

Ad Hoc Work Group

Figure 6-1 Integration Transition Structures

Multiple Acquisitions

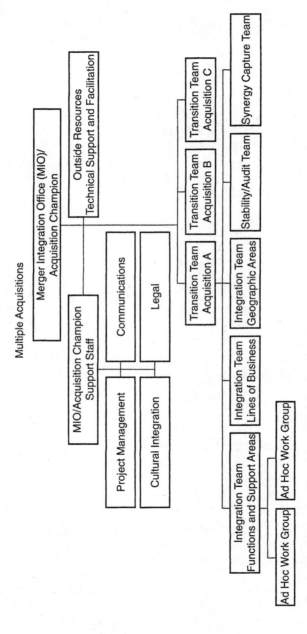

Figure 6-1   Integration Transition Structures (*continued*)

143

chief financial officers). These positions are typically named by the CEOs of the merging companies and report directly to them.

For a company that is making a series of smaller acquisitions it is likely to be an executive of the acquirer (e.g., M&A group, business development, CFO, member of the senior team) who oversees all the acquisitions. The MIO/IC should be provided with support staff to manage the numerous activities, and with outside help to give needed technical support and facilitation (e.g., for the MIO and the transition and integration teams). In particular, several support teams should be created:

1. *Project management team.* This team oversees a master project plan to ensure that all the integration activities are being managed and are on schedule. Essentially, this is the primary control mechanism for the integration process. All transition and integration teams are required to develop and execute project plans in their respective areas. More will be said about project management later in this chapter.
2. *Communications team.* This team ensures that communications to all stakeholders are being managed. The team ensures accuracy and consistency of all information disseminated. See Chapter 5 for a more in-depth discussion.
3. *Cultural integration team.* This team helps analyze and work through cultural differences that may impact the ability of all other teams to successfully perform their duties. See Chapters 3 and 8 for a more complete discussion of cultural issues.
4. *Legal team.* This team provides advice on all legal issues and guides all teams in recognizing acceptable and unacceptable activities and discussions (e.g., antitrust, SEC) prior to closing.

It is the MIO's/IC's responsibility to:

1. Clarify for those involved in the integration the strategic and financial objectives behind each merger or acquisition and the minimal synergies that must be captured (certainly unanticipated synergies should also be sought if they arise).
2. Create and charge:
   a. Transition teams to manage the integration of each acquisition in the case of multiple acquisitions.
   b. Integration teams to manage integration in the case of a merger or an acquisition.
3. Select transition team or integration team leaders for each acquisition.
4. Ensure that the guiding principles (discussed below) are adhered to.
5. Review and approve all major recommendations made by transition teams and integration teams.
6. Ensure cooperation among transition teams when more than one acquisition is being integrated.

7. Provide support to the transition teams and integration teams (i.e., provide resources, clear roadblocks).

Although the terminology differs, the concept of the MIO is basically the same as what has been used in many mergers including Chevron-Texaco, Baxter–American Hospital Supply, and Chase Manhattan–Chemical Bank. The MIO/IC should oversee the acquisition process from the transaction stage through the integration stage to ensure continuity of information and direction and should be led by executives or others with influence in the acquiring and acquired organizations.

Transition Teams

Depending upon the size, complexity, number, and importance of acquisitions being integrated at the same time, one or more transition teams should be created. For small and simple deals, one team may be able to handle several acquisitions. For multiple large deals, several transition teams will be needed. All will report to the MIO/IC, who will ensure that coordination among teams takes place. The teams ensure that each company being integrated receives the proper level of attention and support and that someone is held accountable for managing the transaction. If a company is making a single large acquisition or is involved in a merger, a transition team is not needed. In such instances, integration teams will report directly to the MIO.

It is the transition team's responsibility to:

1. Manage the transition phase of an acquisition.
2. Create and staff integration teams to examine all functions, lines of business, geographic locations, product lines, and activities considered for integration.
3. Ensure integration teams understand the strategic and financial objectives behind their acquisition and the minimal synergies that must be captured (certainly unanticipated synergies should also be sought if they arise).
4. Ensure integration teams are on schedule, and where necessary, are meeting and communicating with each other.
5. Create a standard methodology or process (e.g., best practices) for integration teams to use in making decisions.
6. Provide support to integration teams (e.g., provide resources, clear roadblocks).
7. Ensure cooperation among integration teams.
8. Make prioritized recommendations, including the business case, to the MIO/IC concerning the proposed integration of the acquired organization (e.g., products and services, organizational structure, management processes and systems, staffing, organizational culture, compensation, and benefits).

9. Set priorities for how the integration recommendations should be implemented.
10. Ensure execution of recommendations.
11. Ensure that both the acquirer and the target continue to function effectively (i.e., there is no value leakage) during the transition stage.

The following guidelines should be considered when staffing transition teams:

1. The team should consist of a transition team leader and integration team leaders (discussed below).
2. The transition team leader should:
   - Be an executive or a manager within an acquirer (depending upon the size, complexity, and importance of the acquisition).
   - Have a solid understanding of the businesses being integrated.
   - Understand the models and assumptions driving the valuation and pricing.
   - Be flexible and able to negotiate with a variety of people and departments.
   - Have excellent project management skills.
   - Have played a significant role during due diligence.
3. Involvement of target people on the transition team (e.g., as integration team leaders) should depend upon the size of the deal, the degree of integration required, and the level of involvement desired.
4. The team should meet weekly, or more often if needed, to discuss all aspects of the integration project, to talk about progress, and to ensure that issues do not slip through the cracks. More is said about tracking integration and project plans in Chapter 9.
5. The team should provide the continuity needed for the integration to proceed smoothly and without duplication or omissions of key tasks.
6. The transition team leader should be provided administrative support for managing the logistics of team activities, coordinating integration team materials, preparing presentations, communicating, dealing with cultural issues, and managing the project.

Integration Teams

Separate teams for each area (e.g., functions and support areas, lines of business, geographic area) of the business should be created. Typical functional and support areas examined include:

1. Strategy
2. Production
3. Distribution
4. Marketing

5. Sales
6. Engineering
7. Research and development
8. Human resources
9. Information technology
10. Legal
11. Procurement
12. Finance and accounting

Lines of business typically focus on major product lines. Geographic areas typically range from regions within a country (e.g., Southeast, Midwest), to countries themselves (e.g., United States, France, Venezuela), to continental regions (e.g., North America, Southeast Asia, Northern Europe), to the entire globe. To a large extent, these are dependent upon how the acquirer and target or merger partners have been organized in the past and how they intend to organize in the future. Again, a merger may be the catalyst that changes the way a company will compete in the future. For example, a merger between a U.S. and European telecommunications company could change the focus of two primarily domestic players to that of a global player. As a result, the types of teams that would be created and their focus may be very different than for the merger of two domestic companies.

It is the integration team's responsibility to:

1. Evaluate a specific function, line of business, or other area of each organization in a merger or an acquisition.
2. Identify how specific synergies can best fulfill the financial and strategic objectives of the deal.
3. Examine the viability of the best approach for managing each area and activity after the deal is closed.
4. Make specific recommendations, including the business case, on changes needed in either the acquirer, the target organization, or both to realize objectives, strategies, and synergies.
5. Make specific recommendations on what needs to be done to successfully implement changes.
6. Develop a detailed project plan for executing changes and implement it after it is approved.

All integration teams should be led by knowledgeable executives and managers from both the acquirer business unit and the target, and be made up of key people from both the acquirer and the target who represent diverse operations, lines of business, and geographic areas. Each transition team is typically staffed with between 6 and 10 people. The need for knowledge and representation should be balanced with the need to effectively and efficiently manage team dynamics. It is critical that the integration teams establish solid contact with people in their respective organizations so that the strengths of each company are understood and not overlooked during integration team deliberations.

Stability/Audit Team

This is an independent team charged with maintaining a satisfactory level of service to customers of both organizations during the transition period. The team's responsibility is to monitor employee and customer retention, service, profits, productivity, and other indicators that determine stability of both organizations. This team assures that sufficient attention is being given to the "business" during the integration. There is always a risk that integration activities consume so much time and energy that value leakage can occur.

The team leader of this group reports results to the transition team and to the MIO/IC. The team should include not only employees from audit and operations but also "generalists," who understand multiple functions.

Synergy Capture Team

Another independent team is responsible for identifying and tracking synergies. These include costs, revenues, net working capital, and investments (i.e., the components of earnings and cashflows). This team works directly with the MIO/IC and with the transition and integration teams that are working to identify and document synergies in each area. The focus is to track synergies over time, including the time after closing, to ensure they are realized. More will be said about tracking synergies in Chapter 9.

Ad Hoc Work Groups

Ad hoc groups are made up of key operational personnel from across the acquirer and the target. It is their responsibility to provide integration teams with specific technical advice and solutions to problems as they evolve.

These groups are formed throughout the transition stage as technical expertise is needed and are dismantled when each group's tasks are completed. The members of these groups would be part-time participants from across the acquirer or the target and would be considered "subject-matter experts." Provisions have to be made to ensure that ad hoc team members can be accessed since the integration is not their primary responsibility.

It is the ad hoc work group's responsibility to:

1. Review aspects of integration plans.
2. Recommend changes to plans.
3. Coordinate any conversions or changes.
4. Provide subject-matter expertise.

Developing Teams

To ensure that all teams work in an effective and efficient manner, it is important that time and attention be given early to the formation and development of the teams. Otherwise, the teams will likely waste time, if not flounder. Prior to beginning any work, transition and integration teams should be:

1. Briefed on the merger or acquisition and provided information on the merger partner or acquisition
2. Briefed on what is expected of them and how their day-to-day job will be handled
3. Provided necessary skills training (e.g., project management, best–practices assessment)
4. Provided intercultural sensitivity training and introduced to counterparts from the other company

Building partnership and cooperation among integration teams can go a long way in facilitating the integration process. In particular, it is useful to take members of the teams for an offsite retreat to set the context and ground rules for the management of the integration process. Below is an example of a three-day offsite session I conducted to help get integration teams off the ground prior to beginning transition planning.

Activities

The CEO, president, or another executive presents, in detail, to all attendees the strategic and financial objectives underlying the merger or acquisition and synergies that have been committed to. If these have not been fully developed, it is worthwhile that they be developed or completed prior to major integration activities. A preliminary version should be shared with attendees at the offsite retreat, with their input and revisions sought. The purpose of this exercise is to build an understanding of, and gain commitment to, a shared strategic direction. It is this shared direction that ultimately provides the glue for building the new organization and must drive the integration decision process, rather than expediency or local interests.

An educational session on merger and acquisition integration, the challenges it creates, and approaches for dealing with these challenges is useful. It gives attendees a realistic view of what awaits them and how to effectively manage through it.

An executive of each organization shares with attendees a history of his or her own organization, including its products and services, geographic presence, strategic direction, and organizational culture. To reduce tension, it may be useful to have members of each organization do a humorous skit during an evening to reflect their own culture. The objective here is to allow members of each organization an opportunity to discuss who they are. This helps eliminate stereotypes, "superiority syndromes," and arrogance that people of any one organization might have. In other words, it levels the playing field.

Following this discussion, small groups from each organization are formed and asked to address the following questions: (1) How would you describe your own culture? (2) How would you describe the culture of the other integrating organization? (3) How are they similar and dissimilar? (4) What elements of each organization's culture are most likely to support the strategic direction of the integrated organization? (5) Do we need to have a single culture throughout the integrated organization, and if not, how do we honor each organization's culture? (More will be said about this in Chapter 8.)

After the small groups present, the larger group of attendees can then focus on real versus perceived differences in culture and aspects of culture that are useful to the new organization. Often, many of the differences are perceived ones rather than real ones. This allows the group to eliminate incorrect stereotypes and focus on how to deal with real differences. Once real differences are isolated, then the group can discuss which aspects of existing cultures, if any, are useful to the new organization. Actions for resolving differences, or creating new aspects, can then be discussed.

A workshop using small mixed groups of attendees from the combining organizations can help anticipate, and begin to deal with, factors that might have a bearing on the overall success of the integration process. The groups meet to address the following questions: (1) What factors will support the integration of the organizations? (2) What factors will create roadblocks to effective integration? (3) What actions can be taken now to overcome the roadblocks and to leverage the support?

After these questions are answered, they are shared and discussed with the larger group. Common themes are identified, and actions to manage them are agreed to. Toward the end of the offsite retreat, teams should be given specific charges and ground rules, as noted above.

To facilitate interaction among members of all organizations, time for socializing in the late afternoon and evening should be planned. This may involve informal or formal activities. If formal activities are used, ensure there is a deliberate mix of people from both organizations. This socialization process facilitates working relationships.

Once integration teams have been formed, it is helpful to clearly outline expectations for each team. These should include:

1. The team's charge and scope
2. The team's authority, limits, and duration
3. Those to whom the team is accountable
4. Deliverables and time frames for completing specific work
5. Specific goals and success measures that the team should focus on, including cashflows, earnings, budgets, synergies, and any indicators that drive them (e.g., quality, safety, productivity)
6. Any specific methods the team should employ in conducting its analyses and making its recommendations
7. Budget and other resources needed

8. Composition of the team
9. Team members' roles and responsibilities
10. Team decision process (e.g., consensus)
11. Barriers to team performance (e.g., external political issues) and how they can be cleared
12. Project management approach to be employed in executing the team's work

It may also be useful for each team to have an independent facilitator. The facilitator should:

1. Encourage teamwork among the participants, regardless of company of origin.
2. Facilitate productive meetings ensuring that:
   • Agendas are distributed well in advance of a meeting.
   • Participants understand the issues to be discussed.
   • There is open discussion, and all issues discussed are clear.
   • Conflicts are constructively managed and resolved.
3. Advise team leaders and members of issues that need to be dealt with and items requiring resolution.
4. Be aware of issues, activities, and conflicts with other teams.
5. Ensure schedules are developed and communicated.
6. Continue to ask questions that provide clarity of issues.
7. Provide relevant information and feedback to those facilitating other teams.

The facilitator should be one who:

1. Has good organizational and political skills
2. Is willing to help others obtain results
3. Feels comfortable with limited or no authority
4. Can accomplish results by quickly building relationships and trust
5. Is insightful and analytical
6. Will maintain confidentiality

ARTICULATE INTEGRATION GUIDING PRINCIPLES

The integration of two firms can be complex, with numerous decisions having to be made. These decisions can have a great bearing on the people affected by the decisions. More importantly, they can have a great bearing on whether the strategic and financial objectives underlying the merger or acquisition are realized. Given the complexity of the integration process, and our inability to have a decision rule or tool available for every decision, it is important that a basic road map to guide those making the decisions be established. As such, many successful companies develop a set of integration guiding principles to serve as a road map and ensure that it is employed during the transition process.

In a merger, the guiding principles should be developed by the MIO. These principles foster consistency of actions throughout the entire transition and integration stages. It is incumbent upon the MIO to ensure that these principles are not hollow words but are adhered to throughout a merger or an acquisition.

In an acquisition the principles should be articulated and accepted by the acquiring executives and managers prior to the formal announcement of the acquisition and should be shared with the target through the IC. Below are some examples of guiding principles.

When Baxter acquired American Hospital Supply, it utilized the following principles:

- The organization will be based on doing what is best for the business.
- The best people will be retained regardless of company affiliation.
- The merger will proceed in an orderly fashion, but it must achieve early and visible benefits.
- We will seek decentralization to the extent that it serves our customers.
- The need to do it right will be balanced with the need to do it expeditiously.
- The integration will include participation from executives of both companies at every step.
- Management intends to conduct the merger integration in an unprecedented, model way.
- Employees of both companies will be treated in an open and honest fashion, and will be kept informed about the progress of the integration through constant communication.[2]

When Smithkline and Beecham merged, they committed to creating a new and transformed company. To guide this effort, they articulated the following principles:

- The merger will be one of equals, including shareholders, board members, management, and businesses. This will allow the company to become global without taking on a huge debt.
- Before the merger is finalized, management will plan how the companies will come together and identify the business expectations for the new firm.
- The merger integration will be accomplished as quickly as possible to capitalize on the energy and expectations of employees and before new ways of operating set in.
- The integration will involve as many individuals as possible. Managers understand the challenge and opportunities of their operations much better than a small group of headquarters executives.

Hence they will participate in the hundreds of project teams that will design the new company. Guidelines and standardized procedures will give them a sense of what the new company is trying to become.

- No appointment beyond the members of the Executive Management Committee will be made until the new company's organization structure has been defined. Then the best individuals from either firm will be selected to fill key slots. In the meantime, present members of senior management will observe leading candidates as they perform their current responsibilities and either lead or work in merger task forces.
- It is important to keep employees informed about what is happening, what will happen next, and what the company expects of them.
- Businesses that do not fit the strategic concept of the new company will be sold.[3]

I could go on with numerous examples of statements of guiding principles, but many of the principles used by companies are similar to those above. In general, the statements address the following areas:

- The involvement of people from both organizations in the integration process
- How people will be treated in:
  - Selection and retention decisions
  - Communications
- How the merger or acquisition integration processes will be managed
- The focus of the integration effort
- The focus on customers and strategic priorities during the integration

Although a number of principles can be articulated, I would like to highlight three that I have found to be of particular importance to successful integration. They are the degree of involvement of people in the integration process, the value of using a business and strategic perspective in making integration decisions, and the importance of treating people with dignity, respect, and fairness in decisions. These help ensure a well-managed value-enhancing outcome. It is also important to note that these principles should already be part of the principles that the merging or acquiring companies employ in their normal business activities!

Degree of Involvement

The extent to which people from *both* organizations participate in the integration of the combined organizations must be considered early. Involving the target's people is critical since:

- They have relevant knowledge about the target's situation and its history.
- They may have new ideas to contribute (e.g., best practices).

- Their involvement may be critical to gaining acceptance and commitment to decisions and retention.
- They may serve as important internal agents of change within the target.

In an acquisition in particular, the level of involvement should be determined by whether the target has performed well in the past and by whether the target's management and employees are competent and need to be retained. The level of involvement of target employees is characterized in Table 6-2.

When moderate and high levels of involvement are warranted in a merger, the MIO and integration teams should be jointly led and staffed. When moderate and high levels of involvement are warranted in small to medium-sized acquisitions, IC and transition teams should be led by executives and managers of the acquirer. Integration teams should be staffed with key people from both the acquirer and the target. When little involvement is warranted, a few select people who have necessary insights to manage through the transition or are to be retained should participate on integration teams.

Financial and Strategic Perspective

Those involved in the integration process must understand from the outset that decisions and activities must be aligned with the financial and strategic objectives underlying the acquisition, and should not be undertaken for the sake of expediency and local political interests. Failure to align will result in people and organizational units taking actions that do not support the acquisition objectives and detract from value creation.

Fairness, Dignity, and Respect

As decisions that affect individuals are made, caution should be taken that all managers and employees, regardless of organization of origin and whether they are retained or not, are treated fairly and honestly and with a sense of dignity and respect. Not only does this minimize the trauma experienced by those who are not retained by the acquirer, but it sends a very strong signal to those who are retained what the acquirer truly stands for (see the discussion in Chapter 7). Further, the integrated organization should be staffed with the best people, regardless of organization of origin.

Table 6-2   Level of Involvement of Target People

Performance of Target	Desired Retention of Target People	
	Most	Few or None
Solid	High Involvement	Little Involvement
Turnaround	Moderate Involvement	No Involvement

Similar to the last point, this sends a critical message to all the acquirer and target employees.

The remainder of this chapter outlines the key activities that must be managed for the principles discussed above to be successfully implemented.

DECIDE WHAT TO INTEGRATE AND HOW TO DO IT

After the integration transition structure is defined and communications begun, the MIO/IC must decide how it will manage the integration. There are two critical decisions to make here:

1. What areas of the companies should be integrated?
2. What approaches to integration should be employed?

What to Integrate?

Since integration can cause costly and time-consuming changes, it is suggested that the transition and integration stages engage the "principle of minimum intervention." Only those functions and support areas, lines of business, and geographic areas that are necessary to support the strategic and financial objectives and sources of synergy underlying the acquisition should be integrated.

However, in a transformational merger it is likely that almost every area of the business will be affected. This will necessitate a reassessment of both firms' business strategy and all aspects of the combined organization. As noted in Chapter 2, some mergers are transacted with only a rough understanding of how the organizations will compete in the marketplace and will be integrated. This is more likely to be the case in a merger between large multibusiness companies where there is significant overlap in some divisions and an opportunity to reposition the new combined company. In such cases, all aspects of both companies will be reevaluated during the transition stage, and many of the details will have to be honed.

This means that integration teams must examine each area of the business of both the acquirer and the target and then decide what to integrate. It is hoped that much of this was done during the transaction stage as those involved in due diligence and valuation thought about sources of synergy.

Preparing for the integration decision requires that two activities be performed:

1. The current state (i.e., baseline) of each area should be examined and compared. This includes the area's:
   - Vision, objectives, and strategies
   - Culture
   - Activities performed
   - Systems

- Business processes
- Operating and business models
- Organizational structure
- Positions, descriptions, and head count
- Operating and capital budgets

For the sake of simplicity, a side-by-side comparison of each of these elements should be made. Table 6-3 shows one way to do this. This comparison helps articulate each company's approach and the similarities and differences between the companies. Once these are understood, the teams can then begin to analyze what makes sense for the new company moving forward.

2. One or several scenarios for the end-state organizational design, based on financial and strategic objectives, should be developed. This provides a basis for understanding any gaps between what each organization is currently doing and what the new organization needs to be doing in each area.

For example, a German company involved in sorting and recognition systems used by postal authorities, priority shippers, and retail and distribution acquired a U.S. company after a careful strategic assessment. The acquisition expanded the German company's geographic presence in the NAFTA region, furthered its technological leadership, and strengthened its position as a total system supplier. After examining each company independently, the German company developed a pro forma of what the integrated organization would look like and then began to develop the details behind it. The concept set the stage for the integration teams. As illustrated in Figure 6-2, the primary scenario for the end-state organization was a transnational organization[4] where there would be localization of certain activities and global integration of others. Localization allowed needed responsiveness to the idiosyncrasies of country environments. Global integration allowed certain activities, such as product development, to be

Table 6-3   Assessing the Current Organizational State

Area	Topic	Acquirer	Target	Similarities	Differences
Strategy	Market focus				
Human resources	Medical plan				
Information technology	Software				
Manufacturing	Production process				
Purchasing	Supplier policy				

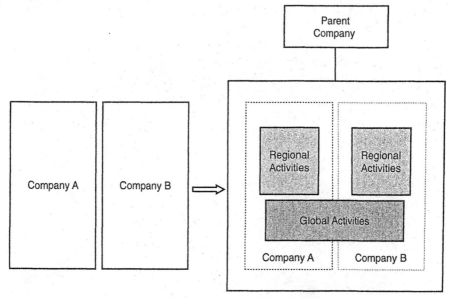

Figure 6-2   Pro Forma Organizational Concept

scaled such that the costs of development could be amortized over a worldwide volume. These activities would require some level of standardization. Thus it became the work of the integration teams to decide which activities would be global and which would remain local and how to realize that. First, the team had to detail the current state of each organization and then examine the pro forma. From there it had to identify the gaps between the two. Once this activity is completed, a methodology for deciding what and how to integrate must be chosen.

What Integration Approaches to Use?

As discussed in Chapter 2, and illustrated in Tables 6-4 and 6-5, integration decisions should be influenced by the financial and strategic objectives underlying a particular acquisition and the sources of synergy that are potentially available.

It is suggested that the areas of the companies to be integrated should be benchmarked to determine best practices and tested against the metrics that are deemed important to achieving the forecasted earnings and cashflows (e.g., variable and fixed cost, customer retention, quality, productivity). This will involve:

1. Using an integration template or best practice that the acquirer has already developed and can apply to new acquisitions
2. Using a best practice that has been developed by a target and applying it to the acquirer and subsequent acquisitions

Table 6-4   Linking Strategic Objectives and Synergies

	Strategic Objective				
Type of Synergy	Consolidate Market within Geographic Area	Extend or Add New Products, Services, and Technologies	Enter a New Geographic Market	Vertically Integrate	Enter a New Line of Business
Cost	High	Low	Low	Moderate	Low
Revenue	Low	High	High	Low	None
Market power	High	Moderate	Low	High	None
Intangible	Moderate	Moderate	Moderate	Low	Low

Table 6-5   Strategic Objectives and Impact on Integration

	Level and Type of Integration		
Strategic Objective	Consolidation	Standardization	Coordination
Consolidate Market within Geographic Area	High	High	High
Extend or Add New Products, Services, and Technologies	Moderate	Moderate	High
Enter a New Geographic Market	Low	Low to high	Low to High
Vertically Integrate	Low	Low	High
Enter a New Line of Business	Low	Low	Low

3. Using a best practice that has been developed by one of the merger partners and that can be used in the combined organization
4. Working in collaboration with the target or merger partner to develop a new best practice

Figure 6-3 provides a decision tree used to make integration decisions for a company that was engaged in an industry roll-up. The decision tree identifies three integration options: forced assimilation, voluntary assimilation, and innovation that the acquirer would need to employ to ensure that synergies were captured.

Gaining Acceptance and Commitment

In any one of these three methods, acceptance and commitment to new approaches will have to be secured. If not, resistance to change may

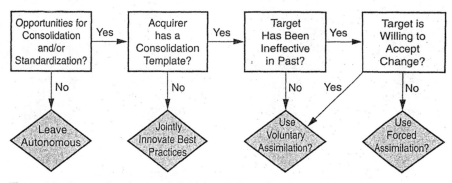

Figure 6-3   Integration Approach Decision Process

become a problem. This may not be a problem, however, if an acquirer intends to replace the acquired people! Thus, the following approaches and their implications should be considered:

Forced assimilation—where a target is *required* to adopt the practices of an acquirer. This is likely to be met with the greatest resistance to change by target people, as they feel like their cultures and practices are threatened. Many target people describe this as "superiority syndrome" by the acquirer and feel as if they are being treated as second-class citizens. However, this may be necessary if the target has been ineffective in the past, requires change, and has not done so willingly. It may also be required if a large acquirer is folding a small target's backroom activities into its, regardless of who has the best practice. In such cases, it may be best to replace target people since their support and commitment may not be likely.

Voluntary assimilation—where a target *voluntarily* adopts the practices of an acquirer or a merger partner (or vice versa). A target may not have been as successful as the acquirer in the past and may be pleased to have a new approach. This is likely to be met with higher levels of support. However, some conflict and problems may still result for those who have to adapt to the changes. Moreover, it will greatly depend upon how the acquirer manages this process. See Chapter 7 for additional insights.

Innovation—where integrating groups decide to abandon existing practices in favor of newer and better ones. Typically, there is no sense of superiority by either the acquirer or the target, and the focus is on defining a new best practice.

To innovate, organizations often employ reengineering or process improvement approaches to develop changes that logically fit with the strategic and financial considerations driving the merger or acquisition. In the merger between Boeing, McDonnell Douglas, and Rockwell, the company utilized McDonnell Douglas's R&D center, Phantom Works, to drive the integration.[5] The center was used as a general technology generator to improve manufacturing processes throughout the entire corporation.

Challenges of adaption here will be similar to those of any work group going through a change process. The process may also require outside assistance or new people with fresh insights and ideas. Again, a merger or an acquisition may create an excellent opportunity to shake things up.

People will only voluntarily assimilate and support innovation when they:

1. Understand the strategic and financial objectives behind the deal
2. Participate in both designing and implementing new approaches
3. See the value each organization brings to the table
4. Understand how the solutions will benefit the combined organization
5. Realize they will personally benefit or not lose from changes

Mapping the Integration

The areas to be integrated can be mapped based on benchmarking, and then the changes in each area that need to be made and the impact of the changes on synergies can be detailed. For example, Figure 6-4 provides a simple representation of the integration of several acquired security monitoring companies by a large acquirer as part of an industry roll-up. The industry was fragmented, with opportunities to grow through both geographic expansion and consolidation within geographic markets. Almost all the players were small, privately owned firms concentrated in narrow geographic markets. There were opportunities to achieve economies of scale through cost reduction and transfer of best practices and innovation. To achieve these, the acquirer examined four core areas of the business: call centers, installation, sales, and customer service. After careful analysis, several conclusions were reached.

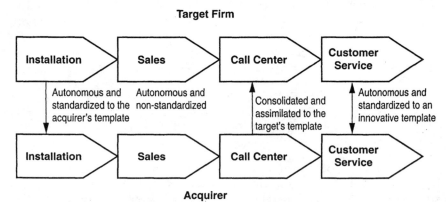

Figure 6-4   Representation of Integrating Acquisitions Selectively

First, many of the acquired companies had their own local call centers. None of them were very efficient, with high fixed costs. Based on a comprehensive study, it was decided that the individual call centers could be shut down and consolidated into two nationally scaled centers. Moreover, these centers could be located in geographic areas where employees could easily be hired and the lowest costs could be achieved. All that was needed was access to a telephone line, a key part of monitoring. The center design was developed as part of the roll-up strategy by the acquirer. As a result, significant efficiencies and cost reductions, and thus synergies, could be achieved. It is important to note that this strategy is quite similar to that used by major acquisitive banks (e.g., Sun Trust, Bank of America), whereby "backroom activities" such as information processing can be eliminated for each bank and centrally consolidated and redundant branches can be consolidated.

It was also found that each firm had a different approach to sales, installation, and customer service. Based on a best-practice study, it was decided that the acquired firms would be standardized to a best-practice model established by the acquirer. The model, which significantly reduced costs and improved response time, eventually became a template for future acquisitions. However, whereas the call center could be consolidated, these functions needed to be locally decentralized. The only consolidation that took place was when multiple acquisitions were made within the same geographic area and there was redundancy in people and physical assets.

Unfortunately, neither the acquirer nor the acquired firms had a very successful customer service capability. Thus, the acquirer used the acquisitions as a window of opportunity to innovate and develop a new approach that became the standard for the new company. This activity was carried out by an integration team, with the involvement of people from all the firms being consolidated.

The decision was made to leave the sales organizations relatively autonomous. A few procedures were standardized, but it was determined that there was enough variance in local markets not to force a standard model. Finally, a standard approach to installation, based on a best-practice template established by the buyer, was transferred to the acquired companies. Fortunately, through training programs, employee visits, and incentives, acquired employees embraced the changes.

It is important to note that the best-practices model identified the most effective organizational structure, activities to be performed, budgets, positions, physical assets, and head count that were needed to run each area. Moreover, the model carefully tracked cost savings in real estate rent and other overhead, salary reduction and elimination for branch operations and corporate staff, other corporate overhead, marketing, and other costs. Some capital expenditure would be needed. All the elements above were factored into both the valuation model and the impact on earnings and cashflow.

The illustration clearly indicates that there are multiple ways in which to integrate organizations and that multiple approaches need to be employed within each merger or acquisition. The approach chosen needs to be driven by both the strategic and financial objectives underlying the deal, but also by the judgment of integration teams as they attempt to learn the best way in which to manage the various parts of the business.

This was the case in the consolidation of the call center operations. The choice of physical location remained open to analysis by integration teams and was based on a sound methodology and goals (e.g., cost, quality, cycle time). For example, a call center could be centralized and performed either at an acquirer business unit; at the target, which may already have a best practice (i.e., center of excellence); or at a new and better location, yet to be determined.

Whether a target can serve as a center of excellence for a function or an activity will depend upon its history and prior success. Keeping an open mind about the capabilities and value that a target may bring will be helpful in finding better solutions to meet financial and strategic objectives and in building the support and commitment of target people.

In addition to practices, consolidation and assimilation of cultures, names, and identities of the organizations also need to be addressed. These are usually far more difficult to achieve than physical asset consolidation.

Managing How Fast You Go

There is considerable debate on how long the integration process should take. Speed can best be defined as the time it takes to make changes in the buyer, seller, or both and thus integrate the firms. Some argue that you should move quickly and integrate as fast as possible. People are expecting change, and delays prolong the uncertainty. As Sandy Weill, Citigroup's chairman and CEO, notes:

> Make decisions faster than you normally might, rather than slower . . . it will help you hold onto the good people and send the right message to everyone.[6]

Speed avoids periods of uncertainty in direction, both in the organization and in the marketplace. It also sets an early expectation that changes will be made and mitigates some of the buildup of political resistance to change.

Others argue, however, that integration should move more slowly, whereby careful assessments of how the organizations can be put together can be made. Moving slowly allows for a well-thought-out and planned integration. This argument is probably due to the incompleteness of the due diligence or preclosing acquisition integration planning process—all the more the reason to get as much analysis and planning completed as possible prior to closing.

Fortunately, there are a few studies that provide insights on this issue. A study by PriceWaterhouseCoopers[7] of 124 medium to large companies that executed a merger or acquisition within the last three years found that companies that managed the transition faster had more favorable gross margins, cashflows, productivity, profitability, and speed to market. Of those surveyed, 89 percent felt they should have managed the transition even more quickly. Unfortunately, there is not much precision in the definition of speed. Respondents simply indicated whether the transition was managed more or less quickly than their normal pace of work. Speed of integration of operating policies was also reported to have an effect on employee reactions. More rapid integration led to greater confidence in company direction, clarity of company direction, product focus, and speed of decision making. Also, more rapid integration was associated positively with acceptance of new vision, employee commitment and motivation, customer relations and communications to employees and customers.

Secondary findings of several other studies do provide some indication of the virtues of a fast versus slow integration process and the context in which one or the other may be expected to lead to greater postacquisition performance. In a case study of three international mergers,[8] a slow integration process was used to minimize conflict between the merging partners. Parity (i.e., balancing of management positions between the two companies), for example, was instituted between the power, responsibility, and authority positions of the combining firms' management teams. However, this process was later blamed for the combined firm's inability to develop cooperation within the board and management levels, along with a common identity necessary for postacquisition performance. The slow integration process used by these firms was actually found to inhibit, rather than enhance, integration.

Another study[9] found that the successful acquisition of Nokia-Data by ICL was the result of selectively and simultaneously utilizing both slow and fast approaches to integration. The study indicates that a key to the success of the merger was allowing time for each partner to learn about each other and for ICL to identify merger priorities. Change was phased in over time, without stripping either company of the areas it valued most. On the other hand, the two companies decided to begin to work on a new range of products, which appealed to the acquired employees who were weary of the acquirer's bureaucracy and potential inability to maintain the acquired firm's responsive decision-making practices. Furthermore, the decision was made to change every Nokia-Data sign in its home country of Finland to an ICL sign on the date of acquisition approval and to engage in press and other media campaigns to leave no doubt about the acquisition. This study clearly indicates that the speed of integration is complex, in that some facets of integration may be best suited for slow speed and others best suited for fast.

Based on research findings regarding the integration of R&D functions among combining manufacturing firms, another study[10] also suggests that speed is a complex issue. In this study it was found that human resources–focused integration plans and actions that help to promote a gradual process in which individuals from two organizations learn to work together and cooperate in the transfer of strategic capabilities improve postacquisition performance. It was also found that the centralization of R&D within the acquirer appeared to quickly provide clear strategic R&D objectives for the combined organization, resolute implementation of burdensome organizational changes, and avoidance of endless discussions on a joint R&D strategy. Speed, thereby, substantially reduced the uncertainty among the acquired firms' R&D professionals.

From a process perspective, a study[11] found that the speed at which integration occurred depends upon whether people were involved in a merger workshop. Those employees engaged in a workshop were able to develop a shared diagnosis or vision of an improved combined entity. This created increased organizational commitment and openness to postacquisition integration and, consequently, quicker integration. In addition, the study suggests that encouraging learning between the merging firms which combines both cognitive learning, based on rational processes, and behavioral learning, based on experimental learning, also improves the speed of integration.

Although the research is not conclusive, it suggests that integration should move purposefully and as quickly as possible. More importantly, speed considerations should be weighed against commitments to delivering earnings and cashflows. Premiums paid for an acquisition and commitments made to achieving synergies within a specified time frame should have a great bearing on speed There is certainly more than one executive who aggressively committed to achieving synergies within one year of the closing of the deal. Doing so becomes a critical acid test of the success of the deal and ultimately that of the executive.

However, one should be realistic about how long it might take to implement change. Some areas (e.g., information systems) may require significant time to integrate, even after integration changes have been agreed to. Experience suggests that fully integrating organizations (e.g., many areas, cultures) can take anywhere from one to five years, depending upon the relative size of the target and the extent of the integration. In the next section I will discuss how to put together an integration plan.

DEVELOP AN INTEGRATION PLAN TO DRIVE IMPLEMENTATION

The integration planning process requires that two key activities take place. First is the handoff between the due diligence and integration teams.

Otherwise valuable information, analyses, and insights gained during due diligence will be lost. Second, a project plan to ensure that the transition and integration activities are successfully completed should be developed and implemented.

Manage Handoff with Due Diligence Team

Optimally, the person serving as the transition team leader would serve as the due diligence team leader for a particular acquisition, and a key person or people from the due diligence team would join the transition and integration teams. In a merger this would be the responsibility of the MIO.

If the transition team leader cannot serve as the due diligence team leader, then:

1. All materials developed during due diligence are given to the transition team leader.
2. Transition team leader is fully briefed on:
   a. What analyses were and were not thoroughly completed.
   b. What was learned about the target.
   c. Any problems or issues that were identified during due diligence that would affect integration.
   d. Assumptions regarding levels and sources of synergies that were built into the valuations and purchase price.
3. The MIO or IC takes responsibility for ensuring the handoff is made.

Again, this is a critical step since many M&A activities are fragmented in organizations, especially large ones. For example, it is very likely that a corporate business development group is responsible for due diligence and an operating manager is responsible for integration. Coordination is not automatic and must be managed.

Develop an Integration Project Plan

During both the transition and integration stages, numerous activities will need to be performed to manage the integration. This requires systematic and disciplined project management. This activity should be coordinated by a support team working within the MIO or directly for the IC. As noted earlier, integration team leaders need to either have solid project management skills or get a quick course prior to beginning their work. It is essential that the transition and integration teams develop and execute project plans that detail:

1. All the analyses and activities that need to be conducted prior to closing
2. Activities that need to be executed after closing, or what some acquirers have labeled "day one" and beyond (i.e., the point at which the acquirer owns the target and can begin implementing changes)

To effectively manage all the details required to plan and execute the integration, it is essential that the transition and integration teams be provided with the following:

- Project management software
- Report templates
- Guidelines for completion of reports
- Reporting time lines
- Appropriate checklists

Project management software should be employed to develop integration plans for each team in the first weeks after the acquisition announcement is made. Each team's plan should roll up through an automated process to the MIO, in the case of a merger, and to the IC and transition team leader, in the case of multiple acquisitions, who will then manage the "critical path." This comprehensive plan will be the document that guides the implementation and monitoring of the transition and integration processes.

The plan should be reviewed and approved by the MIO, IC, and transition team leader. This plan will determine the magnitude of the overall project, the resource needs of the project, and the final project organization structure.

The progress of all teams, milestones, issues to resolve, and changes to be made will be monitored based on updates to the plan. By following a formal monitoring process, management at all levels can stay abreast of the transition-integration process. This type of monitoring allows red-flagged issues to reach management with appropriate lead time for responding successfully.

Key activities to develop project plans include:

1. Major activities to be completed
2. Time frames and milestones for completion of major activities
3. Specific responsibilities for execution of activities (departments and people)
4. Resources needed to carry out activities:
   a. People (existing and additional)
   b. Financial
   c. Timing of need
5. Pro forma and budgetary impact (recurring and incremental impact) from any proposed recommendations:
   a. Revenues
   b. Costs
   c. Capital investments
6. Contingencies and potential impact on:
   a. Employees
   b. Customers

    c. Other key stakeholders

    d. Time frames

7. Contingency plans

8. Known potential roadblocks to be dealt with and solutions for dealing with them

9. Approach for monitoring and managing the integration project plan

Table 6-6 illustrates a "high-level" project plan and time line for managing transition activities for a bank acquisition. All these activities occurred over a five-month period and were completed just prior to the closing. Table 6-7 provides a more detailed project plan for one phase of the project plan, an organizational assessment of a target. This phase was to be completed over a one-week period prior to the closing.

Table 6-8 illustrates a high-level project plan that was used to consolidate call centers. Target company centers were to be closed and consolidated into two national-scaled centers of the acquirer according to the time frame in the plan.

Project plans help ensure that the numerous activities that must be completed to integrate organizations and capture synergies are successfully managed. Project planning provides a coherent basis for organization, accountability, teamwork, communication, and ultimately control.

A FINAL NOTE

Numerous activities must be planned during the transition stage. To the extent that they can be completed prior to the closing, the greater the momentum to implement them after the closing. This requires a coherent and well-organized process, with the proper people from both an acquirer and a target or merger partners involved. It also requires that roles and responsibilities of the key people be clearly spelled out.

Table 6-6 High-Level Bank Integration Plan

ID	Task Name	Start	Finish	Resource Names	September	October	November
1	Project organization	9/3/01	9/20/01				
2	Identify transition approach	9/23/01	12/31/01				
3	Prepare for day one	9/23/01	12/31/01				
4	Manage employee retention	9/23/01	1/31/02				
5	Marketing communication strategy	9/23/01	1/15/02				
6	Bank branch optimization model	9/23/01	11/15/01				
7	Product mapping	11/1/01	1/15/02				
8	Gap analysis	12/31/01	1/31/02				
9	Systems inventory and mapping	11/1/01	1/15/02				
10	Statements/notices/reports	11/1/01	1/15/02				
11	Internal financial controls	11/1/01	1/15/02				
12	Training approach	11/1/01	1/15/02				
13	Equipment surveys	11/1/01	1/15/02				
14	Facilities surveys	9/23/01	1/15/02				
15	Early implementation opportunities	11/1/01	1/15/02				
16	Implementation/testing approach	11/1/01	1/15/02				
17	Implementation scope finalization	11/1/01	1/15/02				
18	Implementation plans	1/15/02	1/31/02				

Table 6-7   Detailed Organizational Assessment Integration Plan

ID	Task Name	Start	Finish	Accountable	May 20, '01	May 27, '01
1	Prepare employee retention and communication plan	5/21/01	5/25/01		▮	
2	Create key dates document	5/21/01	5/25/01		▮	
3	Determine teller system	5/21/01	5/25/01		▮	
4	Establish budget time lines	5/21/01	5/25/01		▮	
5	Identify personnel generalist for transition	5/21/01	5/25/01		▮	
6	Identify MIO staff admin. assistant	5/21/01	5/25/01		▮	
7	Identify staff analysts	5/21/01	5/25/01		▮	
8	Meet with acquired bank management	5/21/01	5/25/01		▮	
9	Name transition manager	5/21/01	5/25/01		▮	
10	Name line executive manager	5/21/01	5/25/01		▮	
11	Name integration team members	5/21/01	5/25/01		▮	
12	Prepare budget templates for distribution	5/21/01	5/25/01		▮	
13	Develop welcome letter for new employees	5/21/01	5/25/01		▮	
14	Select physical office space for transition team	5/21/01	5/25/01		▮	
15	Set up office equipment	5/21/01	5/25/01		▮	
16	Set up communications	5/21/01	5/25/01		▮	
17	Conduct project orientation and kickoff	5/21/01	5/25/01		▮	

Table 6-8 Call Center Consolidation Time-Line

ID	Task Name	Duration	Start	Finish	Accountable	May	June	July	August
1	Dallas	24w	5/21/01	11/2/01	Jones				
2	Houston	24w	5/21/01	11/2/01	Smith				
3	Indianapolis	29w	5/21/01	12/7/01	Jenkins				
4	Kansas City	33w	5/21/01	1/4/02	Green				
5	Chicago	37w	5/21/01	2/1/02	Sloane				
6	Minneapolis	41w	5/21/01	3/1/02	Roberts				
7	Milwaukee	45w	5/21/01	3/29/02	Chavez				

7

MANAGING STAFFING, RETENTION, AND REDUNDANCY

At some point in every merger or acquisition, it is inevitable that executives will have to address issues of staffing, retention, and redundancy. Invariably, there will be redundancy in areas of the organizations that overlap, and executives will have to manage the orderly departure of people from the organization. This will certainly be the case where cost synergies are being sought. Even in cases where an organization is growing through the addition of new products and services or geographic expansion, it is an excellent opportunity to examine the capabilities of people and to decide whom to retain and whom to let go. It is even more critical when executives are looking to transform a company by acquiring new capabilities.

Deciding who the best people are, developing strategies to retain them, and managing the termination of those who are not needed will be essential to building a new, more competitive company. One executive challenged me on the importance of these issues. He told me the people issues were exaggerated. He said that he would rely on attrition to eliminate redundancy. He wasn't going to worry about devising a complicated staffing process and fighting to retain people. I asked him what type of people he thought would stay and what type would leave.

In general, decisions concerning the fate of people in a merger or an acquisition are not easy to make, can be quite political, and can have a dramatic impact on everyone in an organization. Three sets of interrelated "people" decisions must be managed during the integration process, and these are addressed in the remainder of the chapter.

1. Staffing the integrated organization
2. Retaining key people
3. Managing employee redundancy

In making these decisions, two of the guiding principles discussed in Chapter 6 and highlighted below are important.

TREAT PEOPLE WITH FAIRNESS, DIGNITY, AND RESPECT

The success of the staffing process depends upon the extent to which it is perceived as fair.[1] Although people have different definitions of what fairness means, most people involved in a merger or an acquisition would agree that:

- People from both the acquirer and target or from both merger partners are given an equal opportunity to be selected for positions.
- Those who are not retained are given a reasonable opportunity to transition out of or to other parts of the organization.

Not only do these principles have a bearing on those who do not receive a position, but they also do on those who remain with the new organization. How this process is handled sends clear signals to those who remain about what the real values and culture of the new organization are—versus the espoused ones captured in executive speeches and written materials.

This point was exemplified in the merger of two major oil companies. As part of the merger, a number of redundant information technology operations in the southwest United States were to be consolidated. Decisions about whom to retain or let go were made.

Without any advanced notice, a middle-level manager from the target was met at his office by two armed guards. He was informed, for the first time, that he was no longer employed with the company. No reasons were provided. He was instructed not to touch or take anything from his office and was escorted off the premises. He was simply told that human resources would contact him with all necessary information and his personal effects would be sent to his home. Needless to say, he was devastated. He had no chance to say goodbye to friends and colleagues. The 20 years he worked for the target seemed to mean nothing, and he was humiliated. More importantly, there were 18 direct reports that watched this event take place. Within 18 months all of them had left the company. In follow-up exit interviews they indicated that on that day they knew exactly what the acquirer was all about. They did not need any fancy banners and executive speeches about the company's culture and values.

COMPETENCE

If the real objective is to build a more capable organization as a result of a merger or an acquisition, then it is essential that it be staffed with the best people possible. This is of utmost importance when the primary assets being acquired are people. Clearly it is not easy to identify who these best people are. Thus it is incumbent upon merger partners or an acquirer to develop an approach for ensuring that reasonable selection criteria and a process for choosing the best people are established.

STAFFING THE INTEGRATED ORGANIZATION

An organized systematic process for staffing is vital to the integration process, regardless of whether it involves a small acquisition or a large merger. Of all the decisions made during integration, none are more important than those that determine who will fill key positions.

In the case of a small acquisition the process may not be that complex. There may be only a few positions to name. In a large merger the process may indeed be quite complex, with thousands of positions being named, ranging from the CEO to frontline employees. In the remainder of this section I will present a basic approach that has been used successfully in both large mergers and large and small acquisitions.

In a large merger where there is overlap from the top all the way to the bottom of the organization, the process begins by naming the CEO of the combined company, with the approval of the boards of directors. This is often done by negotiation between the two CEOs or lobbying with the board. To avoid this tough choice, many merging companies have attempted the co-CEO role. I will discuss this later in the chapter. Once the CEO is named, candidates for the next level of positions are selected, usually jointly by the CEOs of both companies. It is important to name the top positions and key people as early as possible to stabilize the transition and solidify the basic organizational structure. In the Chevron-Texaco merger it involved 61 people. In the Baxter–Travenol Laboratories–American Hospital Supply it involved 100 people.

After the top positions are filled, the staffing process needs to continue until all the open or new positions in the combined organization have been named. Depending upon the nature of the integration, staffing may range from a few position changes to a complete revamping of the organization. Moreover, key people may leave the organization prior to the closing due to concerns over whether they will have a job or not, leaving unanticipated vacancies. (More will be said about retention later on.)

How positions are filled is vital. On the one hand it is important to be unbiased toward people in regard to organization of origin. On the other hand it can be problematic if the primary focus for staffing decisions is to seek balance between the two organizations. Caution should be given to the notion that balance constitutes fairness.

Some organizations attempt to provide a balance between the number of people retained from each company involved in a merger or an acquisition. Although noble, it usually does not work. When balance is more important than competence, it is unlikely that a new organization that is capable of competing will be created. It also sends a signal to the organization that competence is not the most important criterion for the future. What message does that give people? This point is driven home by Harry Stonecipher, former CEO of McDonnell Douglas. Commenting on the merger between McDonnell, Boeing, and Rockwell, he noted that:

> It's not about making everybody from McDonnell Douglas, Boeing, or Rockwell happy . . . it's about making one new Boeing company with the best people in the best place.[2]

In Chapter 4, the importance of assessing the performance, talent, competence, skills, motivation, and management style of key people during the transaction stage was discussed. The information collected then becomes a critical part of the decision making during this stage.

As the scenarios for the new organization (e.g., objectives, strategy, structure, positions, competencies, head count) are developed, it will become increasingly clear as to how many and what type of people will be needed after the deal closes. Assessments not conducted during the transaction stage must then be done during the transition stage. Again, the earlier these assessments are done, the better, since until people are named to their position, uncertainty will run rampant. Value leakage in terms of quality people leaving will become a major issue.

Typically, the staffing of lower-level positions is often not completed until late in the transition stage or even until after closing. This is the case because a thorough review of people takes time, and many of the positions cannot be detailed in advance due to lack of cooperation or the inability to discuss the organization in detail.[3] While speed is critical to a successful integration, making the right decisions may be more important. After all, such decisions affect people's lives and are the backbone of a successful organization!

Once the top spots are named and the basic organizational structure is put into place, the executives who have been assigned these positions will begin to select their staff. This process will eventually cascade down through the organization. Again, the nature of the integration will determine how extensive this effort is.

Managing the Staffing Process

Figure 7-1 presents a staffing approach that has been employed by a number of successful acquirers. The approach is similar to a general staffing approach used by many firms. What differentiates it in an M&A context is the:

- Sources of candidates considered
- Selection process utilized

Simply put, care must be taken that there is not bias in either the pool of candidates considered or the choice of candidates itself. It is very easy for executives or managers to subconsciously fall victim to bias due to friendships, or to the fact that they have worked with or know someone from their own organization better than from the target or merger partner. This is natural and is likely unless there is an articulated process to counter it.

To ensure objectivity is brought into the selection process and that a thorough pool of candidates is created, a staffing integration team should be given oversight for this effort and report directly to the MIO/IC. The team should be co-led by human resources executives and managers from both companies and interact with other integration teams whose areas are affected by selection decisions. It is important to note that the staffing integration team does not decide whom to hire. That ultimately is the responsibility of the executives and managers who will oversee the retained employee.

There are two key roles this team should play. First, as positions are identified, the staffing integration team ensures that a slate of candidates from both organizations is considered. If a viable internal candidate does not exist, external candidates should be sought. Second, the team ensures that each candidate is given "due process" in the selection decision. This means that all candidates are given serious consideration and their files reviewed. The objective is not to create a bureaucratic process but to create a systematic and fair process.

After the closing, and once the major positions in the organization are named, integration teams should be disbanded. However, there still may be numerous positions that remain unfilled. The hope is that the major positions have been taken care of and the basic organization is in place and capable of functioning. At this point the staffing process will fall in the hands of line management. With HR support, line managers should be encouraged to continue a staffing approach similar to the one outlined above. HR should also ensure that a slate and the rationale for selections are provided prior to decisions being communicated to people. To ensure fairness, one acquirer created a review and appeals board. The board reviewed every employee file to ensure that those who had been identified for one or more positions were considered. Moreover, a rationale had to be provided for people not chosen and why someone else was a better fit. The board's role was to ensure that the process was fair, not to second-guess selection decisions. Regardless of the process, it is still in the best interest of managers to retain the best people they possibly can.

The following is a brief overview of the steps in Figure 7-1:

1. Develop a position description for each position being filled. Include:
   a. Roles, responsibilities, and accountabilities.
   b. Whom they will report to.
   c. Skills, knowledge, and competencies required for the job.

2. Solicit a slate of candidates from both companies participating in the merger or acquisition for each position. Consider candidates from other functions, lines of business, and geographic areas. If no internal candidates exist, engage an external search.

3. Collect information on each candidate. Information can be secured from multiple sources (see Chapter 4 for a more comprehensive discussion). Make sure information tracks with item 1c above. The objective is to collect as much valid information as possible that will help predict a candidate's success in the proposed position. To the extent that multiple sources of information conclude the same thing about a candidate's competence, the higher the probability that an accurate judgment can be made. Certainly this must be weighed against budgetary and timing considerations.

4. Based on the above information, reduce the pool to a list of "viable candidates." The assessment can be based on the consensus of multiple decision makers. It is important that the direct manager of the position to be filled and members of the staffing integration team (or human resources after closing) participate in the decision.

5. Based on the information collected, interview candidates to fill in gaps in information and to further verify information collected. Evaluate candidates with respect to how well they exhibit the competencies required by the position. If the new position requires a geographic transfer, inquire whether the person would be willing to relocate. This can become a problem and should be verified rather than assumed. More will said about this below. In general, it is wise to make sure there are qualified backup candidates in the event the candidate rejects an offer.

6. Using all relevant information, select the candidate. Involve outside consultants if additional information or insights are needed. Once the decision has been made, document it, including the rationale. Table 7-1 presents a simple grid for capturing the selection decision-making process.

7. Before any decision is announced, make sure that:
   a. HR reviews it for Equal Employment Opportunity (EEO) analysis.
   b. Salary and benefit package is put together.
   c. Any other requisite approvals are sought.

8. Once decisions are made, be sure they are clearly communicated to the candidate, then to others as deemed necessary.

9. Once decisions are made, prepare to execute them:
   a. If the candidate has been offered a position, prepare to make a specific and attractive offer, including geographic location, salary, benefits, perks, etc., to recruit the candidate for the job.
   b. If the candidate has not been offered a position and has no role in the new organization, prepare to sever the person from the organization.

c. If the candidate has been placed on hold, prepare to provide the candidate with a temporary role and explain how the decision process will work from here. In this situation the person will be considered for reassignment into vacancies that exist.

d. If the candidate will only be retained for a defined period of time, usually to assist with the transition, explain that the person is needed for a period of time, usually to complete the transition. Prepare an incentive to motivate the person to remain throughout the transition.

As staffing decisions are made, the staffing integration team and eventually the HR organization need to continually update the actual impact of these decisions on total head count and budgets. These will then need to be tracked against forecasted budgets for each function, line of business, and geographic area to ensure they are in line with base-case financial and synergy projections. This information should be shared with the synergy capture team as well.

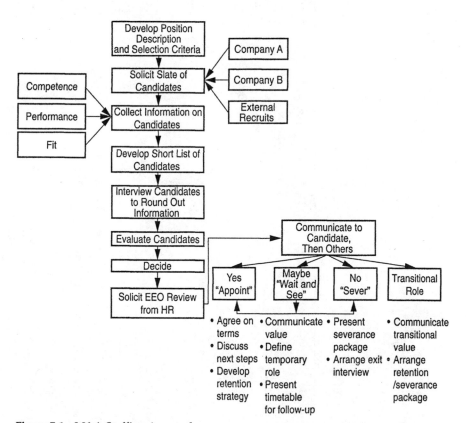

Figure 7-1   M&A Staffing Approach

Table 7-1 Selection Decision Form

Position _____

Location _____

Candidate (Name)	Current Position	Current Location	Predecessor Organization	Rating (Rank Order)	Willingness to Relocate and Accept the Position	Rationale for Ranking	Salary Requirements	Decision*	Action Plan

*Acceptable candidate—make an offer.
Unacceptable candidate for position but consider for another position.
Unacceptable candidate; sever from the organization.
Candidate needed during transition.

A Note on the Co-CEO

The concept of the co-CEO has become a fascination of companies seeking a "merger of equals." In an attempt to deal with egos and to send a signal that neither organization will dominate after a merger, the CEOs attempt to share power.

While nice in theory, it is extremely difficult to implement in practice. By the time executives reach the top spot, they are used to having power and have considerable ego. While the co-CEO approach may be well intentioned, the likelihood that CEOs could share the position for an extended period of time is relatively small. In fact, the *Forbes* 500 study, cited in Chapter 1, pertaining to the top 10 pitfalls in achieving synergy, notes that the clash of managerial egos and styles is the sixth most important factor leading to failure.

Based on an examination of several key mergers, it is apparent that the co-CEO is most likely to work well under a couple of conditions. The first is that it is limited to the time it takes to manage through the transition to an integrated organization. During that period it sends a signal to both organizations that neither company's employees will be treated as second-class citizens. It also provides some stability to ensure that the integration process is managed in an orderly fashion. The second is that one of the CEOs is clearly designated as the leader of the new organization, with the other on a timed retirement or severance agreement. Under these circumstances the likelihood of power battles and ego clashes is diminished. A couple of examples will help illustrate this.

The Case of Citigroup[4]

Sharing power may have been the only way to get the merger of Travelers and Citicorp done in the first place, as both companies' boards were extremely loyal to their CEOs. However, the decision to share power led to balkanization, and the two CEOs inevitably ended up fighting for territory. The ability to share power is not a typical CEO characteristic. CEOs are trained to command by individual vision. They are fond of invoking team spirit—as long as they are captains of their teams. They don't often wield equal power in major company decisions, despite public pronouncement of close consultation.

Sanford Weill

Sanford I. Weill rose to prominence in the 1960s when he started the securities firm Shearson Loeb Rhodes. After selling the firm in 1981, he bought the Commercial Credit Company, which would eventually become, after numerous acquisitions, Travelers Group, Inc.

Weill is a living legend on Wall Street. Born in a middle-class Brooklyn neighborhood, Weill rose to the top using his street smarts and flamboyant personality. In 1998, Weill was the third highest-paid CEO in the United States, receiving $167 million in compensation, largely as a result of his role in the merger. Weill earned a reputation as a tenacious cost-cutter who focuses on the short-term goals of stock prices and earnings. The acquisition-loving leader maintains a close inner circle that is among the most loyal to be found in any major corporation. He values his personal relationships and helped his son, Marc, become chief investment officer at Travelers. Weill's personality and style trickle down throughout the organization he leads and have a tremendous impact on the corporate culture of his company

In February 1998, Weill contacted Citicorp chief John Reed and presented his idea for Citigroup. The rest is history. Sanford Weill, now 67 years old, was named one of *Businessweek* magazine's top 25 managers of the year for 2000. When asked about retirement in 1998, the man who personifies corporate America replied, "I don't have any plans for retirement. That's the responsibility of our board and I enjoy what I am doing."

John Reed

Citicorp had come to reflect the personality and management style of CEO John Reed, who had led the company since 1984 and whose personality and style were manifest throughout Citicorp. The son of a U.S. businessman, he grew up in Argentina, and he was no stranger to international markets. He was reputed to be a loner who spent much time reading and thinking. Wall Street viewed Reed as a visionary, committed to long-term thinking and willing to make the investments necessary to realize his vision. Such thinking was expected at the company that created the first ATM network, and continued investments in biometric identification and Internet technology were indications of that commitment.

Reed generally was perceived as a scientific manager. Rather than developing a cadre of trusted lieutenants, as was characteristic of his counterpart at Travelers, Reed relied on memos, process, and bureaucracy to control his organization. Reed felt that the Citicorp management team was not effective in fostering an entrepreneurial spirit, perhaps, in part, a result of those tendencies.

In laying the groundwork to become CEO, Reed earned a reputation as being undiplomatic, but he performed well enough as head of the company's consumer banking division that he did become CEO. After the merger, Reed would enjoy strong connections to the merged company's board, a fact that would be important as he and Weill competed for the dominant role in the merged entity.

Reed's vision for the merger was to utilize the company's ubiquitous presence and domestic and international experience to extend Travelers' distribution channels in order to achieve cross-selling synergies. Further, he hoped that access to Travelers' strong management would help him cut costs, "cutting through the bureaucracy" and bringing greater "operational discipline" into the old Citibank organization.

The Co-CEO Structure

Many deals fail to materialize because companies are unable to resolve the question of top leadership. However, in the Citigroup merger, an approach was designed to overcome the significant egos of the respective leaders, and merger discussions proceeded. The solution was to share the responsibilities of many high-level roles via the creation of co-CEOs. The co-CEO roles of Sandy Weill and John Reed were the most significant feature of this structure.

This power-sharing approach offered several appealing advantages. As stated above, it answered the question about who would hold the number one position of the merged entity. Without this compromise, the merger would probably have never been consummated, and subsequent increases in shareholder value may have never been realized. Further, the sheer size of the integration task required the contribution of management talent from both firms. By creating co-CEO roles in the new entity, Citigroup successfully retained significant management talent during the crucial early stages of the integration.

Unfortunately many of these advantages provided only short-term benefits and in fact contributed to some problems. The co-CEO approach delayed the inevitable shakeouts and emergence of the dominant leaders throughout the company. Corporate infighting and positioning contributed to internal turmoil. Management focus was distracted from operating issues, and the integration initially proceeded at a less than ideal pace.

At the outset, the co-CEOs stated they would run Citigroup as equals. To remove the inevitable succession question, they even announced their intention to leave the company at the same time. However, most observers immediately predicted problems would soon arise. The chairmen's premerger paychecks showed a 44 percent disparity in Weill's favor. The merger was supposed to even both executives' compensations, but it would be hard for Weill to avoid treating Reed as a subordinate to whom he has given a lucrative raise. Although Weill and Reed did share a common vision for the company, their styles led to differences over execution strategies.

Self-confidence is considered by some to be the indispensable leadership characteristic, and Weill is known for abundant displays of confidence. In March 2000, Weill came to his biblical theme birthday party playing the role (complete with costume) of Moses. The choice presents some interesting analogies. Moses, who led slaves out of bondage and into nationhood, is considered one of the greatest managers of all time. It was now clear that Weill was the one to lead Citigroup to the promised land. Moses's knowledge of the Sinai Desert, developed during his years as a shepherd, enabled him to display a confidence among the wandering Israelites that secured his position of leadership.

Similarly, Weill's history of successfully meeting the challenges of large acquisitions and his resulting insider knowledge of Wall Street made him an effective and confident leader. Further, Weill exhibited the charisma and vision that inspires an organization to action. Weill tends to make decisions based on his instinct rather than through any elaborate review process.

In July 1999, in an internal memo, Weill and Reed announced the splitting of their duties and their decision to no longer make decisions jointly. Weill took over responsibility for the daily operations of the company, while Reed focused on technology and human resources initiatives. This splitting of duties foreshadowed the formal demise of the co-CEO structure. The excellent results of the company changed the dynamics of the board during 2000, giving Weill even more flexibility to do what he wants. Weill's personal attributes were undoubtedly key contributors to his eventual selection by the Citigroup board to be the sole CEO of the company.

The Case of Verizon

When GTE and Bell Atlantic decided to merge to become the largest U.S. telecommunications company, they chose to have co-CEOs lead the new company. Chuck Lee from GTE and Ivan Seidenberg from Bell Atlantic had different styles and different upbringings.

Lee went to an Ivy League school, is 61 years old, and is quite outgoing. Seidenberg, on the other hand, worked his way through night school in New York, getting a bachelor's degree and an MBA. He is 54, quiet, and soft spoken.

The relationship between the two has been described as harmonious. They get a long quite well and share adjoining offices. The lack of conflict and ability to effectively share the co-CEO role is best characterized as follows:

> Lee matter-of-factly credits the harmony mainly to an agreement that he will leave as co-chief executive in just over a year and stay as a non-executive chairman for the next two years after that. (It's an arrangement that ever-so-patient Seidenberg has down pat—during the Bell Atlantic–Nynex merger he struck a similar deal will Bell chief Raymond Smith.) Lee, who spent the last 18 years at GTE, seems content to exit with a bang. "My career's capstone is launching this company," he says.[5]

Once people have been chosen for key positions, the challenge of retaining them becomes a central focus. Failure to manage retention will mitigate all the "great" choices that were made.

RETAINING KEY PEOPLE

Just because people are offered a position in a merged or an acquired organization does not mean they will take it, especially if they are capable and mobile. And even if they do take a position, that does not mean they will stay very long and produce. Assuming they will is a big mistake, especially in the case of people who are deemed vital to the success of the merger or acquisition. These may be people who have valuable and rare skills and competencies, have connections with key constituents, or are viewed as influential leaders by many in their organization. Moreover, the cost of externally recruiting and developing a new executive, manager, or employee can be exorbitant depending upon the level. This of course assumes that a qualified external candidate even exists. As such, acquiring and merging companies must give considerable thought to retaining these people.

As an example, the importance of retention and the problems associated with defection became apparent in the merger between Harris Semiconductor and General Electric Solid State (GESS). Harris's senior management went to great pains to retain senior managers from the GESS organization. Harris was committed to balancing the top positions in the company between GESS and its own people. Harris was located in Melbourne, Florida, whereas GESS was located in Somerville, New Jersey. The new corporate headquarters would be located in Melbourne.

Harris named a GESS person to the VP of marketing position and thought he was committed to joining the new organization. Although the new VP commuted to Melbourne for a number of months, he was never on board. Unfortunately, Harris management thought he was and began building the new organization with the VP as a key part of it. It was not long before the VP left and the position had to be filled again. Clearly the defection was a blow to the new organization and created a loss of momentum and a vacuum in the marketing organization at a time when rebuilding the company's image in the marketplace was a high priority.

Why did this happen? Harris's management assumed that the VP would be thrilled to join the new company and relocate to Melbourne. The weather in Florida was clearly better than in New Jersey, and real estate dollars would go a much longer way in Florida! After all, Harris's management lived there. Why wouldn't anyone else want to? What Harris's management did not consider was that the VP had extended family, aging parents, and long-term friendships in New Jersey. He also was unsure he would fit in the new company and did not want to take the risk of relocating. He initially took the position but was never committed to it. He rented an apartment in Melbourne and commuted weekly while looking for another job in New Jersey. When asked about his plans to buy a house in Melbourne, he hedged and said he was looking. He never let on to what his intentions were, until he resigned.

This story is not dissimilar to others. In Chevron's merger with Texaco, it was decided that the new corporate headquarters would be in San Ramon, California, the home of Chevron. Texaco's headquarters in White Plains, New York, would be closed. Key people from Texaco were offered positions in San Ramon. Many Texaco people declined for many of the same reasons as the GESS VP. In the end only 14 of the top 61 positions at Chevron-Texaco have been filled with Texaco people.

Retaining people requires a sound recruiting effort similar to one that would be used with new hires, with the primary objectives being:

1. To attract people to the merged company and the proposed positions
2. To ensure they are motivated to stay and contribute
3. To ensure they adapt well to their new environment

Management can influence some of the objectives but not others. For example, willingness to relocate may not be easily influenced. Personal situations, such as elderly parents, children in school, and extended family, may preclude a person from relocating. But there are many things that can be influenced. Below are several key actions that management can take.

Significant Role
Most importantly, many people need to feel they will have a significant and meaningful role in the organization after a merger or an acquisition. Unless people have no alternatives and need the money, they will not likely take a gratuitous position. The position offered must be equal to or exceed the responsibilities and challenges that people currently have.

Mentoring and Support
The acquiring company should consider a program whereby people retained from an acquired company are given a mentor in the new company. The mentor helps them learn the ropes and adjust to the new internal work environment. More will be said about this and other approaches for assimilating new people in Chapter 8.

Fit
People will be concerned whether they will fit with the people they work with. As was illustrated in Chapter 4, fit is an important element in the selection decision. It is also important in the retention decision. A lack of fit may create an awkward situation for people and lead to their eventual departure. A study I conducted with two colleagues clearly suggests that differences in management styles between acquiring and acquired executives were significantly related to the latter's departure.[6] This suggests that if a person does not fit, then two choices are possible.

1. Do not select the person, regardless of the person's capabilities, and ensure there are backups or replacements for him or her.
2. Appreciate the person's stylistic differences and help the person feel as though he or she is a valuable member of the organization and management team.

Realistic Job Preview

All organizations and jobs have pros and cons. Typically, when people are recruited, they are often exposed to the pros, only to quickly learn about the cons. The result is unmet expectations, disillusionment, and turnover.[7] While it is understandable that an acquirer wants to put its best foot forward when selling people on the new company, that can be a mistake. If people are given a realistic preview, their expectations are likely to be more consistent with reality and their chances of adapting to the new organization much greater.

Economic Incentives

As someone once said, "People do not take jobs just for their health." Clearly people work for a variety of reasons, of which economics may be the most important one. It may be helpful to provide attractive inducements to people to take positions in a new company and continue to remain and produce. A variety of incentives can be employed, for example, compensation tied to retention for specific time periods or compensation tied to performance.

In planning a retention strategy it is important to realize that some key target people will be needed indefinitely, whereas others will only need to be retained through the transition stage. There are ways of achieving both.

Retaining Key People Indefinitely

Guarantees such as financial incentives or employment contracts may be required for key people, especially if they are being asked to relocate. A standard incentive program is difficult to develop for all people, and each person should be handled on an individual basis. Individualized attention to the retention of key people has proved successful in retention during and after the closing.

The need to tailor a program should be weighed against the need to ensure that perceived equity exists among people within an organization. Inequities between the target and the acquirer people may create conflicts if people are consolidated into the same work units. In this vein it is important to focus not only on acquired personnel but on acquiring ones as well. I have encountered numerous situations where target people were given so much attention that acquiring people felt as though they were second-class citizens.

Incentive programs should be competitive with what other organizations are offering employees of comparable position. If a program is unattractive, people may be motivated to leave, especially if the other elements discussed in this section are not taken care of and there is a strong labor market. This applies in a non-M&A context as well. Incentives to consider include salary, benefits, and other perks. Incentive programs should also provide people with the motivation to remain and produce long term and should include long-term bonus and stock option plans with long enough payout time frames and short-term restrictions to garner commitment. Clearly these will vary depending upon the level of the position being considered.

Retaining Key People through Transition

Different incentives may be required to retain those people who are needed for a limited time. The reality of most M&As is that the elimination of jobs is necessary in order to meet cost-saving goals, which may occur in either the acquirer or the target organization. However, many of the people who hold these jobs may be needed through the transition period.

For example, many acquirers realize that when integrating information systems (IS), people from a target may be needed until the conversion is completed. These people have insights into how their systems operate that are undocumented. They are needed to keep their systems operating in the short term and to provide information that will ease the conversions. Once the conversion is made, they will not be needed. This is often the case in companies such as banks that are consolidating backroom activities. Until the conversion is made, however, loss of people could be disastrous and lead to significant value leakage. There is nothing worse than a company losing its ability to process information. As noted above, CEOs of acquired or merged companies are also retained just long enough to ensure a smooth transition.

To retain people on a temporary basis, an enhanced severance package can be offered. The enhanced package provides additional benefits if people stay through a specific target date or event. If they leave before that date, they forfeit the additional benefits. Providing additional incentive not only will retain key people, but will improve their attitudes as they deal with customers.

The following are incentives that have been found to be effective by successful acquirers:

1. "Stay" packages (monetary incentives) based on staying until a specified target date or event—e.g., up to six months of additional severance for remaining until the target date. If the person leaves prior to that date, he or she forfeits the entire incentive.
2. Stock options awarded for staying for a specified time.
3. Outplacement packages to assist in job search after a specified time.

The Challenges of Relocation

Many people will not relocate in a merger or an acquisition due to the uncertainty associated with a new location. In addition to family issues that prevent people from leaving, there are also concerns about remaining in the new location if they should lose their job. Given the uncertainty in

M&As and the shakeout of positions during the first year after a deal is closed, this can become a significant issue. Provisions for dealing with this, such as specified employment contracts or severance and relocation benefits, should be considered as part of negotiating with an employee. This will likely vary by organizational level.

Economics of Relocating

Most companies have standard packages for relocating employees. These packages are quite useful in retention decisions of acquired employees and should alleviate some of the concerns people have. Packages should include:

1. Relocation expenses (e.g., moving expenses, real estate adjustments)
2. Cost-of-living adjustments to equalize living conditions
3. Relocation support (e.g., assistance in finding housing, schools)

If people are assigned to an international location, this becomes a more challenging issue.[8]

Recruiting the Family

Relocation not only affects the employees being moved, but also affects their families. It is critical to remember that an entire family needs to be recruited in the retention and relocation process. Although this may seem cumbersome, it may be pivotal in the case of a key employee.

MANAGING EMPLOYEE REDUNDANCY

It is inevitable that people will become redundant in a merger or an acquisition and not be retained. Although such decisions must be made, care should be given to how these decisions are executed. If there are redundancies, ensure they are handled firmly but compassionately. Executives want to send a signal to employees and the community that jobs are sacred and that everything reasonable will be done to ensure that no employees needlessly lose their jobs. Although few people who are being let go will be pleased with the outcome, it is possible to minimize trauma by managing the process in a compassionate way. Essentially, this can be accomplished by providing employees with sufficient support (e.g., adequate severance and outplacement) to ease their transition into another employment situation. While support can be costly, most companies would agree it is worth it. It is likely to minimize adverse reactions (e.g., discrimination lawsuits, sabotage) by those who are terminated and is also likely to maintain or enhance a company's reputation in the market. Again, it will send a strong signal to retained employees about the culture and values of the new company. Both are essential in minimizing value leakage and in creating an environment where people are willing to work hard to build the new company.

Something to Consider

Although the staffing process is designed to select the most qualified people for positions, it does not mean that those not selected are unqualified to remain in the organization. Some may qualify for other positions, or with minimal training and development may be able to do so. Further, many people who are selected for positions that require relocation may choose not to accept them and leave the organization. There needs to be an orderly process to handle these possibilities.

As an example, a major telecommunications provider created a process for managing downsizing due to mergers and acquisitions. As part of capturing cost synergies, thousands of redundant managers were to be severed. Further, a number of operations were to be relocated from San Francisco to St. Louis to take advantage of lower geographic-based operating costs. Several options had to be managed.

1. Downsizing without relocation
   a. The most qualified people were offered the same or a comparable position in their current geographic location (defined as within 50 miles).
   b. Remaining incumbents were considered for reassignment to other positions.
   c. Those who were offered and accepted downgraded positions had their salaries "red-circled" (unadjusted) for 24 months from the close of the merger.
   d. Those not offered positions were placed in a "not-selected" process.
2. Positions relocated without downsizing
   a. The most qualified people were offered a position in a new geographic location. In most cases the geographic change was due to the relocation of an operation to capture lower costs.
   b. Incumbents declining the offer were considered for positions in their current geographic area.
   c. Those not offered positions were placed in a "not-selected" process.
3. Positions relocated with downsizing
   a. Qualified incumbents in the current geographic location were offered positions first. These people were offered jobs first to minimize relocation costs and provide continuity and uninterrupted operations.
   b. Qualified incumbents from other geographic areas were then considered.
   c. Those who were offered and accepted downgraded positions had their salaries "red-circled" (unadjusted) for 24 months from the close of the merger.
   d. Those not offered positions were placed in a "not-selected" process.

The "Not Selected" Process

A clear and compassionate process was used for those who were not offered jobs. They were sent a "60-day letter." The letter explained two options they had available. They were provided an opportunity to become part of a pool of people who for 60 days could seek another position within the merged organization while remaining in their current position. They were given priority placement. Essentially, people would self-nominate and apply for a position for which they were qualified.

Positions were posted using an Intranet-based posting process. The Intranet site had a standardized resume-building process. The site became a common vehicle by which those looking to fill positions could recruit internal candidates. Several attributes of the process were notable:

1. All qualified people affected by the merger were given priority over other equally qualified people who were not affected.
2. Company-employed spouses of relocated managers were given priority over other equally qualified employees.
3. During the 60 days the company could proactively offer qualified employees a position.

The order of priority was (1) merger-affected participants, (2) relocated spouses, and (3) the general employee population.

At the end of 60 days the participants were terminated and offered severance benefits. They could also choose to leave with severance at any time prior to the 60 days. If people chose not to participate in the 60-day process, they were terminated and they were eligible to receive severance.

Severance

Severance benefits were offered as follows. No severance was provided for those who:

1. Voluntarily left the company
2. Were terminated for poor performance
3. Were offered a position at the same salary grade or equivalent and required no relocation

All others qualified for the plan.

The severance agreement provided managers with the following benefits:

1. Payment of accrued wages
2. Payment for current year's unused vacations
3. Completion of tuition payments for current courses in which they were enrolled
4. Exercise of vested stock options
5. Severance payments

6. Self-paid medical, dental, and vision care for 18 months after termination of employment under federal law (COBRA)
7. Benefits under the company's Education/Development Support program for reimbursement of up to $5000 paid out over a maximum of one year for approved courses and fees to help gain reemployment

To receive these benefits a manager had to sign a benefit plan termination and waiver agreement. The agreement specified all the obligations of both the employer and manager upon separation. This agreement is typical for many large companies.

The company also had "change in control" contractual provisions for multiple levels of management, otherwise known as golden, silver, and bronze parachutes. Generally, a change in control is defined as a beneficial change in ownership of a company's voting stock or in the composition of the company's voting stock. Changes of control usually provide enhanced benefits. Such contracts originated in the 1980s as a result of hostile takeovers. They were put in place to reduce the fear of job loss by executives and managers of acquired companies and to encourage them to look out for the interests of shareholders.

In addition to severance benefits, the company provided outplacement support to severed employees. This support was contracted to firms that specialize in this area. Such firms established contact with managers and employees as soon as they were notified of their termination. Outplacement firms provide support in resume writing, interviewing, and career counseling and assist in job searches.

Clearly this process followed the guiding principles articulated at the beginning of this chapter. People were indeed treated with fairness, dignity, and respect, and competence was the major driver of staffing decisions. The outcome was an orderly process. Those who left and those who remained did so with few adverse reactions.

What Else Can Be Done?

In addition to the severance and outplacement process, there are a number of other actions that an acquiring or merging company can do to eliminate the costs of redundancy. Many of these attempt to ease the process of involuntary job loss through either less severe or voluntary approaches. These include:

1. Work-schedule alterations:
   a. Part-time jobs
   b. Shortened workweeks
   c. Job sharing
2. Natural attrition
3. Hiring freezes
4. Early retirement incentives
5. Curtailment of promotions and transfers

6. Salary freezes and reductions
7. Temporary leaves without pay

Although these options may minimize the trauma of terminating people, they may not be sufficient to eliminate the redundancy that a merger or an acquisition can create. Certain approaches such as natural attrition and early retirement may lead to the voluntary exit of qualified people who are needed in the new organization. If severance and retirement incentives are too attractive, they may become oversubscribed and may encourage too many people to leave early. To the extent possible, an acquirer or merging company wants to influence those who stay and those who leave rather than leaving it to chance.

A FINAL NOTE

How staffing, retention, and redundancy are managed can have a profound impact on merging companies. They send clear signals to employees regarding what the company and its executives stand for. These, in turn, can have a dramatic impact on the retention and motivation of key people and thus on value preservation, synergy capture, and value creation. Ensure that they are a part of your integration process.

8

TAKING ACTION: MANAGING THE INTEGRATION STAGE

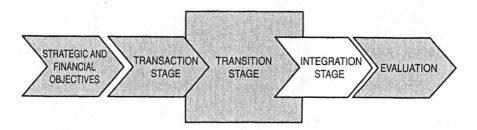

The deal has closed. The combined companies are one legal entity. Key positions have been filled, transition and integration teams have been disbanded, and the executives are ready to rebuild the new organization and work units. The theoretical exercise of planning how the companies will be integrated is over. There is clarity on what the financial and strategic objectives are and how the organizations will function. If not, these need to be completed as quickly as possible by the senior management team after the closing. If so, they need to be reaffirmed and communicated to the organization by the team.

Now the challenge is to successfully integrate the companies, preserve value, and deliver the synergies, earnings, and cashflows that were promised. It is likely that there is a cadre of people from both organizations who interacted during the transaction and transition stages. This includes senior managers, transition and integration team members, and ad hoc work-group members. They already should have had a good opportunity to learn about each other, have had cooperative experience and think well of each other. They already should have communicated this within their own respective organizations as well. In spite of this it is typical that the majority of people have likely yet to interact with counterparts from the other organization. All they have is their impressions from what they have heard, seen, and imagined.

Depending upon the nature of the deal and the synergies sought, the complexity of the integration will vary. In the case of a merger where synergies are being attempted throughout most of if not the entire organization, the integration will be quite complex and pervasive. In the case of a small acquisition where it is being integrated into an existing operation, the integration and ensuing changes will be simpler—except, of course, for those directly affected! In general, the less the synergies being sought, the less the complexity of the integration. Where there is little standardization, combination, or intervention, the less the challenges.

Success requires that executives and managers articulate clear visions, values, goals, and/or strategies for the combined organization. It also requires that they align work units and capable and motivated people from multiple organizations to drive the objectives underlying the merger or acquisition. It requires managing the integration of multiple cultures, innovating, building new teams, and in general managing a complex change process. Unfortunately, this is where many M&As fail. Where does one begin? There are a number of key objectives that must be met and activities that must be managed during the integration stage. These are presented in Table 8-1.

DEMONSTRATING A COMMITTED AND OPEN-MINDED LEADERSHIP

There is no question that the leaders of acquiring and merging companies play a vital role in the integration process. Simply put, they set the tone for the integration and set an example of how it should progress. This is not to imply that they have total control but that they set many things in motion. An excellent example of this is the role that Carlos Ghosn has played in the acquisition of Nissan by Renault. Ghosn is a highly accomplished executive who has had great success leading a number of compa-

Table 8-1 Integration Stage

Objectives
1. Complete analytical activities that were not completed prior to the closing
2. Execute actions to physically integrate the target or merger partner
3. Rebuild the organization into a stronger, more competitive entity capable of realizing financial and strategic objectives

Activities
1. Demonstrating a committed and open-minded leadership
2. Building teams and work units
3. Focusing on financial and strategic objectives
4. Remaining flexible—things change
5. Providing for capable and motivated people
6. Assimilating new people
7. Achieving cultural integration

nies and turning around Renault. He was made president and CEO of Nissan in 1999 and was charged with turning it around while successfully integrating it with Renault.

Nissan faced three main problems. It:

- Had 2.4 trillion yen (22 billion dollars) in debt
- Was unable for many years to show a profit
- Had a continuous decline in global market share since 1990

Ghosn faced a radically different culture in Japan than in either France or the United States, where many of the decisions to transform Nissan would not be embraced. He would have to work within a different culture to win support for his ideas and motivate a new organization to take on and successfully implement the challenges. Most people felt that he faced an impossible challenge.

Proving those people wrong, Ghosn skillfully got the organization and Japanese industry to focus on the issues facing Nissan and the need to turn the company around. He was tenacious in his focus on business objectives and built consensus among those around him on why these were critical for the acquisition and the companies to succeed.

Of importance, Ghosn did not attempt to utilize an ethnocentric approach to changing Nissan (he was born in Brazil, was educated in France, and worked in France and the United States prior to this challenge). As Ghosn commented:

Cultural differences can be viewed as either a handicap or a powerful seed for something new. From the beginning, I said that I viewed cultural differences as an opportunity to innovate in achieving the pragmatic business objectives we had before us. This is risky when you say it before you even start. It's been 15 months since I arrived at Nissan. And now, six months after the start of the revival plan, I can tell you that today cultural differences are seen more as an object of cross-fertilization and innovation in the way we are doing things than as a motive for frustration or reason to disagree. This is due to one thing—the Nissan Revival Plan. When the Renault people came to Japan, the management of Nissan had from the beginning a very strong consciousness about the severity of the situation. There was no room for bickering or fighting or infinite discussions about whose method or whose process we were going to adopt.

The Nissan Revival Plan came very fast and established strong objectives. It didn't leave any room for meditation on the differences about cultures. We were all mobilized and engaged in the revival of the company. What we see today is that differences in culture are being used more and more as ways of listening to what different people can bring to the table to achieve our objectives for the future. So, it is a careful selection of best practices and best approaches. There is enormous pressure on everyone to deliver. In a way it was simple, we just established a point where everybody understood what we had to do to survive as a whole company.

Of course there are frustrations that always exist with language barriers: where you don't operate in an environment of spontaneous communication; where you have to go through a translator (you know that when you go through a translator, about 40 percent of your intended meaning is lost); where you're not sure that what you want to get across to people, on the shop floor or in meetings with customers, is actually being communicated the way you intended it to. These are what I consider small frustrations; if you accept these and other things that perhaps are part of the fact that people don't think or act the same way in France or in Japan, it is easier to deal with such things as language barriers. When you have taken the time to understand that, and when you are really motivated and mobilized by a very strong objective, then the cultural differences can become seeds for innovation as opposed to seeds for dissention.[1]

These comments and the fact that in 2001 Nissan reported its first profits in many years demonstrate the power of a committed and open-minded leader during the integration process. He did not allow cultural differences, which were significant, to become an excuse for failure, although he could have easily done so. He embraced the differences and used them. There is no doubt that the crisis at Nissan helped everyone see the need for change. However, it was still Ghosn's leadership that has made a huge difference. If not, why did it take Nissan 10 years to recover?

Ghosn attributes the success of the turnaround to:

- Focusing on the key priorities, the business goals—"And these are to create value—value in the short and midterm for our customers, our shareholders, and our employees."
- Top management's attitude and behaviors:
  - "Top management is highly visible. What we think, what we say, and what we do must be the same."
  - "We must be committed to the responsibilities we've agreed to. When we don't deliver, we have to face the consequences."
- Four dimensions of leadership behaviors:
  - Be open-minded.
  - Listen to ideas.
  - Focus on the goals.
  - Act very fast.

BUILDING TEAMS AND WORK UNITS

Once the merger or acquisition has been closed, the first order of business is to begin the process of building teams from the senior management level on down. The extensiveness of this activity will depend upon the degree of integration. In a transformational merger it may require a complete rebuilding of all teams and work units. There may be a new mix of people and an entirely new approach to the way the organization is to operate, including products, services, organizational structure, systems, and culture.

Many people will be put together who have never worked together, who are from different organizational cultures, and who bring different personal styles (see Chapter 4). In a small acquisition it may be the addition of a few people to an already functioning team. Even for those who have worked together and for the new leader it is useful to review how the team operates and should operate. To assume that people will effectively work together may be an erroneous assumption. People will be used to different ways of working and will likely be jockeying for a meaningful place on the team and in the work unit. The potential for political behavior, misunderstanding, and conflict under such a scenario is high, and the likelihood of cooperation is low, especially in the case of a complex merger.

A number of key activities should be performed to ensure that people work together and are aligned around the same financial and strategic objectives. Clearly, the alignment process must begin at the senior management level; otherwise it is not likely that managers throughout the organization will fall into alignment. If executives do not set an example for acceptable behaviors, it is not likely that those throughout the organization will consistently do so. Asking people from integrating organizations to cooperate while the senior management team battles is not likely to have the desired effect. One only needs to examine the problems that ensued at Citigroup after the merger. Senior management battled, and so did everyone else. This led to the departure of many good people who felt they did not fit in the new organization.

There are numerous ways in which to build a senior management team. Much of it depends on the style and orientation of the CEO. Some CEOs do not like "soft" team-building activities and are very task-oriented, whereas others have more patience for the "soft stuff." Some CEOs have a directive leadership style, whereas others are more involving and empowering. Regardless, it is critical that CEOs, as well as all leaders, establish ground rules by which a new team will work together and get buy-in for them. It is unlikely that everyone on a senior management team will embrace all the rules, but at a minimum the team members will need to support the rules and live with them. If they cannot, it is likely that they will not have a sustained role in the new organization.

I have worked with a number of newly formed and revitalized post-closing senior teams and have found it useful to begin by defining some basic team processes on how people will work together. Often an experienced outsider to help facilitate the management teams and to coach executives and managers can be of great value. This process is being used to build the senior management team and the ensuing management teams for the top 61 people in the Chevron-Texaco merger. Some useful topics to address as part of team building include defining:

1. What is the role of the senior management team?
2. When does the senior management team meet and for what purposes? Does it meet on a regular basis? Can any member request a meeting of the team, or is that the prerogative of the CEO? Is the team a decision-making team, or is its purpose to provide recommendations to the CEO?
3. How does the team agenda get set? Is it set by the CEO or by members of the team?
4. What is the decision-making process that will be employed by the team? Is it consensus-based? Majority vote? Does the CEO have a vote, or is he or she the final decision maker?
5. How does the team deal with differences of opinion and manage conflict? Is it through open discussion during meetings or behind closed doors?
6. What role does each person play on the team and for specific types of decisions? Does he or she have responsibility for making decisions, approving decisions, or providing resources and support?

Depending upon the CEO's leadership style and the situation, such decisions can be arrived at in a number of ways. First the CEO can just make and announce decisions. Second the CEO can involve the entire team in making them. Third the CEO can declare which decisions are his or hers and make them and which are the team's and let the team make them.

A couple of factors need to be considered when making this choice. First, most executives expect to have some input into the senior management decision-making process. In a study I conducted with two colleagues, for example, we found that executives were willing to support decisions made by the CEO only when their ideas were seriously considered, even if the decisions did not reflect their position.[2] Second, I have found that most executives can live with the approach chosen by a CEO as long as it is consistent with the expectations that have been created. In other words, if the CEO led people to believe they would be involved in decisions and were not, then they had negative reactions. A comment that an executive once shared with me summarized it best:

> I understand that it is the prerogative of the CEO to run his organization any way he wishes. However, I assume that since

he picked me for his team he believed that I was competent and had something meaningful to contribute. Thus, at a minimum, I expect to be heard. Also, I do not have a problem if in the end the CEO makes the decisions. Again that is his prerogative. However, that is fine as long as it is consistent with the ground rules that he sets. Setting one set of expectations and playing by another just doesn't play well with me. If he needs to change the rules, fine, but just give me enough warning so I can adjust.

Once the senior team is able to operate, there are a number of issues that must form the basis of the team agenda. Some of these issues may have been worked out during the transition stage through the work of integration teams, whereas others will have to be worked out during integration. Regardless of the amount of work done during transition, some level of refinement is always needed. Issues that senior management must address or revisit include:

1. The vision and financial and strategic objectives of the merger or acquisition and the firm in general, and how that translates into organizational priorities and objectives throughout the organization
2. How the organization will be designed to support these objectives, including:
   a. Culture
   b. Activities performed
   c. Systems
   d. Business processes
   e. Operating/business models
   f. Organizational structure
   g. Measurements and rewards
   h. Positions, descriptions, and head count
   i. Operating and capital budgets
3. How the integration and change process will be managed
4. What areas are to be affected
5. What are the priorities, especially with respect to the financial and strategic objectives

Once the leadership of the merged organization is in place or some key positions have been filled in an acquisition, the process of team building needs to continue throughout the organization. Many of the team issues described above need to be cascaded through the organization. The focus of the team's agenda will change depending upon the particular area. For example, functional areas, lines of businesses, business processes, and geographic areas will focus on pursuing their objectives and strategies. However, they must be aligned with those developed by the senior management team.

Without alignment there is a risk that the financial and strategic objectives underlying the deal will not be met. The goal, however, is not to turn team building into a bureaucratic process. As long as team goals are clear and aligned and the recommendations of integration teams on consolidation and standardization are being implemented, there should be room to allow each unit some flexibility and sufficient lines of communication to make adjustments in objectives as warranted by changing situations. After all, customers, competitors, and other external elements continually change, requiring flexibility and adjustment.

The Role of Perceptual Filters in Building Teams[3]

As discussed in Chapter 4, a tool such as the Birkman Method can be of great help in the selection of people. In addition, it is also useful in helping acquirers and merger partners understand the issues involved in integrating target people into the new company and also is useful in helping them prepare for that. Armed with these insights, executives and managers can then use the information to build new merged teams or insert individuals into existing teams. The instrument can be administered to the many people who were not assessed during the transaction stage to help facilitate the development of newly created teams.

The use of an instrument such as the Birkman Method allows members of a new team to quickly learn about other members' styles and how best to deal with them. From my experience, this helps shorten the length of time it takes for people to learn about themselves and others, minimizes unnecessary conflict, and facilitates a process whereby diverse individuals can learn to work together and to address the business issues.

Let us take as an example a manufacturer of plastics that acquired a biomedical research firm to help it become the creative and visionary company it once was. The manufacturer (renamed here as Plastico), like the well-established energy companies discussed in Chapter 4, was one of the top four in the world. Competition in Europe and Asia was putting a real squeeze on its profits. The leaders of Plastico felt they had three viable options:

Option 1. They could sell off their least profitable product lines.
Option 2. They could expand further into medical prosthesis and surgical supply products (an area in which they had recent success).
Option 3. They could sell off two losing product lines and acquire a medical-related business.

They chose option 3 and bought a biomedical research company (Glower Corporation), noted for its breakthrough product ideas that created links between physics, engineering, and physiology.

The integration of Glower Corporation would involve the implementation of new structures and processes. Managers of Plastico would be asked to collaborate with team leaders from Glower Corporation to establish new ways of working. As in almost any situation, clashes can occur because people have different sets of expectations about the outcome and different assumptions about how to bring it about. When ideas or methods are really quite foreign, people frequently have an emotional reaction to the other's approach. Those reactions can then lead to stressful behaviors.

Plastico was an old-line, hard-core manufacturing company known for its style as a tightly run ship. Glower Corporation, on the other hand, was run like a freewheeling graduate research lab. It had attracted some of the brightest physicists and biologists in the country, and its culture valued individuality and cross-functional teams. These two organizations would be a test for the very best of integration thinking. It promised to be a stretch for both sides. Plastico had the capital and international infrastructure, but Glower Corporation held the key to new products and increased profitability.

Behind the human element of ingrained differences in approach is the fact that business situations consist of *structural* and *relational* elements. Structural relates to things such as departmental organization, systems, processes, finance, administration, etc. Sometimes the best designed infrastructure and control systems can go awry simply because well-intentioned leaders in different functions take different approaches in an integration project. Relational relates to how people interact with each other.

In Chapter 4, in the insurance company case with Dirk, we saw how perceptual filters play a role in organizational decision making. Here we revisit the maxim that for each party to an interaction, perception is reality. The parties get to that reality through the perceptual filters they use— their expectations and their assumptions. The degree to which there is tolerance and understanding of what each filter contributes to the whole determines the effectiveness of a new structural element (departmental configuration or process).

The specific situation we want to highlight from the integration of Glower into Plastico (renamed Mediplast for this example) was the focused and sustained effort required to meld these two disparate management teams into a unified team. There were the usual corporate change campaigns around vision, mission, goals, and the creation of a new brand led by the marketing department and the office of corporate communications. Despite these traditional efforts to communicate a "new way" at Mediplast, there were nevertheless severe clashes in personality, style, approach, and values.

The CEO of Mediplast was the former CEO of Plastico. He was a man of vision and a risk taker in a culture that had heretofore been somewhat risk averse. He knew it would take something extraordinary to break down the prejudices that the executives of each company held of the other. He believed the whole senior management team had to go through a process that was entirely new. It couldn't belong to Plastico, and it couldn't come from Glower. Something new—that grew out of the combined efforts of both—had to take the place of former conventions and styles. That meant new ways of relating to each other and a new language to create a bond among those who, at the outset of the merger, were like tourists in another's foreign territory.

In a previous company the Mediplast CEO had come to know about our executive process. He called a colleague and me in to help with the integration. We started at the top, with the combined senior management team, leading a program that set the tone and the pace for the rest of the organization. We set in place a three-month cascading team-building initiative that required people at every level in the organization to work on cross-functional teams and to learn a new way of communicating about work and about their interpersonal relationships. Everything from strategic planning, to individual performance appraisals, to watercooler conversations, was influenced by this team-building process.

It started with a 1 1/2-day retreat, which later would be replicated with every work unit. We took the new leaders of Mediplast through a series of exercises aimed first at helping them see the value of understanding their own perceptual filters and those of their colleagues. Within minutes, these exercises brought home the fact that one's own perceptual filter is not the only way of viewing a problem or situation! They were humbled and challenged. Mediplast's senior team members quickly saw how each of them gave off subtle verbal signals to others in terms of both words and body language. They further learned that by paying attention to the clues in the language a person uses to describe something, they could quickly identify the filter the other was using. Armed with that understanding and an ability to interpret "filters," they realized a growing appreciation for others' points of view (see Figure 8-1).

Not all the sailing was smooth. Early on in this retreat, we saw the warning signals of a clash between the head of operations and the head of research and development. Each had starkly different views on how the company should create new-product planning and implementation. The goal of this process was to put Mediplast in the lead against the competition for bringing new products to market.

The operations VP (former Plastico) was a bit like our friend Dirk, whom you will recall from the Healthy Life case recounted in Chapter 4. He saw things through an "operations and technical filter." As the VP of operations assessed the issues involved in designing the new-product planning and implementation process, he focused almost exclusively on the implementation aspects and paid little attention to the needs of the R&D team.

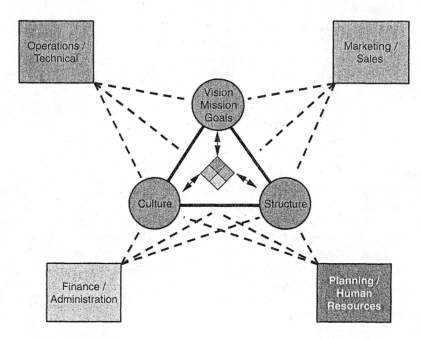

Figure 8-1   Perceptual Filters

His perceptual filter viewed issues though a prism of technology, pragmatism, and an insistence on results and having the facts at hand. He had little patience for experimenting or working the bugs out in a trial. His perception of how to get this process established was simply to "get on with it and get it done."

His R&D peer, from Glower Corporation, was a research scientist, and was known even inside Glower as the ultimate individualist. He filtered his assessment of the task through a long-range planning filter. He constantly referred to the big picture, the unreasonable hurry of those on the implementation side of the house, the complexities of having "fail-safe" products, and the lack of appreciation on the part of others for the creativity and originality of the R&D staff. He assumed that the solution would result from experimentation and then synthesis of the results. His dominant approach was strategic, experimental, and thoroughly thought-out.

The VP of R&D wanted to produce products that would meet customers' needs for utility, durability, convenience, and attractiveness. He insisted that bringing these features together couldn't happen overnight. The VP of operations wanted to get products into production in a staggered process to avoid several products hitting the assembly lines at the same time, a situation that would max out his production capacity and require overtime.

Back and forth they went. The R&D head insisted on multiple performance tests. The VP of operations knew that his bonus was contingent on reducing overtime costs. He pleaded for delivery based on staggered product development. The timing of products coming out of R&D must be precise and on schedule. The VP of R&D, whose bonus was based on reduced defects, insisted he couldn't release products until they met long-range durability tests. Sometimes this delayed the release of new products into the production cycle. The men reached a standstill.

At this point, we asked them to switch positions and describe the situation from the other's perspective. So our "do-it-now" operations and technical filter VP of operations now heard himself championing the R&D position through a long-range analytical-creative planning filter. And as difficult as it was, the VP of R&D had to package his proposal in factual, schedule-imperative ultimatums. Over lunch that day, the men kicked around ideas about what they had learned from taking an opposite problem-solving approach to their normal one. First, they discovered they had learned to appreciate, if not fully understand, an issue from the other's perspective. Next they noted that this exercise helped them become aware of the kinds of inputs on which the sales or control guys would most likely insist. They joked with each other about the predominant filter type each represented, but underneath they were keenly aware that they both held strong tendencies to operate from the premise of having their own rules and wanting others to live by those rules. Like most of us, they thought their rules were the right ones. They discovered how emotionally attached to them they were. Finally, they realized this strong attachment to *their way* of seeing a problem pushed them to just jump right in and start behaving almost automatically, as if a record needle were stuck in a groove. These were important lessons. Though neither fully realized it at the time, these insights represented colossal leaps in understanding and personal growth.

The second half of our workshop focused on the behaviors and the motivational needs of the team. We stressed two key principles. First, that when it comes to behavior, *there is no such thing as normal*. Sounds preposterous! What do you mean, "no such thing as normal"? If we go back to the lessons learned earlier from the experiences with the perceptual filters, it isn't so hard to understand that we see our own behaviors as normal. What we come to understand is that there is normal for me, for him, for her, or for "those" people. When people behave differently from us, in most cases their behavior is simply just that—different. It is usually not right or wrong. It just is.

A second principle is that the way a person behaves is not necessarily indicative of the way he or she is motivated. In other words, *there is no logical connection between the way a person behaves and the way he or she needs to be treated*. To grasp the power of this statement takes a bit of explaining and a few examples. When the meaning sinks in, it is often one of those great "ah-ha" experiences.

Let's revisit the previous example of the VPs of operations and R&D who were tussling over a product planning and implementation process. This example can be used to illustrate the way that a basic understanding of the surface behaviors and the underlying motivational needs of the other helped these two very different personalities forge a productive and congenial relationship. To explain the process of how this happened, we turn first to the 11 different personality components found in the "Strengths and Needs Report" described in Chapter 4. These components identify one's usual behavior, motivational needs, and possible stress reactions (i.e., when motivational needs are not met).

While we worked with the entire Mediplast senior team in this workshop, the CEO had privately told us that for the company change-over process to succeed, the relationship between the more traditional VP of operations and the more rebellious, scientific VP of R&D just had to work. Thus, we provide only the profiles of these two vice presidents to illustrate the process we used to help develop, first, an understanding of differences and, then, ways to work productively with those differences.

By studying the diagram in Table 8-2, which displays their profiles, we begin to see how the "needs/behavior" connection works. It is then quite obvious how team members can either thwart or foster productive contributions from their colleagues. The personality categories that follow are the same we reviewed previously in the insurance company case where Dirk was a prime candidate for CEO. Here, in the case of the two "dueling VPs," we can see at a glance, simply by how their scores align in each category, where are similarities and differences between them. The discussion below elaborates on some of the areas that predictably could produce tension between these two and illustrates some of the lessons the two learned about each other.

Component Scores of Strengths and Needs

Recall the scoring pattern we saw with Dirk: On a scale of 1–99, scores below 50 are considered low and those above 50, high. Generally, the interpretation of scores in the range of 40–60 is dependent on the situation. Scores to the left of the slash (/) in Table 8-2 represent usual or strength behavior. Scores to the right of the slash represent motivational needs. Let's look at scoring patterns of Mediplast's two VPs to see what areas might cause stress for one or the other.

Starting with the personality component on the far left, "Esteem," which has to do with the degree of directness or subtlety in communication, we see that both men's scores to the left of the slash are in the low range, 3 and 13. This means we could expect both the VP of operations and R&D to communicate quite straightforwardly. In other words, their

Table 8-2 Strengths and Needs Report

	Esteem	Acceptance	Structure	Authority	Advantage	Activity	Challenge	Empathy	Change	Freedom	Thought
VP Operations	3/1	93/98	61/61-	83/66	53/53	99/97	99/99	9/9	32/32+	82/88	2/2
VP R&D	13/57	99/11	95/40	25/25	3/65	4/20	77/77	85/9	49/49	82/76	99/90
Average	8/29	96/55	78/40	54/46	28/59	52/59	88/88	47/9	41/49	82/82	51/46

communication style would be pretty much the same. When we look at the scores to the right, we see there is a big jump on the needs side, from 1 to 57. A score of 1 means that the VP of operations is motivated by relationships that are very direct and frank. Given that a score of 13 means that the usual behavior of his R&D colleague is to be direct and frank, we would anticipate few conflicts. Our VP of R&D, on the other hand, will communicate in a frank and open manner only when he feels assured of the respect of the other party to the communication. If he isn't assured that his ideas are valued, he may be overly sensitive to perceived criticism, be embarrassed, or get his feelings hurt. His stress behavior would be to shut down or withhold his ideas. So right away, we have a red flag that goes up, indicating that the way the VP of operations addresses the VP of R&D will be important if they are to have a productive relationship.

Moving next to "Acceptance," or the preference for social involvement in work versus the desire to work independently or with just a small team, we see, again, common styles in "usual behavior" in that both VPs are highly sociable and tend to be skilled in meeting people easily. However, if we look at the motivational need scores to the right of the slash, we see a huge difference in needs. Our VP of operations needs the support of a team around him to stimulate his gregarious and outgoing behavior. Quite the opposite, the VP of R&D needs a great deal of time to himself, away from the social pressures of work if we expect him to be communicative and attentive. The lesson here for the VP of Operations is to give his R&D pal time to withdraw and be alone.

We can skip over the component "Structure" (which indicates how insistent one is with planning and details) because the ranges are essentially similar, and we could expect slightly similar behaviors and responses. This brings us to "Authority." Here we can see at a glance big scoring differences for each officer. The VP of operations has high scores for both usual behavior and needs, meaning that he is very directive, aggressive in thinking, and quick to take a stand; he wants the same from his environment. He needs a situation where he can direct others and where there are strictly enforced lines of authority.

The VP of R&D's behavior is quite the opposite. His style is to suggest rather than actively direct. He avoids open clashes and is outwardly pleasant and agreeable. He prefers an environment where authority is clearly defined and delegated and where he, himself, is managed through persuasion rather than being told what to do. Immediately, another and much larger red flag goes up. The VP of operations must come to realize that his pattern of dominance will not engender productive response from his colleague. If the VP of R&D is treated in an authoritarian way, he will resist that direction and have difficulty confronting that style. Between the two, there will be an issue of who is in control.

Next, we will skip over "Advantage" (which relates to competitiveness and materialism) to "Activity." This component gives us a picture of how each will use his personal energy. The VP of operations, with scores in the high 90s on both usual behavior and needs, personifies someone who is physically active, forceful, and competitive. He needs lots of things to do and opportunities to be active physically. On the other side of the ledger, we find the VP of R&D with a usual behavior score of 4, indicating he is very much a thinker and a delegator and is efficient in using his energy. He needs lots of time to reflect and to analyze, he needs the stimulation of new ideas, and he needs unhurried work conditions. Yet another gigantic red flag is raised. The tendency for the VP of operations will be to see the VP of R&D as someone who is slow and doesn't move at the pace needed for the project. R&D will see his operations counterpart as moving so quickly, he may be prone to make mistakes. Under stress, both will tend to magnify their natural tendencies.

Finally we leapfrog over "Challenge" (the way we relate to the demands of work), "Empathy" (the degree of emotion or feeling we put into or need from our day-to-day work), "Change" (the degree of focus or novelty we give to or want from work), and "Freedom" (an indicator of conventionality or indivdualism), to "Thought" (the amount of time we take or need for certain kinds of decisions). Here we find the largest red flag of all. The VP of operations has extremely low scores for usual behavior and motivational needs. A configuration of 2/2 indicates a style of making quick decisions and needing an environment that is clear and unambiguous and that provides opportunities to take immediate action. Contrast that with the 99/90 of the VP of R&D, where we have the profile of an analyst who needs to think through decisions very carefully, and we have potential for a real clash around the issue of timing.

As we explain what these and the other scores in their profiles mean, our goal is not to have either VP change himself, because this effort is not about changing who you are. It is about becoming aware of the other's needs and how a shift in behavior can motivate positive and productive work from the other. The resultant solution for Mediplast's planning and implementation process can be enriched by:

1. Both VPs facilitating communication that is direct but respectful between each other
2. Both VPs being committed to the team and by the operations VP allowing the VP of R&D to have space to think and reflect and be alone
3. The VP of R&D recognizing that speed and movement is an imperative for his colleague in operations
4. The VP of operations realizing that his style of direction will thwart the creativity of the R&D leader

Our hope is that both will learn patience and acceptance of their differences.

As we reviewed the component scores with the entire team, the senior managers had their own unique "ah-has" about themselves and their colleagues. From this point of insight, we paired up each officer with a partner the CEO had assigned to handle a "cross-functional" initiative. Along with this pairing came the charge to identify the areas where they found the greatest difference in their strengths and needs. Whether it was communication, organization, directiveness, action orientation, or decision-making style, they each chose one target at which to direct their own improvement campaign. They agreed that when one missed the other's motivational needs, the other would provide feedback in terms of what approach could have worked better.

At the Monday morning "management meetings," Mediplast's CEO would ask each officer to report on how well he or she met the designated behavior target and then what they each learned about themselves and their counterpart. The fact that the counterpart was present kept each senior manager focused on the facts. Often the reported interactions and lessons learned injected humor into the management meetings, but the overwhelming result seemed to be an increasing degree of individual humility and receptivity to others' points of view and styles.

This kind of reinforcement is expensive—to the tune of two hours per month of ten executives' time over a three-month period. Why did the CEO do it? He knew that it was not the technology or the financials that would meld these disparate companies into a unified whole, but the relationships the key officers had with one another. This would set the tone for the entire company and for interactions with customers. He felt it would be the differentiator, and he was willing to support that financially.

There were several side benefits from the team-building process. One was incorporating some new "relationship" elements into the annual 360 degree performance reviews and the bonus determinations. As the process cascaded down and was institutionalized at each level, the two very disparate organizations gradually united into one that was now very new.

Another benefit was the way officers used their knowledge and "people-reading skills" in the team-selection process. Given the heavy emphasis on cross-functional teams, an executive heading a team could use his or her self-knowledge to describe to an incoming team in both behavioral and needs terminology what behavioral outputs were desired from the new team as well as what each team member could expect to get from the team leader. Fluency with this new corporate "language" allowed team leaders to frame questions and listen to responses in a new way—a way that captured the factual as well as the emotional essence of a work situation.

Many executives and lower-level management team leaders used another element of our process to illustrate their points clearly and simply to a new team. This element was the leadership style grid, which a team leader can use to characterize the key interests, strengths, motivational needs, and stresses of each team member (see Table 8-3).

In each of four categories—interests, usual behavior, motivational needs, and stress—the initials of each team member pinpoint, in the relevant quadrant, the location of either their dominant interest, style, need, or likely stress reaction. For example, a team member who has strong interests in taking action would have his or her initials somewhere in the "Expeditors" quadrant. For interests in persuading or selling, initials would be in the "Communicators" quadrant; for planning, in the "Planners" quadrant; and for handling administrative details or systems, in the "Administrators" quadrant. The leader could easily identify where there were surfeits or deficits of strength on the grid. This could mean that for a certain project, team members might be asked to work outside their interest or most productive areas, the fallout being that it might be more difficult to motivate them to do something in which they were less interested or productive. Of course, the ideal was to put people on projects that tapped into their interests, strengths, and needs.

The grid also proved a handy way to identify stress. For example, if a team member was becoming overly domineering, a colleague would know that was typical of "Expeditors" stress behavior. One thing that helps move people out of stress is to keep them busy. A colleague could ask if it would help to have some additional things to do, or simply give the stressed person something to get done by a certain deadline. By learning what the typical stress behaviors of each quadrant were, and ways of helping the person stuck in stress move out of it, the team members contributed to both self-management and team management.

Both the grid and stress reaction scores, which are part of the components in the "Strengths and Needs Report," were used frequently by Mediplast's officers and staff to get themselves or others back on a productive track when they found their needs were not getting met. The grid gave them labels to use in describing stress behavior, and the stress-

Table 8-3   Leadership Style Grid

"Expeditors"	"Communicators"
"Administrators"	"Planners"

reactive scores from the components gave them measures of intensity and descriptions of how to deal with a specific stress situation. The newly integrated teams got pretty good at working with stress behaviors. They used examples from work situations to support the 360 degree performance review category that addressed "managing self and others."

Over the year, as we worked with Mediplast to operationalize new policies and practices, we saw many descriptions of quadrant behavior and samples of terms sprinkled throughout performance reviews. There was not a single management meeting that didn't make use of the terminology. What seemed to please Mediplast executives and staff alike was that the skills they were applying to work relationships were helping them listen better, see others' perspectives, and manage stress in their home lives as well. This resulted in no turnover among the senior managers and an effective cascading of team development throughout the new organization. It's pretty hard to put a dollar value on that side benefit.

The lesson we learned was that our "intervention" to unite two groups into a single new one was appropriate for this situation. What made it a part of the teams' nervous system was the vision of the CEO and his insistence on holding people accountable for using the lessons they learned. It is this kind of focus that differentiated this integration from so many I have seen.

While our process is useful in building cooperation among team members, the focus of a team's efforts during the integration stage is critical. Cooperation without proper focus will not result in value-creating outcomes. The next section discusses two key objectives that teams need to focus on: financial and strategic objectives.

FOCUSING ON FINANCIAL AND STRATEGIC OBJECTIVES

A recurring theme throughout this book has been the importance of financial and strategic objectives. Again, these are pivotal to the value-creation process. Nowhere is it more important than during the integration stage. It is in this stage where objectives become operational and people and teams need to focus on achieving them. Regardless of whether the deal is a small acquisition or a large merger, people's attention must be focused on these objectives. People need to be continuously reminded of their importance and the precedence they must assume during the integration stage and beyond. Failure to attend to "the business" and to deliver on these objectives will be disastrous for everyone, from the CEO to frontline employees.

Not only must broad-based objectives be set for the organization, but they must be translated into objectives that people throughout work units (e.g., functional and support areas, lines of businesses, business process-es, geographic areas) can manage and control. Although higher-level objectives are important, work-unit objectives are pivotal for driving indi-vidual and team behavior.

In some cases, this process will require certain units to continue to focus on the same sets of objectives and maintain the same level. For oth-ers it will require new objectives and levels. The key is to ensure that all individual and work-unit objectives and levels of achievement are aligned with the broader objectives. Moreover, people need to be mea-sured for these objectives and be held accountable and rewarded for achieving them. It is easy for people to take their eyes off these objectives as they become focused on the integration process itself.

REMAINING FLEXIBLE—THINGS CHANGE

Someone once told me that M&As are like marriage. No matter how well two people have planned their lives together, people and situations change and continuous adjustments have to be made. If not, the likely result is a divorce. In a merger or an acquisition it is the same. No matter how much due diligence or integration planning is done, it is almost certain that over time adjustments will have to take place. As noted in Chapters 3 and 6, due diligence and transition planning are inexact processes due to time constraints and access and availability of informa-tion. Regardless of how well they are conducted, many things will be overlooked and unanticipated.

PROVIDING FOR CAPABLE AND MOTIVATED PEOPLE

In building a merged organization it is essential that the capability and motivation of people be developed to meet the demands of the new orga-nization. Capability is their ability to carry out a task; motivation is their desire to do so. Even though a careful process may have been used to select the most capable people for positions, it is no guarantee that people will be ready to step in and perform. This is especially the case if new sys-tems, structures, work processes, and the like have been adopted. It will take time for people to learn and adjust to and accept the changes. As Figure 8-2 indicates, there are a number of elements that management must employ to ensure that motivation and capability are captured.

1. Once people assume positions in the new work unit, their roles and responsibilities must be clarified. Even the most motivated people will fail if they are unsure where they need to focus their energies.

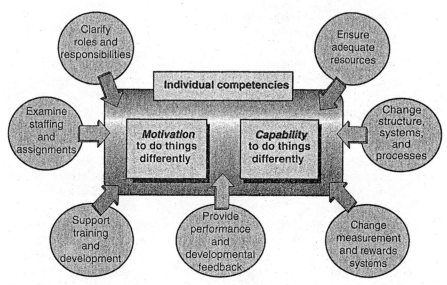

Figure 8-2   Creating Capable and Motivated People

2. Care must be taken to ensure that people are placed in the right positions. This requires matching the right person to the right job.
3. Training and development are pivotal. Highly qualified people will need training and development to meet the needs of new positions that are created, technologies that are employed, and systems and work processes that are introduced. If done properly, integration teams should identify such needs as part of their work.
4. It is important that a performance and developmental feedback process be established. Without feedback, people will not know whether they are meeting expectations or not.
5. Measurement and reward systems may be among the most powerful elements in shaping behavior. What is measured and rewarded is what people will focus on.

As an integrated example that captures all these elements, a large equipment manufacturing company used a merger as an opportunity to significantly change its after-sales service approach. Before the merger neither company did a very good job at servicing customers. A customer service integration team was created, and after careful study of best practices a new approach was developed. The team concluded that numerous aspects of the organization would have to be transformed.

1. The type of people required to staff the customer service organization would have to change. More agreeable, patient, nurturing, and technically sophisticated people would have to be hired as customer service representatives. Few people in the existing organizations qualified.

2. The people would have to be trained in a very specific protocol that helped to soothe unhappy customers and to provide technical skills to solve problems over the telephone.
3. A sophisticated information system would have to be created that would allow the representatives to access a customer's complete file to ensure that customers got personalized treatment. Moreover, the system would have to contain self-paced diagnostics that would provide all representatives with the capability to solve simple problems over the phone. This could significantly cut costs and improve customer satisfaction and retention.
4. The company would have to arrange with local service centers to provide customers with overnight repairs if problems could not be fixed over the phone.
5. Inventories of replacement equipment and logistics would have to be put in place to send customers new equipment overnight if items 3 and 4, above, did not work. Although this could increase net working capital, it was concluded, after study, that it would be more than offset by customer retention.
6. Representatives had to be empowered to make decisions to solve customers' problems without taking time to go through the hierarchy for approval. This would certainly reduce cycle times for decisions and minimize the time of people involved.
7. Representatives had to be motivated to make all of the above elements work. To that end, the performance of representatives was carefully measured and tracked, and the representatives were given incentives, recognition, and more decision-making authority based on outstanding performance.

Clearly, many organizational elements need to be aligned to ensure peoples' capabilities and motivation. Failure to achieve one element would have led to failure. What good would a motivated and well-trained person be without the proper systems? Conversely, how effective would the system be without the proper person using it and interacting with a customer?

ASSIMILATING NEW PEOPLE

In many situations, acquired people will be brought into an existing organization. Not every acquisition results in a transformation with completely new ways of doing things. For example, I worked with a major highway construction company that was growing geographically through the acquisition of small, privately held firms. The acquirer was a very well run organization that had developed best practices for its operations over a number of years and was not looking to transform itself. It was only interested in successfully acquiring and integrating new firms. With the exception of some accounting functions that were consolidated, most of the target firms' operations were geographically decentralized. Due to transportation costs, paving operations needed to be located close to where the construction work and available raw materials were located. In almost all cases, however, the targets' operations were not of the standard of the acquirer and had to go through changes.

The acquired people were pleased to have been bought by the acquirer. In fact, they knew that the acquirer sought to keep all qualified people, since the acquirer itself did not have enough people to staff the new geographic areas.

The acquirer had a reputation for being among the best companies in the industry and was known for treating its people fairly. The acquired people were receptive to the changes. After the deal was closed, the executives of the acquirer visited the targets' operations to meet with the people and to learn as much as possible about their concerns and issues regarding the acquisition. Their primary concern was whether they could successfully assimilate and succeed in the new organization. The acquirer went to great pains to ensure that would happen.

It is safe to say that acquired people who have been retained want to succeed in the new organization. The faster they can reestablish their careers and perform effectively, the better. It is therefore critical that acquiring companies create a process that quickly assimilates acquired people in an organized way.

I conducted focus groups with managers and employees of several acquired telecommunication companies that highlight this point. Many noted the importance of successful assimilation. Some of the more typical comments included:

- "I needed an orientation on company benefits, open job opportunities, access to computers, access to records and files needed to do my job."
- "I tried to get into a management position. I asked people, but no one could tell me whom to talk to."
- "I had no information about where, what, and when I was going to start my job."
- "Our managers are having trouble getting us what we need [ID cards, business cards]."
- "The acquired company has too many acronyms and nobody explained to us what they mean."
- "There was no employee orientation. I did not know where to get information or help."
- "We need someone from benefits to come talk to us."
- "We lost our four weeks of vacation and had to start from scratch."
- "We don't know how their [acquired company] systems work."
- "There was a lack of training. The computer was not accessible on day one. The hardware did not always work, and when you asked for help, you got the runaround. Reference books were not up to date."

- "HR provided us with no direction. We did not know what forms needed to be filled out. We needed guidance and did not get any help. We had to train ourselves, the hard way."

One company that has successfully assimilated acquired employees is Cisco Systems. Cisco, which has acquired more than 50 companies in a seven-year period, has created a SWAT team of 36 full-time employees that is responsible for the assimilation of acquired firms.[4] The team relies on a swift and systematic process to ensure that new employees are shepherded and adapt to the new organization.

Key to Cisco's process is the philosophy that people are the primary asset in its acquisitions; people must get integrated first, not products; and employee retention and continued motivation are critical.

After Cisco makes an acquisition, the SWAT team engages in a number of key activities. The activities described below attempt to minimize uncertainty and to provide employees with a road map for adapting quickly to Cisco.

1. Employees are provided with quick and honest communications concerning job roles and titles and changes that are planned in the acquired firm.
2. Acquired employees are immediately provided with a folder of basic information about Cisco, the phone numbers and e-mail addresses of Cisco executives, and charts comparing their benefits with those of Cisco. More importantly, afterward there are two days of follow-up question-and-answer meetings.
3. Technically, employees are provided with new photo ID cards and new business cards. E-mail and voice-mail systems are also quickly converted so that acquired employees can access Cisco systems.
4. In some deals Cisco has guaranteed that no jobs would be lost for one year without the approval of the acquired executives.
5. In some cases Cisco will increase salaries, amend expense allowances, and honor commitments to sabbaticals to keep acquired employees whole.
6. Effort is given to retain acquired entrepreneurs by giving them a role in the new organization and significant challenges and opportunities.
7. Acquired employees are given Cisco stock options. Certainly the rise in Cisco's stock price was an attractive motivator for retaining people. Unfortunately, Cisco's stock price at the time of the writing of this book has become far less attractive.

Other companies that have developed assimilation and orientation programs for new hires have used them during acquisitions. These can easily be adapted to an integration situation. Again, the purpose is to ensure that employees are quickly integrated into the new work environment and allowed to succeed.

One company developed a program that involved the human resources organization, an acquired employee's immediate manager or supervisor, and key employees within the existing work unit. The role of each is presented below:

Human Resources. Provides acquired employees through orientation meetings with a complete overview of benefits and compensation packages. This includes a clear overview of the packages and the steps needed to utilize them, as well as e-mail addresses and telephone numbers of human resources staff available to handle questions.

Manager/Supervisor. Has primary responsibility for facilitating the assimilation of acquired employees.

Key Employee Partner. Has primary responsibility of guiding an acquired employee through the orientation process.

Employee. Has ultimate responsibility for managing his or her own orientation, with the support and guidance of others.

ACHIEVING CULTURAL INTEGRATION

- "We-they"
- "We're better because. . ."
- "We bought you, therefore. . ."
- "We are superior"
- "You're second class"

These words are the "fighting words" that are at the heart of culture clash and the causes of significant conflict. They are words often heard by acquired employees. They denote a lack of respect and the feeling of siege that is likely to take place during integration. This may especially be the case when companies that have been bitter rivals in the marketplace merge. Examples of this include the mergers between Boeing and McDonnell Douglas and Lockheed and Martin Marietta.

This was driven home to me when Harris acquired General Electric Solid State (GESS). GESS in itself was the product of a previous acquisition by GE. Jack Welch, GE's CEO at the time, acquired RCA primarily to get NBC. All other parts of the RCA business, along with some of GE's businesses, were put up for sale since they did not meet Welch's goal of being either the first or second leading competitor in their markets. GESS and RCA Solid State were among them. Both organizations were on the trading block for three years before Harris bought them. Little investment was made in them during that period, and there was little attempt to carefully integrate them. Over that time the relationship between GESS and RCA was strained and conflicted. There was little cooperation. RCA was treated as an outsider. When asked to describe the integration of GESS

and RCA, an RCA executive told me, "GESS's idea of synergy and integration was to take a GE lightbulb and stick it up the rear end of the
Nipper." The Nipper, of course, is a famous symbol of the RCA organization. These were fighting words that did not foster a smooth integration.

During the same acquisition it was decided that the Harris name
would be the new name for the corporation. Essentially, all references to
GESS and RCA would eventually disappear. As part of this effort, signs
on facilities, business cards, and the like would all become Harris. This
was not an overly complex technical challenge. However, it was a huge
cultural and psychological challenge. One day as part of this effort, a team
of Harris people showed up at an RCA facility ready to change the signs.
(For three years GESS never removed the RCA signs.) A Harris person
requested that the sign be replaced. No problem! He also noted that there
was a statue of the Nipper (that infamous dog) in the reception area and
had him removed. Several hours later the employees at the location
threatened to walk out of work if the statue were not returned. In fact, the
Harris manager had to build the dog a house and lay the dog to rest in it
to avert a crisis.

These seem like rather silly behaviors, especially from "mature
adults." However, they do capture the significance of culture, history, and
most importantly pride. I have found over and over again that people are
proud of their companies. They are also capable and willing to change.
However, these examples demonstrate that how acquirers handle things
can have a profound impact on how those acquired react. The issue with
the Nipper was not about the statue but about what it represented. The
people at RCA felt that this Harris manager did not respect or value them.
Thus, from day one there was not going to be cooperation. As someone
once put it, "If we were not very good or effective, why did you buy us?
What does it say about you?"

The impact of culture clash has been well documented in both
research and practice.[5] Many successful acquisitions have failed because
of the acquiring company's inability to manage the conflict caused by cultural differences. While such differences may vary, it is almost inevitable
that two companies' cultures will never be the same. Left unattended,
such conflict will almost certainly occur. Figure 8-3 depicts the four stages
of culture clash.

The process innocently begins when people begin to note the differences between the two companies. This is quite normal, since such differences become apparent when employees are exposed to ways that are
different from their own. The issue then becomes how such differences
are handled. If unmanaged, they are likely to be magnified. As people
spend more time together, they are forced to confront different ways of
doing things. Such differences can become sources of conflict as people
disagree on everything from how to make decisions to how to handle conflict. Conflict often escalates to the point where stereotyping and put-

downs occur. Acquiring firms often adopt superiority syndromes and treat acquired people as second-class citizens.

When this occurs, acquired people typically become defensive trying to protect their pride, their ways of doing things, and their interests. The net result is that conflict rather than cooperation ensues. Promised synergies and swift integration never materialize. Shareholder value is never created. Good employees leave. Customers become frustrated and start dealing with competitors.

Although culture clash is a common by-product of integration, it can be successfully managed. Rather than conflict, cultural synergy can be created. However, it takes sound leadership, as in the case of Carlos Ghosn, and a well-managed process to do so. Figure 8-4 presents the stages of successful cultural integration. The process begins with a managed flow of information between acquiring and acquired or merging employees. The objective is to provide a constructive forum whereby the parties get "accurate" information about each other. Through such information, inaccurate perceptions are eliminated and real differences are brought to light. Rather than differences being seen as a problem, cross-fertilization is encouraged, and the best features of both cultures are highlighted. The opportunity for cultural synergy and best cultural practices is created. At this point a well-managed process for working through differences is necessary.

Cultural Mirroring: A Useful Approach
Cultural mirroring is a useful tool to help two integrated groups work through cultural differences and facilitate cooperation. Essentially, it is a

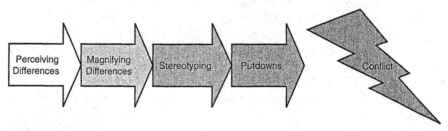

Figure 8-3 Culture Clash

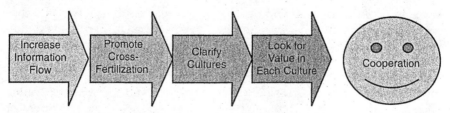

Figure 8-4 Cultural Cooperation

process whereby executives, managers, or employees from the groups are brought together as part of building a team to increase information flow, clarify cultures, and work through differences. Each of the merging groups is asked to:

- Describe your own unit's culture.
- Describe the other unit's culture.
- Describe how you think the other unit would describe your culture.

It is important to note that each group is asked to focus on its work unit's culture rather than on the organization as a whole. As noted in Chapter 3, although organizations have cultures, they may not be the same as that of a division or a functional area. Since groups (e.g., top- management team, R&D, sales) are often integrated, it is their culture that is likely to have an immediate impact on people's thinking and behaviors. Where an organization has a strong culture, it will likely pervade a group's culture.

Several methods can be employed to develop the cultural profile. First, group members can be given a definition of culture and asked to answer the questions above. Second, the group members can be given a list of cultural dimensions and asked to describe themselves and the other organization. For example, the member of a group may be asked to describe how decisions are made in their organization (e.g., centralized or decentralized). Third, the participants can be given a survey instrument that asks them to describe themselves and the other group. The last option gives them a more systematic approach to assessing similarities and differences in culture and the importance of each dimension. As an example, the participants who filled out the cultural profile survey in Chapter 3 describing their own organization were also asked to do it a second time to describe their perception of the other organization's culture. As illustrated in Table 8-4, there were some significant differences between self-descriptions and the other group's descriptions for 10 of the cultural dimensions. Clearly there were misperceptions of the other company's culture. The two groups discussed each dimension. First they clarified differences between their own self-perceptions and the other group's perception of them. This eliminated stereotypes. Second, they isolated actual differences that existed between them, which served as a basis for discussion on how to deal with the differences. More will be said about this issue later.

Based on an open-ended series of questions, the lists that follow reflect the results of the research and development organizations of two pharmaceutical companies that were merging. Prior to the closing it was anticipated that the R&D units would be merged to create a critical mass. There would be an opportunity to better focus the two organizations, eliminate redundancy, and increase collaboration. The net result would be lower product development costs (i.e., cost synergies) and a stronger pipeline of future products (i.e., intangible synergies). The senior management of

Table 8-4 Cultural Profile

	Always	Often	Elements of Both	Often	Always	
	1	2	3	4	5	
Centralized decisions		x, X		y, Y		Decentralized decisions
Fast decision making		y, Y		x, X		Slow decision making
Short-term focus		x, X, Y	y	y		Long-term focus
Individual orientation	X	x	y	Y		Team orientation
Confrontation of conflict		x, y, X		Y		Avoidance of conflict
High-risk tolerance		y	Y		x, X	Low-risk tolerance
Focus on results		x, y, X	Y	X		Focus on process
People held accountable	Y	x, y		X		People not held accountable
Horizontal cooperation		y, Y	X	x		Silo-oriented
High trust among people		y	Y	x, X		Highly political
Bureaucratic		x	X	y, Y		Entrepreneurial
Open and honest communications		x, X, Y		y		Guarded communications
Fast communications			x, y	X, Y		Slow communications
Direct face-to-face communications			y, X, Y	x		Indirect communications
Resistant to change		x	Y, X	y		Open to change

x = Acquiring firm's self-perception   X = Target firm's perception

y = Target firm self-perception   Y = Acquiring firm's perception of target firm both organizations believed a priori that the cultures of the two groups were relatively similar, that there would be few problems in combining them, and that cost and intangible synergies were inevitable. Opportunities for synergies were confirmed by the R&D integration team. However, senior management's early conclusions about cultural compatibility were questioned. The integration team leaders believed that the differences were greater than anticipated. But they also believed that whatever differences existed could be worked out after the closing. This belief is quite typical of many M&As.

After the closing, preparation for integrating the groups began. To facilitate the integration, I was asked to conduct a cultural mirroring exercise to create a cooperative environment in the new R&D organization. The mirroring first began with a self- assessment as follows:

Culture: Self-Description

Company A
- Basic research/discovery mentality
- Strongly held beliefs about research freedom; passion about the role of science in improving life for people
- Emphasis on:
  - Patents
  - Publications
  - Credentials

Company B
- Search-and-develop mentality
- R&D leads toward a commercially viable endpoint rational drug design
- Emphasis on:
  - Submission
  - Results
  - Successful product in marketplace

Culture: Description of Other

Company A perceived Company B as:
- Commercially focused
- Local/parochial perspective
- Not true science
- More a development shop

Company B perceived Company A as:
- Nondirected/nonaccountable
- Global presence/international
- Not as successful overall

In addition to the self-assessments, I conducted an independent assessment of each culture utilizing interviews, company documents, and observation. The assessment yielded the following:

An Objective View of Each Company

Company A

- Keys to career progression:
  - Length of service (tenure mentality)
  - Performance
- Freedom at work to pursue academic and personal research interests as long as basic job gets done
- Research drives the business
  - Long-term focus (7–10 years)
  - Publications and patents build firm's credibility and reputation
  - Which attracts and retains top scientific talent
  - Which extends human knowledge in areas of unique interest
  - Which leads to blockbuster discoveries
- Decision making and accountability
  - Decentralized structure leads to dispersed authority and decision making
  - More difficult to determine who is accountable for what
  - Lack of clarity may encourage individual effort, entrepreneurship, and creativity (necessary in R&D environment)
- Structured by scientific discipline/geography

Company B

- Keys to career progression:
  - Performance against goals
  - Being seen as team player
- Work time very goal directed and time very focused on key priorities
- Market needs drive the business
  - Shorter-term focus (5–7 years)
  - Less patience with scientific process
  - Reliance on some basic research
  - Focus on licensing, joint ventures, co-promotion as technique to ensure new-product flow
  - Fastest way to market is the way to go, since window of opportunity is narrow
- Decision making and accountability
  - Centralized structure leads to focused authority and decision making

- Clarity of structure, measurement, and direction
- Accountability is clear
- Clarity and business management orientation may meet project deadline at expense of creativity and entrepreneurship
- Structured by therapeutic category/major function

As both the objective assessment and self-perceptions indicate, the two R&D groups were not at all alike. Simply put, Company A's culture appeared to be very academic, whereas Company B's was much more applied. Could these two organizations be successfully integrated, and could synergies be created? If the two groups were left to do it on their own, the likely outcome would have been conflict. After the assessments were conducted, each group shared its perspective, as did I. The groups realized that there were many fundamental differences that would have to be worked out if they were to have a chance to successfully work together.

Whether through the use of open-ended questions or a cultural survey, the mirroring exercise creates a constructive forum for an open dialogue on discussing differences and finding a constructive way for dealing with them. Once actual differences are isolated, the key is how to reconcile them. Many experts on intergroup conflict and cooperation always point to the importance of common goals as a way of aligning the interests of separate groups. I agree! As such, it is useful to focus merging groups on the following sets of questions:

- What are the unit's major objectives, and what are the means for achieving them?
- What cultural attributes would best enable the unit to achieve its objectives and strategies?
  - What cultural attributes that neither group has should be adopted?
  - What cultural attributes that are detrimental to the unit should be eliminated?
  - What cultural attributes have no impact on the functioning of the unit but are important to each group?
- What actions should be taken to ensure that important attributes are retained, new attributes are adopted, and detrimental attributes are eliminated?
- What actions should be taken to ensure that attributes not important to the unit, but important to a group, are respected by the other group?

These questions allow the participants to focus on the future needs of the work unit rather than on their parochial interests. Through effective participation and facilitation, people can move forward and rebuild the new unit. This is not to argue that conflict has been eliminated, but that a process for effectively managing it and building cooperation has been established. In the end the test of this process will be whether the unit is successful and whether its members benefit from it.

Recently, a colleague and I conducted a study to assess the impact that cultural mirroring had on the integration of employees of two companies.[6] The research was conducted in six similar manufacturing plants of two merging companies: three from the acquiring firm and three from the acquired firm. Two plants remained independent, two were integrated and participated in the cultural mirroring process, and two were integrated but did not participate. The employees participating in this study were highly skilled. Of those participating in all phases of the study, 120 of 240 employees were from the acquired firm and 116 of 175 employees were from the acquiring firm.

The acquiring firm was a major strategic business unit (SBU) within a larger *Fortune* 500 parent company. The acquired firm was a stand-alone business that had been a competitor of the SBU prior to the acquisition. Both firms manufactured consumer products, and the acquired firm was slightly larger than the SBU in terms of sales and number of employees.

The negotiations that took place between the CEOs of the two firms were considered to be friendly, and the deal was made. Both firms felt that the acquisition was key to their competitiveness and profitability. The acquiring firm paid a premium for the acquired firm and believed that it needed to realize some operational synergies to financially justify the deal.

Neither firm was a dominant player in its industry. Although the firms competed against each other in several market segments, each firm was a leader in several of its own segments. Thus, the acquisition was somewhat complementary and provided both firms with an opportunity to expand the number of segments (i.e., customer groups and product lines) in which they participated. There were also operating synergies (e.g., operating economies of scale, reduction of redundant staff) that could be captured in manufacturing, sales, and general and administrative staff. The acquisition also improved the R&D capabilities of both firms.

A comprehensive integration plan had been developed prior to the closing. Due to premiums paid and the inherent belief that synergies needed to be secured quickly, the CEO established a very aggressive "First 100 Days Program" in which he expected significant integration would take place. However, he also felt that involvement of both firms in designing and executing the integration was critical to its success. To that end, he created an integration transition process that was staffed by key managers and employees in both organizations.

It was also agreed upon that the CEO of the acquired firm would retire shortly after the deal was completed; he would serve as a consultant until his firm was fully integrated into the acquiring firm's SBU. Prior to his departure the acquired firm's CEO, who was 63 years old, agreed to enthusiastically endorse the acquisition.

The study was begun two weeks prior to the formal announcement of the acquisition. At this time (time 1) employees in all plants participating in the study were administered an employee survey by plant personnel managers. Participation in the survey, which was not unlike ones done previously by both companies, was voluntary. The survey was administered on company time, and all results were kept confidential. The completed surveys were collected and sent directly to the researchers. Both firms' plant and personnel managers felt that employees knew that the acquisition was taking place prior to the formal announcement. Although negotiations were held in secrecy and no official announcements had been made, rumors concerning the acquisition and the name of the acquiring/acquired firm were circulating prior to the announcement.

On the day of the announcement, employees were given basic information (e.g., name, location, size, products) on the acquired/acquiring company. This information was communicated via letters to employees from their respective senior managers. No specific information concerning plants or individuals to be affected was provided. Two weeks later (time 2) the acquisition was closed. Within one week of the closing, employees were provided more specific information concerning the acquisition. Senior management of both firms, using letters and videotapes, provided employees with information concerning the strategy behind the acquisition, the vision for the new company (division), and basic plans for the integration. Employees in each plant were also told whether their plant was going to remain independent or be combined. In the two cases where the plants were to be shut down, most individuals in both firms considered these plants to be less efficient than the acquiring firm's plants. The employees were informed that attrition would primarily be used to reduce redundancy. A sufficient number of employees reaching retirement within six months had already given notice that they were leaving, avoiding a reduction in force at the time of the study. All other employees would be given an opportunity to either relocate or be considered for other jobs within the company.

Since employees' identities with their previous company were important and since both companies' products were well regarded in the marketplace, the name chosen for the new division was a hybrid of the two. A plan to change facilities' signs, stationery, and the like to reflect the new name was communicated to all employees and initiated right after the closing. Employees in the acquired company were also fully informed of and placed in the acquiring company's benefits plan with full seniority. As it turned out, the acquiring company's plan was superior to that of the acquired company. All these issues had been worked out prior to the closing by high-level integration teams and factored into the valuation models. Prior to the acquisition, both companies competed for the same employees in the marketplace.

During the next month, a first wave of employees from the acquired plants was transferred to and placed in a work unit within the acquiring plants. It was anticipated that the acquired plants would continue to operate during the ensuing three to six months while they were being shut down. Since both acquired and acquiring plants were located in the same city, no employee relocations were required. During this time no formal interventions other than information sessions for acquired employees on benefits and compensation were conducted.

One month after the closing (time 3), a second survey was administered. This survey permitted an initial assessment of the effects of the merger and combination on the work forces. One month was chosen as an appropriate period because it would provide sufficient time for the initial wave of acquired employees to be transferred to acquiring plants and for all employees to react to events.

Two days after the survey administration (time 4), an intervention to facilitate joint intercultural learning and problem solving was begun (using the cultural mirroring approach described above) at one combined plant. Finally, a third survey was administered six weeks later (time 5). This allowed for a short-term assessment of the effects of the intervention.

The results of the study indicate that those participating in the cultural mirroring process reported greater adaptability to and support for the merger than those who did not participate. Specifically, those who participated reported greater:

- Understanding of the other unit's culture
- Willingness to support the merger integration process
- Commitment to the organization
- Cooperation with those from the other organization
- Performance
- Trust in management

Although many executives, academics, and consultants continually note that culture clash can create value leakage, failure to achieve synergies, and loss of shareholder value, few present any approaches for mitigating its effects or taking advantage of cultural differences. The results of this study support mirroring as an approach that works.

Although tools such as mirroring are promising, they do not guarantee success. Executives and managers must also be prepared to deal with individuals and groups that may have their own agendas and interests in a situation. In such cases, lack of cooperation may be more the result of conflicting interests rather than learning and understanding. Failure to deal with and align them may offset any benefits that can be garnered from intercultural learning.

A FINAL NOTE

The integration stage is where synergies, earnings, and cashflow are realized. Prior stages have been nothing more than theoretical exercises to forecast what these might be. Whether they are realized or not depends heavily on the ability of executives to rebuild teams and develop capable and motivated people who are willing to drive the integration and the new organization. Failure to do so is likely to relegate a merger to the scrap heap of the many others that have failed to create value for investors.

9

EVALUATING THE ACQUISITION INTEGRATION PROCESS

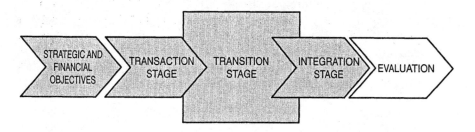

Continuous assessment and improvement are key elements in the success of a merger or an acquisition. Due to the complexity of the numerous activities to be managed during integration and the occurrence of many unanticipated events, it is easy for the process to get off track and for results not to be realized. To ensure progress requires a conscious and concerted effort to keep track of several key elements, along with answers to the following questions:

1. What impact is the integration having on key indicators of business performance? Are the synergies that were hypothesized during the valuation being realized?
2. Are the activities and milestones developed in the integration plan on target?
3. What key issues are emerging during the integration that must be dealt with?
4. What has been learned during the merger or acquisition that can be used to improve subsequent merger or acquisition integrations.

MEASURING KEY INDICATORS

The ultimate goal of a merger or acquisition is to deliver the financial results expected, namely, earnings and cashflow. However, there are a number of other measures that serve as leading indicators of financial outcomes, and they need to be measured as well. These indicators are no different from those that any well-run company would employ as a normal part of doing business.

Three levels of measurement and their interrelationship are presented in Figure 9-1. Level 1 includes financial outcomes. Level 2 consists of the component measures of these outcomes: revenues, costs, net working capital, and capital investments. And Level 3 is composed of the organizational indicators: the customers, employees, and operations that drive the components.[1]

Measurements should be taken on a regular basis to ensure that they have not declined and that forecasts are met. Measurements should be taken in all areas being integrated and in both the acquirer and target or in both merger partners. The measurements should be based on benchmarks to ensure that the changes brought by the integration are yielding the financial and strategic objectives intended and are not creating unintended side effects that might result in value leakage. When feasible, comparisons should be made in one or several of the following ways:

- First, indicators should be tracked to determine whether changes are occurring over time. It is helpful if measurements are taken prior to integration to establish a baseline. To the extent that the acquirer or seller has a history of using a key indicator, this will be easier. For

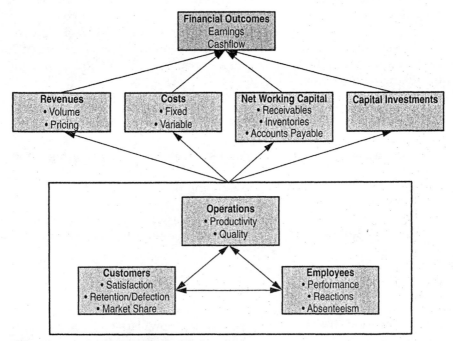

Figure 9-1   Key Indicators of Performance

example, Chapter 5 detailed a communications study a colleague and I conducted. Using premerger and postmerger measurements, we were able to establish that a communication intervention helped improve employee reactions to a merger. This was a critical determinant in the decision to continue the intervention throughout both the acquiring and acquired companies.

- Second, comparisons between similar types of units being integrated and not being integrated allow a more precise causal assessment of whether the integration is having a direct impact on an indicator. In Chapter 8, I reported a study that a colleague and I conducted to examine a cultural mirroring intervention. We employed a comparison-group methodology and were able to determine whether the intervention was impacting employee reactions or not. The results gave us the confidence to roll out the project on a larger scale, and it has worked successfully throughout the company.
- Third, comparisons against valuation forecasts and expectations help determine whether the integration is on track or not. Again, the ultimate test of the success of the deal is whether the valuation projections have been met or not.

Consistency with Financial Projections

Earnings and cashflows are the primary financial outcomes that need to be tracked since valuation models are built on them. Particular attention should be given to the components of these measures, namely, revenues, costs, investments, and net working capital. The extent to which these components are on track will determine whether value is being created or not. Further, specific attention needs to be given to tracking synergies.

A Note on Realizing Synergies

Since valuation and pricing decisions are often based on synergies, it only makes sense that such synergies be clearly documented and monitored to ensure they are realized. As I argued in Chapter 2, the better we can document synergies, the higher the probability that valuations and pricing will be accurate.

Documentation should begin during the transaction stage and be monitored through the integration stage. Not all synergies, however, will be known with precision early in the M&A process. Several, such as general and administrative overhead cost synergies, may be easy to identify; but others, such as revenues and intangibles, may not be.

Often, especially in large mergers or acquisitions, rough estimates of synergies may be made during the transaction stages, with the details to be identified by integration teams during the transition stage or found by managers during the integration stage. This is often due to the size of the transactions and the acquirer's limited time and access to complete in-depth analyses of the target.

In one merger I was involved in, it was estimated that $800 million in revenue enhancements could be accrued by cross-selling products. This estimate was based on numerous assumptions about the sales organizations, distribution channels, and customers. The challenge would be to truly find and realize the $800 million. After the deal was closed, it was discovered that some of the assumptions underlying the synergies were ill-founded, and a gap between the forecast and the reality was emerging. It turned out that the sales organization of the target was not quite as capable as the acquirer had thought, and the potential cross-selling of certain products was not as strong as was imagined. Through documentation the acquirer was able to identify certain shortfalls early. Fortunately, some unanticipated synergies were found that allowed the firm to reach the $800 million. Key to the success was the vigilant monitoring of the synergies and the growing awareness that new sources would have to be found if the $800 million was to be reached.

Prior to closing, integration teams have responsibility for finding synergies. The synergy capture team has responsibility for interacting with integration teams to continually remind them of the "numbers" they have to reach and for monitoring each synergy and the roll-up of all the synergies.

Following closing, operating managers have primary responsibility for monitoring and realizing synergies as part of their budgets, profit and loss statements, cashflow statements, and balance sheets. Ultimately these are the critical documents that will determine whether value for investors was created.

It is also useful for teams and operating managers to develop a spreadsheet to track specific synergies. It helps identify the impact of specific synergies. Table 9-1 illustrates a spreadsheet for documenting and tracking synergies, regardless of whether they are functional or support areas, lines of business, or geographic areas. The spreadsheet should be updated weekly. It should include synergies that have been validated and documented, those that are awaiting validation, and those that have been newly identified since the last tracking report. Validated synergies are those that are virtually certain. Those awaiting validation look good but need to be confirmed. New ones have just been suggested and need to be tested. Only validated synergies "can be taken to the bank." The table identifies the synergies—the net impact they have on cashflows and earnings in the first four quarters after closing and then the next four years. Earnings and cashflows are tracked since they are employed as the central elements in valuation and pricing decisions (see Chapter 2). The table also identifies possible overlaps with other areas that are performing this same exercise. It is important that synergies are not double-counted and are thus not overestimated.

Table 9-2 illustrates a spreadsheet that can be used by a synergy capture team to monitor the synergies reported by all the integration teams. The synergies are again broken down into validated, awaiting validation, and newly discovered. In conjunction with the individual-area spreadsheets, synergies can be easily monitored. For ease of use, all spreadsheets can be managed electronically and maintained on a secure Intranet site. This allows easy access to spreadsheets by those who need to access them.

Customer Reactions

Ensuring that customers are not adversely affected during the integration is an essential element in the success of a merger or an acquisition. Losing either profitable customers or a percentage of their business may have a dramatic impact on earnings and cashflows (i.e., value leakage), especially if the customer represents a large percentage of the company's revenues and profits. In most M&As the objective is either to retain or to grow the customer base. Sometimes, unprofitable customers will be deliberately pruned. Therefore it is essential that customer indicators be continually examined.

Several indicators should be employed: customer satisfaction, retention, acquisition, and market share. Satisfaction measures capture multiple dimensions (e.g., product quality and features, after-sales service, delivery speed, new-product development, price). The dimensions examined should be directly linked to the market key success factors (i.e., the criteria that customers use to decide whom to buy from). Decreases in satisfaction may be a leading indicator of customer defection, loss of market share, and thus volume loss. The impact will be lower revenues, assuming prices do not increase, and higher costs as a company needs to acquire new customers to replace the lost ones.

Retention and defection rates of customers by market segments should also be tracked. The rates are a good leading indicator of market share. These data could be examined on a weekly or monthly basis to determine if any changes and trends are occurring. Certainly the loss of a major customer should raise a red flag. Moreover, the percentage of business coming from each customer should be examined to see whether the levels are increasing, decreasing, or remaining the same. These are important measurements since many cashflow projections are based on certain assumptions about the retention and addition of customers. For example, in security monitoring, customer retention-defection rates were considered key to earnings and cashflow. Given that fixed costs were a very high percentage of the cost structure of this business, the loss of a key customer had a direct impact on both cashflow and earnings. Retention rates were measured and tracked from due diligence through integration.

Keeping track of market share and sales volume, segment by segment, is also useful. It allows a company to directly examine its competitive position within its markets. Often during mergers and acquisitions competitors

Table 9-1 Tracking Synergies by Area

Integration Team _____ [Net cashflows (CF) and earnings (E) are reported in $ millions]

Source of Synergy	Status	Q 1 CF/E	Q 2	Q 3	Q 4	Year 1 Total	Year 2	Year 3	Year 4	Year 5	Known Overlap with Other Integration Teams
Cost savings											
1. Fixed manufacturing overhead (supervision)	Validated	$3.0/3.0									
2. Shared marketing expenses	Awaiting validation	$1.5/1.5									
Revenue increase											
1. Cross-selling product A with target's sales force	Awaiting validation	$1.7/1.7									
2. Cross-selling product B with acquirer's distributors	Awaiting validation	$2.3/2.3									
Market power improvement											
1. Raw material costs	Validated	$.9/.9									
2. Price increase	New	$.7/.7									
Intangible gains											
1. Improvement in plant operating procedures	Awaiting validation	$.4/.4									
2. Smaller inventories	Awaiting validation	$1.0/0									
Total integration team synergies		$11.5/10.5									

Table 9-2 Tracking All Synergies

Total Synergies [Net cashflows (CF) and earnings (E) are reported in $ millions]

Source of Synergy	Status	Q 1 CF/E	Q 2	Q 3	Q 4	Year 1 Total	Year 2	Year 3	Year 4	Year 5
Cost savings	Validated	$3.0/3.0								
	Awaiting validation	$1.5/1.5								
	New									
Revenue increase	Validated	$4.0/4.0								
	Awaiting validation									
	New									
Market power improvement										
3. Raw material costs	Validated	$.9/.9								
4. Price increase	Awaiting validation									
	New									
Intangible gains										
3. Improvement in plant operating procedures	Validated	$1.4/0								
4. Smaller inventories	Awaiting validation	$.7/.7								
	New									
	Validated	$3.9/3.9								
	Awaiting validation	$6.9/5.9								
	New	$0.7/7								
Total synergies		$11.5/10.5								

attempt to disrupt the relationship between an acquirer and its customers. This happened in many markets to major banks being acquired. Smaller credit unions were mounting campaigns to dissuade retail customers from continuing a relationship with their existing bank based on the grounds that service would deteriorate throughout the integration and afterward. This implies that a company needs to do more than just maintain customer relationships. It has to make an extra effort to ensure that its business does not erode.

It would be desirable if measurements could be taken prior to an acquisition, at one point during the transition, and on an ongoing basis after integration. For the most part, preacquisition measurement will depend upon the extent to which the target's management previously conducted such assessments. Interviews with key customers, focus groups, surveys, and archival records are useful approaches for collecting customer data.

Employee Reactions

Employees can have a dramatic impact on productivity and customer satisfaction, especially in service businesses or ones in which intellectual capital is a source of value to the company. Therefore, it is important to track how employees are adapting and reacting to the acquisition. Too often this is a neglected area. Similar to the approach used to measure customer satisfaction, employee assessments made at multiple times and with the use of preexisting measures may better allow changes and trends to be spotted.

There are a number of types of reactions that could be measured, but the following are among those that I have found most important:

- *Reactions to a merger or an acquisition.* Do employees understand what is going on in the merger or acquisition and the changes that are taking place? Do they understand what is expected of them and how they can contribute to the new organization? This may have a direct bearing on employee productivity, absenteeism, turnover, and safety.
- *Satisfaction and morale.* How do employees view the new organization? Are they satisfied with various aspects of the organization and leadership (e.g., communications, compensation and benefits, involvement in decisions, recognition)? This may have a direct impact on employee turnover, absenteeism, safety, and customer relations.
- *Commitment to the new organization.* Are employees committed to the new organization? This may have a direct impact on employee turnover and willingness to put in extra effort on behalf of the organization (e.g., spend extra time on teams and task forces).
- *Willingness to support the integration.* Are employees willing to support the integration process and changes associated with it? This may have

a direct impact on the extent to which employees support changes and how successfully and quickly the integration is completed.

- *Intention to remain in the new organization.* Are employees thinking about quitting the organization? This may have a direct impact on actual voluntary turnover.
- *Employee performance and productivity.* Are employees continuing to produce? Depending upon the company and the nature of the job, numerous measures can be employed (e.g., sales per employee, patents, output per unit of time). These may have a direct impact on revenues (e.g., for the sales staff) and costs.
- *Safety.* Are employees focusing on safety, or are they focusing their attention elsewhere? This may have a direct impact on costs, absenteeism, and turnover.
- *Absenteeism and voluntary turnover.* Are employees taking time away from work or leaving the company voluntarily? This may have a direct impact on the caliber and loyalty of the remaining work force, productivity, quality, and work flow, among other elements. It will also have an impact on costs due to recruiting and hiring of new people and the time it takes for them to ascend the learning curve.

In general, these measures provide warning signs of organizational and financial problems that may emerge from the integration. They need to be monitored and responded to. Interviews with key employees, focus groups, surveys, and archival records are useful approaches for collecting employee data.[2]

Operating Measures

Operating measures should be tracked for each functional and support area, product line, and geographic area of the business. An array of measures can be employed which are idiosyncratic to the company and the area being measured. Normal operating measures (e.g., productivity, quality, safety, innovations, order-processing time, delivery time) that drive earnings and cashflows should also be continually monitored. These provide warning signals that earnings or cashflow problems are emerging. Most of this information can be gleaned from company records, to the extent that a company collects the necessary information and organizes it in a useful fashion.

Once measurements are taken, they need to be analyzed to determine if gaps are emerging. Gaps in leading indicators may provide ample time for corrective action before they have a direct impact on financial results. Gaps in financial results may leave little time and require a crisis response. Once financial results are not realized, the probability of having overpaid for an acquisition has risen dramatically. Table 9-3 presents a simple format that can be used to conduct such an assessment.

Table 9-3　Measuring Success

Key Performance Measure	Baseline Measures/ Expectations/ Benchmarks	Follow-Up Measure	Gaps	Causes	Action to Be Taken to Close Gaps	Responsibility
Financial projections						
Customer reactions						
Employee reactions						
Operating measure						

TRACKING THE INTEGRATION PROCESS

In addition to tracking key indicators, it is important to assess how the integration process is progressing and to identify and solve any emerging issues that may impinge upon it. The objective is to ensure a continuous process of learning and improvement. As such, project activities and milestones identified in Chapter 8 must be continually monitored. So too should issues that arise throughout the integration.

Managing Activities and Milestones

Project plans define both the activities to be carried out and the milestones for achieving them. Transition and integration teams need to continually monitor these to ensure that proper progress is being made. When milestones are not being met, corrective action needs to be taken. If milestones are central elements in a critical path, they may hold up the entire project execution. If this occurs, the timing of changes being implemented and forecasted earnings and cashflows could be compromised. This may result in failed synergies or value leakage. Companies such as Cisco and Bank of America have become very adept at developing and tracking project plans as part of their integration strategy. In fact, Bank of America is quite comprehensive in training its integration teams in project management.

Tracking Key Issues

It is also useful for transition or integration teams to keep track of issues created by gaps in either the key indicators or project plans. Issues will always arise regardless of how well the integration has been planned. No two deals are identical, and there are always unanticipated events. The key is how fast the acquirer identifies and responds to them.

Most successful acquirers create a formalized process of issue tracking and resolution. Simple issues may be tracked and resolved by an integration team. Complex ones may need to be elevated to the transition team or to the MIO/IC for resolution. They may involve the commitment of significant resources or be politically sensitive, requiring a higher level of authority for resolution. Each transition and integration team should formally track key issues. A few key suggestions on how to do that are as follows:

1. Transition and integration teams should meet and debrief on a periodic basis (e.g., weekly), after a major integration activity or stage in the process is completed, or when a critical issue arises. Periodic team meetings should have a portion of the agenda dedicated to identifying and resolving issues. Basic ground rules for what constitutes an issue, who can call a meeting, and what meeting format the team will employ (e.g., face-to-face, virtually) must be established by each team.

2. Team members should be encouraged to keep track of and document current integration issues that need to be resolved in the near future. Team members should also keep track of issues they have resolved and how they did so. This may help someone else who is facing the same issue. Members should also be encouraged to keep a diary noting (a) things that were done well, (b) areas of concern or things that need to be improved, and (c) recommendations on how to correct problems or improve the process for the future. More will be said about this below.

Table 9-4 presents a simple form for tracking immediate issues that can easily be posted on an Intranet. The form identifies an issue, its priority, a plan of action for resolving it, the person responsible for managing it, its date of solution, and its status.

Presented below are issues that were identified by a company (which I call AB) engaged in the roll-up of the security monitoring industry. Several small companies were being simultaneously acquired and integrated. Many backroom activities, such as monitoring were being consolidated, whereas branch (field) operations were being left geographically dispersed but standardized. As firms were being integrated, the acquirer kept track of key issues that needed to be resolved. Issues were divided into three categories: technical, political, and cultural. If they were not managed, they could significantly affect the company's operations, employees and customers, and, ultimately, financial results.

Technical Issues

1. Initial HR meeting with the branch employees is inconsistent from location to location. At some branches the discussion was too high level and did not include enough detail to reassure the very stressed acquired company employees. In other locations the meeting deteriorated into a detailed discussion of health or vacation benefits and left the acquired company employees discontent and unmotivated about AB. In other cases the meeting digressed into a micromanagement discussion about the operations of each functional area. In these cases the employees were so scared about the degree of change that was going to occur that they could not get excited about being a part of AB.
2. The initial communication to the customers is on AB letterhead, so the customers do not even open it in many cases. In other cases, the communication is sent to the wrong contact at the customer's organization. Therefore the accounts payable department does not understand why it has a bill from AB.
3. In Toronto, the initial HR packets included information about benefits that did not apply to Canada (e.g., 401K, paid medical benefit options). Also, HR requested the employees' social security number when it is illegal for an employer to request that information in Canada.

Table 9-4 Tracking Issues

Integration Team	Issue	Priority (High, Medium, Low)	Plan of Action	Responsibility	Solution Date	Status
Human Resources	Communicating benefits information	Medium				
Operations	Conversion of a product from the target's operations to the acquirer					
Information Systems	Bottleneck in generating customer invoices	High				

4. Window stickers and yard signs need to be distributed immediately to the acquired company's customers. The window stickers and yard signs are one of the most powerful and inexpensive advertising methods that support AB's branding. The XYZ branches that were acquired have large customer bases, and the task of changing all the signs is time-consuming for the local branches. This task could be handled centrally from Corporate. If not handled centrally, at least distribute the decals to the local offices of the acquired company so that they can make an effort to get the decals and signs out to the customers.

5. The branch employees need to attend another meeting with HR personnel from Corporate to better understand their benefits. Most branches were visited by HR early after the announcement of the acquisition. However, employees were still in shock at that point and were not necessarily thinking about the specifics of their new benefits. Now the branch employees need to attend a second session with HR to have the opportunity to ask the questions that were not asked at the first meeting. Many benefits and processes to receive benefits may have seemed clear to them at the initial meeting but since that time the employees have encountered problems or confusing processes. (The employees at XYZ do not have their prescription cards or their PPO books for their new benefits, and they cannot use their old benefits.) This follow-up meeting would allow the employees to get answers to questions that have come up since the acquisition. These meetings could go a long way in improving employee morale and reducing frustration.

6. AB needs an inventory, including all branches, of what has not been assimilated from the branches' perspective, from past acquisitions. Avoid distributing a survey to the branches to complete, which would just be creating work for them. The branches need someone from Corporate to visit each branch. Or the Corporate staff could do it by phone as long as the process does not require excessive time commitments from the local management. This initiative needs to be positioned properly. Corporate should emphasize that this inventory is not a "report card" on the branches, but a tool to help Corporate understand what the branches need at this point. If not positioned correctly, the branches will not accurately disclose the extent to which they have not assimilated. The branches need a project team to visit the locations that have not completed the assimilation process. The team will support the local management from various branches by:
   • Developing project plans and time lines.
   • Troubleshooting and assisting in problem solving in system conversions.
   • Developing and distributing customer communications.
   • Conducting training on AB standard procedures.
   • Conducting cultural training.

7. Employees in the branches need employee manuals and standard operations manuals for functional areas. AB may believe that this has been completed in the past, but no one out there seems to have any manuals.

Political Issues

1. On the initial conference call with XYZ to announce the acquisition, remarks were made by AB's management about the closing or sale of certain branches. This was the first that the general managers of these branches had heard of these decisions. (After further analysis, many of these branches were not actually sold or closed, but the damage was done.) This appeared to be caused by AB's corporate managers trying to establish power and control at this initial contact.
2. Staffing is a major concern right now because many general managers have two or more new locations to integrate into their facility. Everyone is aware that only one manager is needed for each department. Managers from all the companies are concerned and asking questions about staffing the management positions. Originally, Corporate told the GMs to not worry about the two new acquisitions until after the first of the year. So the managers were going to have to wait three months to find out about the status of their jobs. This problem is the result of senior management's delay in announcing organizational structure for the new organizations and markets.
3. Significant time, talent, energy, and money have been spent in short-term solutions resulting from senior management's lack of commitment to final solutions. The payroll system is one example (converting XYZ into fictitious job codes in order to meet the contractual obligation, just to convert them again when management has made a decision about the structure of the organization). Giving network connections to buildings that will not be used in the future is another. This type of duplication of work is always a strain on morale, but coupled with the current lack of communication will only increase tension among the employees.

Cultural Issues

1. Initial meeting with XYZ managers was very stiff and formal. The executive management of AB was seated at a head table, with the XYZ personnel seated in a classroom setting. The managers felt that AB management acted superior and condescending.
2. The regional managers feel it is impossible to "make plan" this year. The initial plans discussed for 1998 are more outrageous and impossible to meet. However, the regional managers go ahead and agree to the plan because they are too scared not to, even though they know they will not meet goals. Unrealistic goals and unrealistic time frames are the status quo. They do not feel comfortable in the AB environment and are uncertain about how to be successful in the AB organization.

3. False statements were made by AB managers. For example, in Texas employees were told that everyone would have a job. The general manager just found out that 40 additional employees will be fired by year-end to "make plan" for 1998. The acquired company employees are accustomed to an environment of openness and honesty and have a difficult time deciphering the messages from AB corporate office.

4. Employees want to be a part of a winning team. The initial reaction to the acquisition announcement (after the shock wears off) is excitement about being a part of a successful organization. However, this attitude soon turns to frustration because the communications from Corporate tend to focus on the negative ("You're doing it wrong," "We do not do it like that at AB," "Why have you not made your plan this quarter?" etc.). Throughout the entire assimilation, Corporate needs to emphasize the positives about AB. Regularly scheduled "morale builders" need to be organized. Recognition for effort and attitude needs to become a part of the assimilation process.

5. The "distance" between the Corporate staff and the field is disturbing. The Corporate staff jokingly refer to the field employees as "those people in the field," but the reality is that a wall exists between these two groups. This wall discourages the field from contacting Corporate staff for help in resolving issues and hinders Corporate staff from visiting the branches. The "us and them" syndrome that has been created at AB is having a negative impact on the effectiveness and efficiency of the integration process.

IMPROVING THE INTEGRATION PROCESS

It is very easy in corporations aggressively making acquisitions to reinvent the wheel many times. Typically, acquisition processes are fragmented, whereby many units and different people become involved in the process over time. This often adds to the confusion. As such, the knowledge and experience accumulated across a corporation dissipates as people who have been involved in an integration either resume their normal jobs or leave the organization. Moreover, new people, with prior acquisition experience, join a corporation. Rarely do people with experience meet to systematically debrief and share with others what they have learned.

As part of a continuous improvement process, not only should issues identified by teams be analyzed and addressed, but knowledge on how to improve the integration process should be institutionalized to improve the process for those working on future deals. Since integration begins as early as the transaction stage, the continuous improvement process should include those involved in due diligence, valuation, integration planning, and integration itself. Including people involved in different M&A activities not only will lead to improvements in specific activities but will also ensure that key interrelationships and handoffs among the activities are improved as well.

Once data are collected and analyzed, it is important that the information be shared and used to improve upon the way the acquirer manages future acquisitions. To accomplish this requires that the knowledge developed move from individuals and teams to the organization. The following are activities that successful acquirers have used to do so:

1. At the completion of the integration, a document summarizing the information contained in Table 9-5 should be prepared by each team leader and submitted to the head of the MIO or the IC. The document can be prepared in written form or shared electronically. The document should include a list of those who were involved in the process, their areas of expertise, and how they can be reached by those who are interested in following up.

2. Building on the last point in step 1 above, an electronic database containing information on all people who have been involved in integration should be created. This establishes a network of identifiable integration resources in the organization. As in step 1, be sure to capture the names of people, their integration experience, and how they can be reached.

3. The MIO, IC, or someone who has been designated as responsible for the integration process should solicit input from a variety of sources to improve or develop best-practice frameworks, guidelines, interventions, tools, etc., that are being used by the acquirer to integrate acquisitions and to document these improvements. This is especially important for companies that are serial acquirers and for large companies that may have personnel from many areas and hierarchical levels involved in the process. This may be accomplished through a variety of approaches.

   a. Enlist a team of knowledgeable people inside and outside the company to improve the integration process.

   b. Conduct an annual one- or two-day "Continuous Integration Improvement" conference for all the acquirer's (and acquired) people who have been directly involved in acquisitions. The purpose would be to bring people together to share knowledge. The conference could begin with outside experts sharing the latest ideas and methods and culminate with thematic workshops and small groups to improve specific acquisition processes.

   c. Conduct focus groups of team leaders or members.

   d. Create case studies as part of merger integration debriefings. Cases should be shared with people inside the combined organizations.

   e. Develop and circulate debriefing documents and handbooks.

   f. Develop best-practices Intranet sites.

Table 9-5 Improving the Integration Process

Integration Team	Topic	Things That Were Done Well	Things That Need to Be Improved	Recommendations and Next Steps	Accountable
Marketing	Training	• Training materials were of good quality • Product training was done well • People received solid coaching on products • Training was done on time	• Need more leadership training early • More information on culture/values and marketing strategies of the acquiring bank presented early in the training	• In future develop leadership-training program and get influential leaders to support it • Revise training program to lead with culture and ensure that all participants understand the "language" that each organization uses	
Human Resources	Employee Assimilation	• Developed an assimilation document for newly acquired employees	• Better initial training to ensure employees understand the acquirer • More two-way communications to ensure that all questions concerning assimilation are answered		

4. Individuals who might be involved in future acquisition activity should be provided with best-practices training on how to conduct integration activities. This is also an excellent opportunity for those who have previously been involved in acquisition activities to serve as trainers and to provide mentoring to those who have not.

A FINAL NOTE

It would be best if the integration process unfolded as planned in the transition stage. Unfortunately, the uncertainty of changing events and the lack of complete information to plan perfectly precludes this. That is why it is critical that executives and managers measure, track, assess, and adjust throughout the integration process. It is this flexibility that helps ensure that the strategic and financial objectives hoped for are indeed realized.

10

PERSONAL STRATEGIES FOR PROSPERING DURING THE INTEGRATION PROCESS

M&As can be challenging for those involved. The period during any M&A is surrounded by personal uncertainty that affects everyone from the CEO to frontline employees. During the transaction and transition stages there is a great deal of uncertainty since many decisions affecting people have not yet been made or implemented. As a result, people worry about whether they will have a job, and if so, what it will be and where it will be located.

For example, early on in the Chevron-Texaco merger, it was announced that $1.2 billion in recurring costs (i.e., synergies resulting in lower costs and improved earnings and cashflows) would be eliminated from the combined organizations. This translated into a proposed 7 percent cut in the combined work force, or the loss of roughly 4000 jobs. As mentioned earlier, it was also decided that Texaco's headquarters in White Plains, New York, would be shut down and that Chevron's headquarters in San Ramon, California, would remain as the headquarters for the combined companies. After a well-orchestrated selection process, some corporate staff from Texaco would be offered positions in San Ramon, whereas others would not. For those who were not retained, or did not want to relocate, severance packages would be provided.

This example is typical of many mergers and acquisitions where synergies are sought. They can be very disruptive for those involved. Given that M&As are a common part of the business landscape affecting millions of people each year, it is essential that executives, managers, and employees prepare themselves to prosper, rather than suffer, during these times. The remainder of this chapter gives insights for doing so, all of which are derived from the tens of thousands of merged and acquired people I have been involved with and the ideas of others who have written on this topic.

PSYCHOLOGICAL PREPARATION

The Serenity Prayer

God grant me the serenity
to accept the things
I cannot change,
courage to change
the things I can
and the wisdom
to know the difference.

Reinhold Niebuhr

These powerful words of wisdom are at the heart of psychological preparation for M&As, and other changes you may face during organizational transformations. Many changes are outside of your control—circumstances that you cannot influence. As such, it is essential that you understand what you can and cannot control and focus on the former. I like to use the term *sphere of influence* to describe people's area of control. (At the end of the day, the only things you can really control are your own thoughts and behaviors.) You may be able to influence others, if you are lucky, but rarely do you control other people.[1] It is the thoughts you have and the behaviors you engage in that will ultimately determine how you deal with the events of a merger or acquisition—whether you prosper or whether you are victimized by them.

Get Comfortable with Uncertainty and Change

The first step in psychological preparation is to realize that M&As are pervasive and that they can easily happen to your organization. Second is to realize that M&As result in change for many people. As noted in Chapter 5, people go through a variety of stages in coping with change. Only one stage, acceptance, is constructive and allows people to move on with their lives. The other stages, while often part of the process, delay effective coping and action.

The bottom line is for you to become comfortable with changes and transitions and to prepare for them. Part of becoming comfortable is to view change as an opportunity rather than a threat. For it to be an opportunity, however, requires that you know how to take advantage of the opportunity and that you are not vulnerable to the events taking place.

Create Options for Yourself

An essential element in preparation is to create options, which minimize your dependence on an organization and on a particular situation. When someone has no options and is dependent, he or she becomes vulnerable. When vulnerable and dependent, coping with uncertainty becomes more difficult. The result is more stress and decreased happiness. So here are some suggestions to create options.

Continually Think about and Create Career Options

Often the greatest limitation is an unwillingness to consider and create options, because you are either afraid or unwilling to change. Many people have more options than they think.

Do Not Become Institutionally Dependent

It is important to realize that you can and should be able to work in another organization. In fact, the evidence suggests that most people will have worked for seven companies before they retire.

Maintain External Visibility—Maintain Contacts

Maintaining a network of contacts inside and outside an organization is critical. Contacts provide a valuable source of options for people wanting or needing to make changes. Make sure that you cultivate your network and provide help to others within it when they need it. This strategy will pay off when you need help.

Maintain Marketability—Return Recruiters' Calls

Recruiters are a valuable source of job options. However, they only benefit if they place a person in a new job. Although they do not expect everyone they call to make a change, they will maintain contact with you if they believe there is some chance they can market you. So return the calls and keep an open mind.

Avoid Overspecialization—Develop Marketable Skills

Be careful of the types of assignment that you take on in a company. The more able you are to develop skills, competencies, and experiences that are of value to other companies, the better able you are to have external options. Of interest is that a number of companies encourage and support the idea that it is important to make people employable, whether it be with their current company or another one.

Maintain Credibility and Reputation

Your personal reputation is one of the most valuable assets you have today, and it can have a dramatic impact on your relationship with others whom you may need to rely on. This includes not only your skills and competencies but your reputation for trustworthiness and integrity. The following example nicely illustrates this.

An executive I worked with told me a story about a person he volunteered with on a charitable fund-raising campaign. The person had made a serious commitment to raising funds. As such, the charity and the executive came to depend on this person. At the beginning of the fund-raising effort the person made a solid contribution. As the campaign progressed, his involvement seemed to diminish. He started missing a number of key meetings and often did not return phone calls. Further, he did not live up to his fund-raising commitments. The executive suspected that work or family obligations were an issue. But not even a phone call to explain!

A year later the person went to interview for a job. He had recently lost his job as part of a merger. Ironically, the person he interviewed with was the executive. During the interview the executive asked him what had happened during the fund-raising campaign. The person told him how corporate and family pressures took over his life and how sorry he was. The executive, while sympathetic and understanding, did not offer him a job.

Learn How to Find a Job

It is amazing how many people do not know how to find a job, perhaps because they have not had to in many years. Worse yet, they do not think they will have to in the future. They feel quite secure and believe that it is an act of disloyalty to their company. What they do not realize, however, is that it is an act of loyalty to their families and themselves. Whether you change jobs or not, it is good to know you have the capability to do so.

As part of the options—creating process, learn how to find jobs, prepare a resume, and take an interview. These are not difficult things to learn how to do. Numerous books and courses are available on such topics. In fact, a number of companies provide their employees with such resources. Many companies will provide these as part of relocation programs during mergers, acquisitions, and restructuring. If your company does not, make sure you learn on your own.

Keep Your Bags Packed

This metaphor addresses your psychology rather than your luggage. Simply put, do not have such a deep psychological commitment to your company and job that you feel you cannot leave it. I do not want to encourage you to "job hop" or to perform poorly but to ensure that you have a healthy psychological detachment from your company. This means that if an opportunity comes along that's better for you, and/or your family, allow yourself the freedom to entertain and possibly act on it. Again, you should not be afraid to entertain and exercise options. And companies should not be afraid of people doing so. Leaders should create a work environment that motivates people to stay and produce.

Diversify Your Self-Identity

There is an old saying that we should all pay a great deal of attention to:

"Don't put all your eggs in one basket."

This saying clearly points to the importance of diversification of risk. As important as it is to diversify your investment portfolio, it is just as important for you to diversify your self-identity. Investment advisers preach diversification, so that if one investment goes bad, the entire portfolio does not become worthless. Unfortunately, people do not always see the wisdom of this advice, especially when the one investment they have made is doing quite well. Just witness the euphoria surrounding the run-up of e-commerce stocks in the late 1990s. While the stocks were going well, diversification looked like a poor strategy. Unfortunately, things can change with the downtick of a stock. Witness the number of people who lost a fortune when e-commerce stocks took a beating at the beginning of the new millennium.

Well, the story is quite the same for self-identity. Many people have tied their self-identity to only one thing, often their career and their company. They have everything vested in this one "investment." While the company is doing well and their careers are moving along, everything is just fine. But if there is a merger or acquisition that changes things, the potential impact on their self-identity is severe. Consider the following story.

During the early 1990s I was involved in integrating the merger of two oil companies. I had come to know a senior-level financial executive in the company that ostensibly was being bought. The executive had worked for his company for 25 years. He was quite dedicated and gave the company his total commitment. In fact, he often worked seven days a week and traveled extensively on behalf of the company. During this time his career blossomed and he was compensated quite well for it. Unfortunately, his personal life did not do so well. The extended time away deteriorated his relationship with his wife and two daughters. This led to a divorce and subsequent alienation with his daughters.

The executive seemed to have coped with the events of his life until it was announced that his services were no longer required. He was "made redundant." One day he showed up in my office to share the news with me. It was a rainy day. He was in a suit and tie. Strangely though, he was wearing sunglasses. Shortly after we began our conversation he started to cry. He removed his sunglasses. His eyes were red, indicative of a long bout of crying. After he regained his composure, he became angry. After so many years and so many personal sacrifices, how could the company do this to him! As he was sitting there, I noticed that he was still wearing the company's lapel pin.

Several years later I ran into him only to find a lost soul who had yet to find much happiness. He had nothing to look forward to and was still devastated.

Although this is an extreme example, it does illustrate how lack of diversification is dangerous, especially in a rapidly and constantly changing world. This is not to argue that work is a small or unimportant part of life. On the contrary, it is a major element that is critical to our psychological and financial well-being. Moreover, it is a part of our life that demands significant time and energy if we are to do it right. However, it is not the only thing in our lives. Given the amount of change facing corporations and people today, overinvolvement with an organization can leave people too vulnerable to the events that bring change. When such events happen, it is valuable for people to have other elements in their lives that they can draw satisfaction and happiness from, other things that will allow them to deal with events and to move on. What those other things are is for each person to decide. So ask yourself: "Have I put all my eggs in one basket?"

FINANCIAL PREPARATION

Americans are notorious for not saving. Perhaps this helps explain the strong economy we witnessed during the late 1990s. The spending afforded people a certain lifestyle. For some it was a period of luxury, whereas for others it allowed them to survive.

Unfortunately, the lack of savings and other investments has created a situation where people do not have a cushion that minimizes their financial vulnerability in the event of a job loss. For many, this has not been a problem because of the economic growth and low unemployment that had, until recently, characterized the U.S. economy. It is amazing how many people have forgotten about the corporate restructuring of the 1980s or are ignoring the financial challenges that a number of companies in early 2001 are facing. More and more we are hearing about job loss due to M&As and to cost cutting as revenue growth and earnings have slowed.

Without a cushion, people are less able to withstand job loss. Thus, it is essential for people to have a "cushion" to reduce their vulnerability to changes. It provides a twofold benefit. First, it minimizes the financial crisis of a job loss. Second, it is easier for people to change jobs in a merger or acquisition if they are not happy with their new situation; e.g., they do not like the new culture or their new boss. If nothing else, at worst, they will have added money for their retirement!

It is beyond the scope of this chapter to provide advice on financial strategies. However, numerous books and courses are easily available that address these. A personal commitment to face this issue and start a process of investment is the most critical step.

AVOID THE RUMOR MILL

As noted in Chapter 5, people need to make sense out of the world they live in. In the absence of information, they will use the rumor mill and their imaginations to do so. Too much imagination and reliance on rumors can be dangerous. Often the information is negative and exaggerated. The rumors distract you and often mislead you. Estimates indicate that the rumor mill is accurate 50 percent of the time. The problem is that it is virtually impossible to distinguish the accurate from the inaccurate information. So it is best to seek information from your manager or to do your own research to understand the events taking place. In the absence of information, continue to focus on doing your work and creating and preparing to execute other options. Try to be patient, although it may not be easy to do so. Not only will this minimize your dependence, but it will allow you to control your own destiny. Both create a positive psychology.

DIAGNOSE THE SITUATION

When rumors or a formal announcement of a merger or acquisition hits, don't panic and overreact. However, don't underreact either. It is a good time to assess your personal situation and prepare to respond. As noted throughout this chapter, preparation will give you the capability and the wherewithal to act. It will give you some control over your situation. Now is the time to assess your situation to determine the likelihood that you will be affected, and if so, how.

Your assessment should focus on two issues: the buyer and your current situation. Assessment of the buyer will help you understand what the buyer's motives are in acquiring your company and how the buyer has handled previous mergers and acquisitions. Assessment of your situation will help you understand your personal vulnerability.

Assessing the Buyer

The Internet has made it very easy to gather information on a company, especially if it is a highly visible company or its stock is publicly traded. There is significant information to be had based on Securities and Exchange Commission filings, analysts' reports, and articles in business publications and national and local newspapers. Not only is general information on the company available, but so too is information on previous and current mergers and acquisitions. Such information addresses issues such as how an acquirer has handled or plans to handle staffing decisions and reductions in force, severance, conflicts between acquirers and targets, culture clashes, and sources of synergies, among many others. Pay particular attention to where operations are likely to be located, the staffing decision process to be used, policies on geographic transfers, severance packages, and compensation and benefits packages.

As an example, a large part of the assessment of the hospital management corporation provided in Appendix 3-1 was conducted through Internet searches. I was amazed at how much information was available in local newspapers in areas where the company operated. With a little bit of time, you will be able to learn a lot.

Assessing Your Situation

Once you understand more about the acquirer, and perhaps the merger itself, you will be able to begin to size up your personal situation. Some key questions that will help you understand your vulnerability include:

- *Is my position tied to key executives in my current company?* You may be vulnerable if your position is dependent upon a particular executive who is not retained after the deal is done. Conversely, you may be in a strong position if the executive has been named to a key postclosing position. For example, when SBC bought Ameritech, it retained the president of the Ameritech Directories business. Due to its success, the Ameritech organization's business model would likely survive.
- *Am I in a line versus staff position?* Staff positions are almost always vulnerable in M&As. One of the easiest sources of cost reductions is the elimination of redundant staff, especially at the corporate level.
- *Am I in a corporate or division position?* It is important to understand the acquirer's philosophy concerning centralization and decentralization. For example, in the merger between Sandoz and Ciba Geigy to form Novartis, Sandoz had a decentralized organization and philosophy concerning staff, whereas Ciba Geigy had a centralized organization and philosophy. The message was clear. Corporate staff would be eliminated, with positions that remain being located in the divisions. This left many Ciba Geigy corporate people vulnerable, especially those who could not or did not want to move.
- *Am I in a position that is redundant with that of the acquirer?* Beyond staff positions, certain jobs may be rendered redundant as manufacturing operations, sales organization, and R&D laboratories are combined to reduce costs and improve productivity.
- *Am I in a specialized position?* I will never forget a comment made to me by an employee of a target company who gleefully noted: " I did my homework on the acquirer and they have no one in their organization that does what I do." Unfortunately, this person did not realize that the acquirer did not place any value on what the person did and had moved way beyond the capabilities of that person's position. Understanding what are important capabilities in the acquirer's business model is crucial.

- *Do I have weak or outdated skills and competencies?* In today's environment this is the greatest source of vulnerability. Many acquirers will make a reasonable attempt to staff the new organization with the best talent they can find, regardless of company of origin. With relatively low unemployment, retaining the best talent is key to competitive success and profitability. As noted in Chapter 4, many companies attempt to examine personal competencies in addition to past performance in making staffing decisions. Those who are out of date are likely to be most vulnerable. In some instances, people who are outdated may be retained for a period of time just to provide continuity during the transition period. In fact, they may be offered attractive severance packages if they stay through the transition.

CREATING, CHOOSING, AND EXECUTING YOUR OPTION

Once you have assessed your situation, you need to consider what your options are likely to be. You can either do this early or wait until the acquisition unfolds. The earlier you prepare, the more time you will have to execute. For example, one 53-year-old merged executive told me that he saw the handwriting on the wall, even before the actual closing. The companies were waiting on antitrust clearances and shareholder approval. In the end, he realized that his company was being acquired. The acquirer had announced that the target's headquarters were to be closed and those who were asked to stay would be transferred to the acquirer's headquarters located on the other side of the country. Although he had a chance to stay, he decided that he needed to create other options for himself.

Fortunately, he was prudent throughout his career and saved and invested enough to withstand a loss of income for a sustained period of time. Thus he had the ability to be patient and look for an opportunity that he might enjoy. He quietly contacted executive search firms to identify new employment opportunities. He entertained thoughts of starting a new company—something he had never considered before. The idea rather excited him. He did not wait for a decision to be made about his career and then wonder what he might do. He started the ball rolling early.

Further, he did not panic and overreact. He decided to delay his decision until he "knew the score." He wanted to see how his options materialized before he made a choice. But he knew he was in control because he had some choices. Although he could afford to do so, he clearly was not ready for retirement.

In general, a merger or acquisition will present you with three broad situations. (1) You will be invited to join the new organization and you will choose to stay. (2) You will be offered a position but choose not to stay. (3) You will be let go. How you handle these situations will impact your psychological and financial health and your reputation. This section presents three personal scenarios and strategies for dealing with them: staying and prospering, exiting voluntarily, and exiting involuntarily.

Staying and Prospering

If you are invited to remain and you decide to stay with the combined organization, it is wise to adopt a positive attitude. Joining, but grumbling, not only will make you unhappy, but will eventually wear down those around you. Someone once gave me some good advice concerning this issue: "If you are going to be in the game, then play it well and succeed in it. If you do not like the game, then get out of it and move on to another game." I have found this to be sound advice that is applicable to a merger situation. Given that advice, below are some key strategies that will help you succeed in the game.

Stay Focused on Work and Be a Producer

Staying focused on work has several key benefits. First, it helps you avoid being caught up in all the angst that often surrounds a merger. Second, it sends the right signal to management that you want to be part of the new organization and are ready to make a contribution. Actions speak louder than words.

Do Not Take Sides—Weigh Politics Carefully

It is often not clear during the early stages of a merger who has won and who has lost. I have witnessed many people who have allied themselves with specific executives in a merged organization, thinking that it would help them advance their careers. Unfortunately, the staffing of merged organizations takes some time to shake out. During the first year following the closing there is often a shift in leadership as people who have taken key leadership positions have changed. Some decide after a period of time that they really don't fit. Some never intended to stay in the first place. They stayed long enough to reap certain severance benefits. Trying to figure out who the winners and losers are and aligning with them can be lethal. It is best to commit to performing and trying to stay as neutral as possible for as long as possible.

Get on board the New Culture

As noted earlier, join the new game as quickly as possible and attempt to learn how it operates and what it takes to succeed within it. Sometimes managers will assist you in this effort, whereas other times you will have to figure it out for yourself.

Avoid the Rumor Mill

Since we all need to make sense of what is going on around us, it is tempting to seek information through the rumor mill. This is especially the case when uncertainty has been prolonged and there has not been much information from management. As noted previously, however, the rumor mill is filled with a glut of inaccurate information that is often negative and exaggerated. It is more likely to worry you than to provide you with useful information. It is best to seek information from your immediate manager and to rely on trusted sources of information that you have had experience with before. In many cases you will just have to be patient and deal with the uncertainty since answers to questions may not yet be known.

Continue to Assess Management—Actual and Symbolic Communication

Someone once said that talk is cheap. During mergers and acquisitions, many statements are often made by management. Some are true and some are not. It is important that you focus on management's actions as well as words. When you see inconsistencies, pay attention to the actions. They are a more accurate reflection of what is going on. Also, watch changes in actions over time. What was intended at the beginning of the merger may not be what is realized later. Situations change, and initial commitments cannot be kept. More than once a well-intentioned manager made a statement that "nobody would lose their job due to the merger." Unfortunately, the manager could not keep that promise over time. As information and actions evolve, you will get a better feel for your situation and whether you want to remain in the organization.

Make It Known You Want to Stay

One of the challenges of selecting people in a merging organization is knowing who will take and keep a job if offered it. Sometimes offers are not made because it is assumed that the person is not interested. As such, another, perhaps less qualified, candidate is offered the position. Thus, it is in your interest to let your manager know that you are interested in a career in the new organization.

Don't Become Paralyzed—Continue to Evaluate Internal and External Job Opportunities

Never become too comfortable. Always be prepared to make a change if it is necessary. Although it is not always easy, there are many opportunities that can greatly improve your situation. You may not like a job you took in the new company. If that's the case, examine opportunities in different areas of the company, or look on the outside. In today's environment there are plenty of opportunities for qualified and motivated people.

Keep Your Resume Updated

That says it all. It always pays to keep your resume updated. You never know when you will need it.

Prepare for and Embrace Change—Stay Flexible

It is clear to most of us that the pace of change in the world we live in is accelerating. It is doubtful that organizations and jobs will stay constant.

Moreover, it will require us to make rapid changes. Flexibility is a good attribute for people to have during these times. In a merger, in particular, there will be a lot of change after the closing. No matter how good the due diligence and integration planning processes were, there is still much learning that will take place between the merging firms. It is inevitable that opportunities and threats were not completely understood prior to the closing. There will be unanticipated synergies and some that were exaggerated. There will be key executives who agreed to stay indefinitely, only to leave after six months. The net result is that things will continue to change, and they will have a direct impact on you. Failure to be flexible and make needed adjustments can lead to many frustrations and poor adaptation.

Seek Social Support

A merger or an acquisition, just like any other major event, can be quite overwhelming. As such, it is easy to lose perspective and experience negative feelings. Sometimes sharing our ideas and feelings allows us to vent and blow off steam. Sometimes it helps us put things back in perspective. All of us lose perspective at times, especially when we are caught up in an emotionally demanding and traumatic situation. After all, the worst that is at stake in most organizations is just a job.

Most people tell me how important it is to have others to talk with about what is happening to them. What is also interesting is that they almost always note that such people are not from their work environment. It is very difficult to reveal your true feelings to colleagues. Although we may have excellent relationships with colleagues, organizations are still political environments. It is best to talk to people whom you trust and who have no vested interest in your work situation. These should be people whose only interest is your well-being.

Exiting Voluntarily

Although you have been given the option to stay you may not choose to. There could be many reasons why. These may include the need to move to a new geographic location, changes in the nature of your job, the culture being adopted by the merged organization, and the like. Moreover, after remaining in the new organization for a period of time, you may decide that things have not turned out the way you anticipated. Perhaps commitments or promises made by the management of the merged organization have not been kept. Before making and executing the decision to leave, there are some things to consider.

Seek Professional Outplacement Help

If you choose to leave voluntarily, it is likely that the company will not provide you with professional outplacement help. Essentially you will be on your own. If you have worked for your company for a long time, you may not be comfortable or conversant with finding a new job. Certainly, there are numerous books and minicourses on how to prepare for and find a new job. As well, there are numerous employment and search firms that can help you. These resources will help you prepare a resume, prepare for interviews, and conduct an orderly and productive job search. Much of this today is done on the Internet. It is a wise person who takes advantage of resources!

Examine Severance Packages Closely

Many companies have severance packages available for people who have not been retained due to elimination of redundant positions. Furthermore, if people have been offered a job more than a certain distance from their current one (e.g., 50 miles) or a job not equivalent to their current level of responsibilities, they may qualify for a severance package. Although such packages vary by company, most take into account length of service and position in the current organization. A little patience may pay off and provide you with an attractive nest egg that can give you some time to decide what you want to do. The key here is not to overreact. Often people become impatient and leave their organization quickly, only to miss an attractive opportunity.

Quietly Conduct a Job Search—Don't Showboat

If you decide you want to leave, search for a job and do so quietly. There is no need to make a show of it or to destabilize those around you. Some people need to make a show to demonstrate to everyone how fortunate and "valuable" they are. There is no need to rub it in. Not only does it bother other people, but it will often damage your reputation. You never know whether you will want to come back to the organization, or encounter these people in other situations where you need their support—e.g., a letter of recommendation.

Don't Threaten to Quit Unless You Are Prepared to Do So

It is important to realize that at some point all of us are replaceable in our jobs. Testing that limit may not be such a good idea. I once had a colleague who overestimated his value to the organization. He thought he was undervalued and underpaid and decided to leverage our manager for a raise. So he undertook a poorly thought-out strategy. He went to the manager and told her that he was looking at another job that paid significantly more than the current one he had. After some thought she told him, "You would be crazy not to take the other job." End of negotiation! Unfortunately, he did not really want the other job and was not prepared to leave. But he only had a weak alternative and thus was not in a real position to negotiate. He wound up leaving and has not been happy in his new job. Ultimatums often do not work on sophisticated people. If you do use them, then you better be sure of your value and have a viable alternative to a negotiated solution.

Consider Internal and External Opportunities

Frequently in mergers there are opportunities to transfer to other divisions or operations if the one you are in is not working out. Thus be sure to explore both internal and external opportunities. Most companies will provide job postings of such opportunities and create formal processes for seeing them. Today, jobs are often posted on a company's Intranet.

Time Personal Finances and Your Job Search
Do not overreact. You may regret it. As someone once said, "Timing is everything in life." So is leaving an organization. Be sure that you have enough financial resources to buffer the income loss from leaving your job. While your work situation may seem unbearable, significant financial problems are likely to be worse. That is why waiting for a severance package may be useful. In general it is easier to find a job while you have a job. For one thing, you do not have to explain why you are currently unemployed. For another, having an income allows you to be more patient in deciding what you want to do next. As your income dwindles and your financial needs become more challenging, your choices in jobs diminish.

Examine Transition Benefits (COBRA)
In addition to income, benefits are also an important issue to consider. Federal law requires a company to allow employees who have exited an organization to participate in a company's health plan at the group rate up to 18 months after they have resigned. While this is a huge discount over going it alone, the individuals must pay both their normal contribution and what the company used to pay for them.

Don't Be Negative about Your Past Employer in Job Interviews
The worse thing people can do when interviewing for a new job is complain about their previous employer. It clearly suggests that if and when you leave your new employer, you are likely to do the same thing. What company in its right mind would like that? Second, there are always two sides to a story. Thus whose fault is it that there was a problem? Why leave questions about whether you or your employer was the problem? The best thing is to communicate that you are looking for a new or better opportunity and to be prepared to explain what that opportunity is. Focusing on moving forward tells a new employer that you are part of solutions rather than problems.

Seek Social Support
As noted in the last section, seek social support to help you see things in a clear light. It is particularly important in this situation. Typically, people are more negative about their current job than a new one. This is because they are much more familiar with their current situation and see all the "holes." Most new jobs look brighter than they really are. Moreover, prospective employers do not always provide a completely realistic job preview. Perhaps if they did, fewer people would be interested! It is thus important to seek others who are likely to be more objective and challenge you to think more realistically about your assumptions and the pros and cons of each alternative. This should improve both your comfort level and the probability that you are making the right choice.

Exiting Involuntarily

The final situation is one in which you may not have a choice. You have not been retained by the merging or acquiring firm. Although this can be difficult for you to cope with, it is not the end of the world. In fact, for some it may be the beginning of a new life. It may be the impetus that you need to make changes that you have not been willing, or able, to make in the past. Regardless, it will be challenging and will require adjustments on your part. Here are some things to consider.

Maintain Self-Esteem, Learn, and Move On

In addition to potential economic challenges, not being retained can be a blow to your ego. Nobody likes being rejected. However, one has to move on. Of course, people deal with transitions differently. Some people pass through different stages before they successfully accept what has happened and move on. Some people take longer to do so. Regardless, the only way to manage in such a situation is for you to maintain your self-esteem and to plan and execute alternatives.

Even in seemingly hopeless situations the human spirit is strong enough to find a way to survive and even prosper. Since you cannot change the past, the only way to gain from it is to learn from it, and to use what you have learned to move forward. Thus, although you need to move forward and keep your head high, it is important to ask a fundamental question: Why was I not retained? Was it because I did not have the competencies and skills required in the new organization? If so, how can I ensure I stay current in my next job? Was it because I did not manage my politics carefully? If so, perhaps I may be a bit less naïve in the future. Was it because I was unwilling to take a different job or relocate? If so, perhaps I need to examine my future willingness to change or the flexibility of my personal and family situation. Regardless of the reason, it is important to learn and not repeat mistakes. As someone once told me, "No matter how difficult the situation and negative the outcomes, there is always something positive that can be gained from it, a lesson."

Don't Become Hostile—It's Over

Coming to the point of acceptance is critical. As noted in Chapter 5, many people become angry when faced with a traumatic event. If you do, be careful. The work environment is a poor place to demonstrate such anger. Ranting, raving, and complaining accomplishes absolutely nothing positive. Often, all you do is burn bridges with other people whom you might run across or need in the future. They may be the sources of future jobs, letters of recommendations, and the like. If you are angry, work it out elsewhere, and do so constructively. The key is to accept that a decision has been made, it is final, and all you can do is move on.

Learn about In-House Transfers

Even though your position may have been eliminated in a merger, there may be job opportunities in other departments or divisions of the companies. As noted in Chapter 7, many companies will post such jobs and give priority to existing employees. However, priority will usually be given to those who have the competencies and skills needed in those jobs. So before you conclude that the only opportunities are on the outside, learn about internal opportunities.

Learn about Outplacement Opportunities

As mentioned earlier, often companies will provide outplacement support for people not being retained due to redundancy. The source of such information is usually the human resources department, but do not hesitate to ask your direct manager. He or she may be in the loop. Outplacement support will vary by company and often by your level in the organization. Such support may include resume writing, assistance with interviewing skills, and job postings. Some companies will even outsource outplacement, at their expense, to a specialist firm. If you have not sought work in a number of years and are not sure how to do so, take advantage of this opportunity. Also, there are many Internet-based services that you can use to post your resume.

Learn about Severance (Salary and Benefits)

As with outplacement, companies typically offer severance packages for redundant employees. Such packages will vary by the number of years of employment with the company and with position. However, the benefits often cap at some maximum value. Although a variety of formulas are used to determine severance benefits, typically redundant employees are given their monthly salary times the number of years of service. Some companies cap the benefit at two years' salary. That is not a bad buffer to provide time to regain employment. Again, as noted previously, it is useful not to overreact early during a merger and leave. You may miss a valuable opportunity.

Seek Professional Psychological Counseling

If you are having problems dealing with the situation and are unable to cope, it may be useful to seek psychological help. There is a point where all of us have difficulty dealing with situations, and friends are not skillful in helping us. Seeking professional help is often stigmatized in our society as a sign of weakness or inadequacy. This may especially be the case for men, who have often been raised to be "tough." Actually seeking help is a sign of strength. Strong people can admit that they have a problem and realize they can't handle it by themselves. Even "normal" people lose perspective and are unable to help themselves. Professionals can guide you in understanding the causes of your problems and feelings and help you explore and choose alternatives that can solve them. If you do not know of any sources of help, you can seek advice from your company's human resources professional, your doctor, the American Psychiatric Association, or the American Psychological Association.

Counseling may also provide you with an opportunity to explore what you are truly interested in and what you may be best at doing. There are numerous tests psychologists and counselors use to help people explore their interests and capabilities. They are easy to take and usually not very expensive.

Focus on Finding a New Job (Prepare to Wait)

Solving problems is among the best ways for you to deal with stress, disappointment, and trauma. Seeking a job is an excellent way for you to solve the problem of job loss. With that said, however, you must be realistic. Many people who have lost their job on Friday hit the pavement on Monday seeking work. They have decided to accept their fate and move on with enthusiasm and energy. This is clearly commendable. However, when they do not find a job by the end of the week, they become depressed. Why? Because they have unrealistic expectations of how long it might take to find work and did not realize that many things were outside of their control. The nature of the job you are looking for, the economic environment, your work experience, and the geographic market you are focused on may greatly impact the length of your search. Fortunately, throughout the 1990s and the year 2000, the economy was sound, unemployment relatively low, and the need for skilled people high. These all made the job search much easier and shorter. However, the environment changes, as it did in the year 2001. The bottom line: Be realistic, but be deliberate.

Seek Social Support

Once again, social support remains a critical element in moving forward. Support networks can help you put things into perspective. They can also provide a sounding board as you explore and evaluate new job opportunities. A dispassionate view during this time can help you uncover your own assumptions to ensure that you do not take a position hastily. Often, people are not realistic about new jobs, especially when they feel desperate. Nor do interviewers always tell people all the gory details. Also, people, in their eagerness, often overestimate the positives.

A FINAL THOUGHT

Whether you prosper during a merger or an acquisition is a function of whether you are prepared to deal with it. Prepare now! Create options and do not be afraid to execute them when the time is ripe. Doing so will minimize your dependence upon events that are outside your control. And doing so may open your life to things you never imagined you could or would do. Be among the survivors, not the victims.

ENDNOTES

Chapter 1

[1] Information regarding the merger of Daimler-Benz and Chrysler from Daimler-Benz AG, Investor Relations, 7056 Stuttgart, Germany.

[2] Taken from From the Chairman, *GTE Together*, Vol. 17, Fall/Winter 1998.

[3] For the sake of brevity, hereafter I will use *mergers* and *acquisitions* interchangeably. I recognize that from a statutory perspective the nature of the transaction of the two forms may vary. I will distinguish between the two when necessary.

[4] See Thomson Financial Securities Data, 2001.

[5] There are numerous studies that have examined the relationship between M&As and a variety of measures of performance. Since there are too many studies to review here I suggest you read the following sources for an overview: A. R. Lajoux, *The Art of M&A Integration*, New York: McGraw-Hill, 1998; D. M. Schweiger and J. P. Walsh, "Mergers and acquisitions: An interdisciplinary view," in K. M. Rowland and G. R. Ferris (Eds.), *Research in Personnel and Human Resource Management*, Vol. 8, Greenwich, CT: JAI Press, 1990, pp. 41–107; and M. A. Hitt, J. S. Harrison, R. D. Ireland, *Mergers and Acquisitions: A Guide for Creating Value for Shareholders*, New York: Oxford University Press, 2001.

[6] The ideas in this section were originally developed by E. N. Csiszar and D. M. Schweiger, "An integrative framework for creating value through acquisition," in H. E. Glass and B. N. Craven (Eds.), *Handbook of Business Strategy*, New York: Warren, Gorham & Lamont, 1994, pp. 93–115.

[7] A continuing stream of research by practitioners and academics points to the importance of integration in M&A value creation. These include several studies by major consulting firms such as Coopers and Lybrand, Mercer Management Consulting, A. T. Kearney, and Hewitt Associates, which are reported in J. R. Carleton, "Cultural due diligence," *Training*, November 1997, pp. 67–75; and J. S. Lublin and B. O'Brien, "When dis-

parate firms merge, cultures often collide," *The Wall Street Journal*, February 1997. A study of *Forbes* 500 executives on why synergies are not realized cites 5 organizational issues as among the top 10 (study reported in Towers Perrin internal document). A comprehensive review of academic research identifying integration as an important element in M&A value creation is presented in D. M. Schweiger and J. P. Walsh, "Mergers and acquisitions: An interdisciplinary view," in K. M. Rowland and G. R. Ferris (Eds.), *Research in Personnel and Human Resource Management*, Vol. 8, Greenwich, CT: JAI Press, 1990, pp. 41–107; and D. M. Schweiger and P. Goulet, "Integrating acquisitions: An international research review," in C. Cooper and A. Gregory (Eds.), *Advances in Mergers and Acquisitions*, Vol. I, Greenwich, CT: JAI/Elsevier Press, 2000, pp. 61–91. Also see S. Chatterjee, M. Lubatkin, D. M. Schweiger, and Y. Weber, "Cultural differences and shareholder value: Explaining the variability in the performance of related merger," *Strategic Management Journal*, Vol. 13, 1992, pp. 319–334.

[8] M&A agreements can be structured with such clauses to protect the acquirer against certain liabilities. Insurance policies and escrowed funds can also be employed. However, it is most prudent if the acquirers do their analyses and identify key issues a priori and understand the risks they are assuming. Relying on indemnification often requires a civil lawsuit, of which the results can be quite uncertain.

[9] D. Rankine, *A Practical Guide to Acquisitions*, Chichester, UK: Wiley, 1998.

[10] See, for example, J. P. Kotter, *Leading Change*, Boston: Harvard Business School Press, 1996.

Chapter 2

[1] For example, see R. F. Brunner, K. M. Eades, R. S. Harris, and R. C. Higgins, "Best practices in estimating the cost of capital: Survey and synthesis," *Financial Practice and Education*, Vol. 8, 1998, pp. 13–28, who found that 89 percent of the firms they studied used DCF or a similar approach. It is important to note that increasingly firms are relying on a real-options approach to valuation (T. A. Luehrman, "Investment opportunities as real options: Getting started on the numbers," *Harvard Business Review*, Vol. 76, No. 4, 1998, pp. 51–67).

[2] The total value includes both the equity and debt portion of the firm's capital structure. To determine the equity portion of the firm, the debt is subtracted from the total valuation.

[3] T. Copeland, T. Koller, and J. Murrin, *Valuation: Measuring and Managing the Value of Companies*, New York: Wiley, 1995.

[4] Although beyond the scope of this book, it is important to note that there is much debate concerning the use of terminal values and which approach is best. As such, the value of a firm can vary greatly depending upon which approach (e.g., P/E multiple, perpetuity value) is chosen (see E. L. Morris, "Why acquirers may need to rethink terminal values," *Mergers & Acquisitions*, July/August 1996, pp. 24–29). Further the weighted-average cost of capital can also greatly affect valuation and can vary depending upon the percentage of debt and equity used to finance an acquisition.

[5] In practice, a number of pro forma statements would be developed reflecting different assumptions about sales growth and costs and net working capital as a percentage of sales. For the sake of brevity, only one stand-alone forecast is presented. The purpose of this example is to illustrate the impact of proposed synergies rather than a full treatment of valuation.

[6] M. L. Sirower, *The Synergy Trap*, New York: The Free Press, 1997.

[7] R. G. Eccles, K. L. Lanes, and T. C. Wilson, "Are you paying too much for that acquisition?" *Harvard Business Review*, Vol. 77, No. 4, 1999, pp. 136–146.

[8] This has been clearly documented in research by D. B. Jemison and S. B. Sitkin, "Acquisitions: The process can be the problem," *Harvard Business Review*, Vol. 64, 1986, pp. 107–116.

[9] With that said, it is also important to recognize that it is not always easy to identify and quantify all synergies prior to closing. Unless you can identify enough, however, the risks of doing a deal may become quite significant.

[10] Hilton Hotels Corporation *Annual Report*, 2000.

[11] For a more detailed treatment of the concept of integration and how others have defined it, see D. M. Schweiger and P. Goulet, "Integrating acquisitions: An international research review," in C. Cooper and A. Gregory (Eds.), *Advances in Mergers and Acquisitions*, Vol. I, Greenwich, CT: JAI/Elsevier Press, 2000, pp. 61–91.

[12] Return on net assets and return on capital employed are identical.

Chapter 3

[1] For excellent sources of information, see S. Foster Reed and A. Reed Lajoux, *The Art of M&A: A Merger Acquisition Buyout Guide*, Burr Ridge, IL: Irwin, 1995.

[2] D. B. Jemison and S. B. Sitkin, "Acquisitions: The process can be the problem," *Harvard Business Review*, Vol. 64, 1986, pp. 107–116.

[3] P. Very and D. M. Schweiger, "Creating value through mergers and acquisitions: Key challenges and solutions in domestic and international deals," *Journal of World Business*, Vol. 36, 2001, pp. 11–31.

[4] For an excellent discussion of culture see E. Schein, *Organizational Culture and Leadership: A Dynamic View*, San Francisco: Jossey-Bass, 1985.

[5] See J. P. Kotter and J. L. Heskett, *Corporate Culture and Performance*, New York: The Free Press, 1992.

[6] The importance of cultural differences has been documented in a study of 350 European mergers and acquisitions. The study found a strong correlation between cultural differences and the success of the integration (D. Rankine, *A Practical Guide to Acquisitions*, Chichester, UK: Wiley, 1998). As noted earlier, a study of *Forbes* 500 executives found cultural differences to be the number one pitfall in achieving synergies. A study that several of my colleagues and I conducted compared the cultures as reflected in the top-management teams of 35 acquiring and acquired firms. We examined the impact that cultural differences would have on the stock performance of the acquiring firms. Comparing the performance prior to and after the deal was closed, and controlling for normal fluctuations in the stock market itself, we found that there was a strong negative relationship between cultural differences and stock price. In fact it explained over 30 percent of the variation in stock price! Simply put, the greater the difference, the worse the performance (S. Chatterjee, M. Lubatkin, D. M. Schweiger, and Y. Weber, "Cultural differences and shareholder value: Explaining the variability in the performance of related merger," *Strategic Management Journal*, Vol. 13, 1992, pp. 319–334).

[7] Many approaches and tools are available for assessing culture. Unfortunately, there is little standardization among them. Rarely, do they capture the same dimensions. Thus, the results are not always comparable, making analyses of differences difficult if not impossible. In a merger and acquisition it is best to attempt to use the same or comparable instruments.

[8] Numerous studies have addressed the impact of both national and organizational cultures on M&As. For a thorough review of these studies, see D. M. Schweiger and P. Goulet, "Integrating acquisitions: An international research review," in C. Cooper and A. Gregory (Eds.), *Advances in Mergers and Acquisitions*, Vol. I, Greenwich, CT: JAI/Elsevier Press, 2000, pp. 61–91.

[9] My colleagues and I have studied the impact of these particular dimensions on various aspects of integration. Using a survey instrument, we found that these dimensions were significantly related to postacquisition stock price (S. Chatterjee, M. Lubatkin, D. M. Schweiger, and Y. Weber, "Cultural differences and shareholder value: Explaining the variability in the performance of related merger," *Strategic Management Journal*, Vol. 13,

1992, pp. 319–342.) and executive turnover (M. Lubatkin, D. M. Schweiger, and Y. Weber, "Top management turnover in related M&A's: An additional test of the theory of relative standing," *Journal of Management*, Vol. 25, 1999, pp. 55–68). These studies provide some evidence of the validity of the dimensions and the survey instrument.

[10] A mulitvariate analysis of variance (MANOVA) was conducted across all the dimensions to test whether there was a general cultural difference between the firms. Afterward an individual analysis of variances (ANOVA) for each dimension was conducted between the groups to determine which dimensions were significant. Where significant, the results indicated that the differences between the organizations were greater than the differences within each organization.

Chapter 4

[1] The importance of assessing key people has been documented in a study of 350 European mergers and acquisitions. The study found a strong correlation between the extent of due diligence concerning management and key people and the success of the merger or acquisition (D. Rankine, *A Practical Guide to Acquisitions*, Chichester, UK: Wiley, 1998).

[2] As with cultural assessment, the acquirer's human resource group may have already performed these analyses for the acquirer's organization. To the extent possible, such analyses can be used for the target, or the existing methodology can be applied to the target.

[3] I would like to thank Victoria Emerson, who contributed many of the ideas and materials in this section. She has considerable consulting experience using the Birkman and has worked with me on a number of mergers and acquisitions such as the ones described in this chapter. I would also like to thank Birkman International for their permission to utilize the Birkman Method in this section.

Chapter 5

[1] The digital dilemma, *The Economist*, July 22, 2000, pp. 67–68.

[2] See D. M. Schweiger and A. S. DeNisi, "Communication with employees following a merger: A longitudinal field experiment," *Academy of Management Journal*, Vol. 34, No. 1, 1991, pp. 110–135.

[3] For an excellent discussion of this issue, see T. J. Larkin and S. Larkin, *Communicating Change: Winning Employee Support for New Business Goals*, New York: McGraw-Hill, 1994.

[4] Since multiple companies were being acquired simultaneously, multiple transition teams were created. Each team was responsible for each

acquisition. Due to limited staff and the sizes of the acquisitions, several people served on multiple transition teams. The transition communication leader interacted with the leader of each transition team to ensure each acquisition was receiving effective communications.

[5] E. Kubler-Ross, *On Death and Dying*, New York: Macmillan, 1969.

[6] Clearly, many physical illnesses produce the same reaction, and people should see a medical doctor before concluding it is a psychological problem.

[7] See N. K. Schlossberg, "Taking the mystery out of change," *Psychology Today*, 1987.

Chapter 6

[1] The material presented here is adapted from *GTE Together*, Vol. 17, Fall/Winter 1998.

[2] This material is presented in Robert J. Kramer, *Post-Merger Organization Handbook*, The Conference Board, Research Report 1241-99-RR.

[3] This material is presented in Kramer, *Post-Merger Organization Handbook*.

[4] For an excellent discussion of the transnational organization, see C. A. Bartlett and S. Ghoshal, *Managing across Borders: The Transnational Solution*, Boston: Harvard Business School Press, 1998.

[5] "Building a new Boeing," *The Economist*, August 12, 2000, pp. 61–62.

[6] M. Murray and P. Beckett, "Recipe for a deal: Do it fast," *The Wall Street Journal*, August 10, 1999, pp. B1, B4.

[7] PriceWaterhouseCoopers, "A survey of mergers and acquisitions," 1997.

[8] R. Olie, "Shades of culture and institutions in international mergers," *Organization Studies*, Vol. 15, No. 3, 1994, pp. 381–405.

[9] A. Mayo and T. Hadaway, "Cultural adaptation—the ICL-Nokia-Data merger 1991–92," *Journal of Management Development*, Vol. 13, No. 2, 1994, pp. 59–71.

[10] T. J. Gerpott, "Successful integration of R&D functions after acquisitions: An exploratory empirical study," *R&D Management*, Vol. 25, No. 2, 1995, pp. 161–178.

[11] F. Leroy and B. Ramanantsoa, "The cognitive and behavioural dimensions of organizational learning in a merger: An empirical study," *Journal of Management Studies*, Vol. 34, No. 6, 1997, pp. 871–894.

Chapter 7

[1] Numerous studies point to the importance of fairness in human resources decision making and its impact on people's reactions. For a detailed treatment of this issue, see M. A. Konovsky and J. Brockner, "Managing victim and survivor layoff reactions: A procedural justice perspective," in R. Cropanzano (Ed.), *Justice in the Workplace: Approaching Justice in Human Resource Management*, Hillsdale, NJ: Lawrence Erlbaum, 1993, pp. 113–153; E. A. Lind and T. Tyler, *The Social Psychology of Procedural Justice*, New York: Plenum Press, 1988; and J. Greenberg, "The social side of fairness: Interpersonal and informational classes of organizational justice," in R. Cropanzano (Ed.), *Justice in the Workplace: Approaching Justice in Human Resources Management*, pp. 79–103.

[2] "Building a new Boeing," *The Economist*, August 12, 2000, pp. 61–62.

[3] For example, antitrust guidelines prevent direct competitors that are merging to discuss information that might lead to possible collusion. This may include information on products, costs, pricing, etc. Without knowledge of how these are to be dealt with, it may be impossible to specify all the organizational positions and the number and type of people required.

[4] I would like to thank my graduate students Carolina Jaramillo, Glenn McGuffen, and Joe Pearson for their work in helping to develop this section. Several excellent sources were used in their analysis. These include "The top 25 managers," *Businessweek*, January 8, 2000; "Citicorp-Travelers merger: Troubled times ahead?" Reuters, April 8, 1998; "Citigroup: Is this marriage working?" *Businessweek Online*, 1999; and "Alone at the top: How John Reed lost the reigns of Citigroup to his co-chairman," *The Wall Street Journal*, April 14, 2000.

[5] From Scott Wooley, "The new Ma Bell," *Forbes*, April 16, 2001, p. 70.

[6] M. Lubatkin, D. M. Schweiger, and Y. Weber, "Top management turnover in related M&As: An additional test of the theory of relative standing," *Journal of Management*, Vol. 25, 1999, pp. 55–68.

[7] There is a long line of research in industrial and organizational psychology to support this conclusion.

[8] For an excellent source of information on facilitating expatriate assignments see S. Lomax *Best Practices for Managers and Expatriates*, New York: Wiley, 2001.

Chapter 8

[1] V. Emerson, "An interview with Carlos Ghosn, president of Nissan Motors, Ltd," and industry leader of the year (*Automotive News*, 2000), *Journal of World Business*, Vol. 36, No. 1, 2001, pp. 3–10.

[2] A. Korsgaard, D. M. Schweiger, and H. Sapienza, "The role of procedural justice in building commitment, attachment, and trust in strategic decision-making teams,"*Academy of Management Journal*, Vol. 38, 1995, pp. 60–84.

[3] I would like to thank Victoria Emerson, who contributed many of the ideas and materials in this section. She has considerable consulting experience using the Birkman and has worked with me on a number of mergers and acquisitions. The case presented in this section is one such example. I would also like to thank Birkman International for their permission to utilize the Birkman Method in this section.

[4] This section is drawn from the work of D. Bunnell, *Making the Cisco Connection*, New York: Wiley, 2000, and S. Thurm, "Under Cisco's system, mergers usually work: That defies the odds," *The Wall Street Journal*, March 1, 2000, pp. A1, A13.

[5] A number of excellent theoretical and research articles and books have examined both corporate and national cultural differences on mergers and acquisitions. A few of them are S. Cartwright and C. L. Cooper, *Managing Mergers, Acquisitions and Strategic Alliances: Integrating People and Cultures*, Oxford: Butterworth-Heinemann, 1996; R. Greenwood, C. R. Hinings, and J. Brown, "Merging professional service firms," *Organization Science*, Vol. 5, No. 2, 1994, pp. 239–257; M. R. Lubatkin, R. Calori, P. Very, and J. Veiga, "Managing mergers across borders: A two-nation exploration of a nationally bound administrative heritage, *Organization Science*, Vol. 9, No. 6, 1998, pp. 670-684; M.L. Marks and P.H. Mirvis, *Joining Forces*, San Francisco: Jossey-Bass, 1998; A. Mayo and T. Hadaway, "Cultural adaptation—the ICL-Nokia-Data merger 1991-92," *Journal of Management Development*, Vol. 13, No. 2, 1994, pp. 59-71; P. Morosini, S. Shane, and H. Singh,"National cultural distance and cross-border acquisition performance," *Journal of International Business Studies*, Vol. 29, No.1, 1998, pp. 137-158; A. Nahavandi and A.R. Malekzedah, "Acculturation in mergers and acquisitions," *Academy of Management Review*, Vol. 13, 1988, pp. 79-90; R. Olie, "Shades of culture and institutions in international mergers," *Organization Studies*, Vol. 15, No. 3, 1994, pp. 381–405; A. L. Sales and P. H. Mirvis, "When cultures collide: Issues in acquisition," in J. R. Kimberly and R. E. Quinn (Eds.), *Managing Organizational Transitions*, Homewood, IL: Irwin, 1985, pp. 107–133; P. M. Very, M. Lubatkin, and R. Calori, "A cross-national assessment of acculturative stress in recent European mergers," *International Studies of Management & Organizations*, Vol. 26, No. 1, 1996, pp. 59–86; and Y. Weber, O. Shenkar, and A. Raveh, "National and corporate cultural fit in mergers/acquisitions: An exploratory study," *Management Science*, Vol. 42, No. 8, 1996, pp. 1215–1227.

[6] D. M. Schweiger and P. Goulet, "Facilitating cultural learning during an acquisition: A longitudinal field experiment," unpublished paper, 2001.

Chapter 9

[1] For an excellent overview of integrated measurement, see Robert S. Kaplan and David P. Norton, *The Balanced Scorecard*, Boston: Harvard Business School Press, 1996.

[2] For many of the measures noted, there are well-validated survey instruments and interview and focus group protocols available. I have used a number of them successfully in both research and consulting.

Chapter 10

[1] Unless, of course, we resort to psychological or physical threats. Such control, however, requires the constant presence of the threat and is not a very useful way of managing an organization.

INDEX

Note: Locators in **bold** indicate tables and charts; company names in "quotes" indicate pseudonyms.

Abitibi Consolidated Sales Corporation, 50
ABN AMBRO, 30
Acceptance stage, in Kubler-Ross's Five-Stage Model, 124–125
Access to information, 11–13
Acquirer issues (*See specific topics*)
Acquisition premium, 8
ADT, 37
Alcatel, 35
American Hospital Supply, 145, 173
Ameritech, 3, 31, 37, 256
Amoco, 3
Anger stage, in Kubler-Ross's Five-Stage Model, 124
AOL, 3, 39, 42
Arco, 3
Assessment and assessment stage
    cultural issues in transaction stage, 50–61, **59, 62**
    personal strategic diagnosis of M&A, 255–257
    of possible target, 10–13
    staffing key positions, process for, 72–100
Assimilation, approaches to, 157–160
AT&T, 3, 35, 37

Bank America, 3
Bank Boston, 140
Bank of America, 239
Bargaining stage, in Kubler-Ross's Five-Stage Model, 124
Baxter, 145, 173
Beecham, 140, 152
Bell Atlantic, 1, 3, 139, 182

Berkshire Hathaway, 40
Birkman Method, staffing assessment, 78, 80, 200
Boeing, 159, 174, 217
BP, 3
Business plans, 76

Cashflow
    discounted cashflow (DCF), 20, 22–27, **24–26**, 30
    models, 29, 229
"Catholic Healthcare Systems," 55, 64–69
CEO (chief executive officer), 179, 197–199
Champion of integration, 47–48, 140–145, **142–143**
Change, employee strategic preparation, 250–251
Chase Manhattan, 145
Chemical Bank, 145
Chevron, 3, 56, 145, 173, 183–184, 198, 249
Chief executive officer (CEO), 179, 197–199
Chrysler Corporation, 1, 3, 42–43
Ciba Geigy, 3, 56, 256
Cisco, 35, 104, 216, 239
Citgo, 39
Citicorp, 3, 180
Citigroup, 31, 179–182
COBRA, 262
Columbia/HCA, 37
Commercial Credit Company, 179
Communication issues
    articulation of integration guiding principles, 151–155
    audience salience, 111–112
    customer retention management, 127–128

ABOUT THE AUTHOR

David M. Schweiger, Ph.D., is the Buck Mickel/Fluor Daniel Professor at the Moore School of Business at the University of South Carolina, adjunct professor at EM Lyon in France, and president of the strategic management consulting firm Schweiger and Associates. He has assisted executives of numerous companies in successfully managing the M&A integration process. The coauthor of *Strategic Management Skills*, Dr. Schweiger is the international strategic management editor of *Journal of World Business*. His work has been widely published in professional journals, including *Strategic Management Journal, Academy of Management Journal, Human Resource Planning,* and *Organizational Dynamics.*